Higher Education and Employment

An International Comparative Analysis

International Institute for Educational Planning

Higher Education and Employment

An International Comparative Analysis

(An IIEP Research Probject)

Bikas C. Sanyal

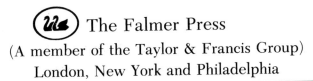 The Falmer Press
(A member of the Taylor & Francis Group)
London, New York and Philadelphia

UK   The Falmer Press, Falmer House, Barcombe, Lewes, East Sussex, BN8 5DL

USA   The Falmer Press, Taylor & Francis Inc., 242 Cherry Street, Philadelphia, PA 19106-1906

First published 1987

Library of Congress Cataloging in Publication Data

Sanyal, Bikas C.
  Higher education and employment.

  Includes bibliographical references and index.
  1. Education, Higher—Economic aspects.
2. College graduates—Employment. 3. Comparative education. I. Title.
LC67.6.S26 1987 378 87-10699
ISBN 1-85000-251-7
ISBN 1-85000-252-5 (pbk.)

Jacket design by Caroline Archer

Typeset in 10½/12½ Caledonia by
Imago Publishing Ltd, Thame, Oxon

Printed in Great Britain by Taylor & Francis (Printers) Ltd, Basingstoke

Contents

Preface

This book on the relationship between higher education and employment represents the global review or 'synthesis' of the experience gained by the International Institute for Educational Planning (Unesco) through a series of 21 national case studies, carried out under the direction of one of its staff members, Bikas C. Sanyal. This research programme was based on joint endeavours between the IIEP and representative national institutions and was spread over a period covering two Medium-Term Plans of the Institute (1978–83 and 1984–89). Throughout this period, the IIEP guided each case study, acting as a catalyst, while national institutions played a more direct and active role.

Although the issues and findings of most of the case studies have already been published and disseminated individually, it was felt that given their implications for educational planning in general, this unique collection of information, analyses and results could provide the basis for some methodological lessons. The IIEP's Governing Board agreed that a synthesis of the case studies was not only desirable but necessary, especially as the unemployment or underemployment of higher-education graduates has become a universal issue, challenging all countries whether 'developing' or 'developed' and irrespective of their political ideology.

The effects of economic stagnation on the one hand, and an unchecked expansion of higher education on the other, are at the centre of the problem. At the higher levels of education marked discrepancies occur between the expectations of graduates of different specializations and the actual absorptive capacity of the labour market. These imbalances lead to unemployment and underemployment of certain types of graduates or to scarcity of others. In qualitative terms, the content and performance of higher-education systems are not geared to the rapidly changing needs of society, which in turn are marked by the scientific, technological and economic demands of development.

The high unit and opportunity costs of higher education, the specific social and political weight of its institutions and students, and the responsibility of the higher-education system in guiding and enhancing other levels of the school system make it imperative that a special effort be directed towards the analysis of both imbalances and discrepancies as well as the search for possible means to correct them.

The overview presented in the following pages attempts to contribute to this analysis by drawing some lessons of a general nature, much as the individual case studies on which it is based attempted to provide specific answers to specific issues. Although national data collected from different sources do not make for easy international comparability, the materials collected in the course of these studies provide a comprehensive data base which allows for some broad conclusions that are generally applicable to the higher-education planning process. Thus this book attempts to identify the determinants of demand for higher education and to analyse the transition from higher education to work, as well as the actual mechanisms of the employment system. In so doing, it seeks to derive implications for planners and researchers involved in higher-education planning.

The IIEP has been very fortunate in obtaining the full co-operation of a large number of different agencies in the countries studied, not to speak of the dedication of the members of the national research teams. Without their help the studies and this synthesis could not have been produced.

It is our hope that the academic community and practitioners dealing with the problems of employment for the educated will derive tangible benefit from this overview.

The IIEP is most grateful to the Governments of Canada, the Federal Republic of Germany, Norway, Sweden and the United Kingdom for the financial support they have provided for the research project.

Sylvain Lourié
Director, IIEP

Acknowledgement

The author acknowledges the contributions made by all the research team members who co-operated with him in conducting the national case studies. The list of names would be too long to mention them individually. However, they are cited in the references given whenever their work is quoted in the study. In addition thanks are also due to those investigators and clerical staff whose names do not appear as authors but whose sincere efforts contributed greatly to the successful completing of the studies.

The total number of anonymous individuals surveyed in carrying out this research exceeds fifty thousand and without their co-operation too the case studies could not have materialized. I am taking the opportunity to express my grateful thanks to them here.

However, special mention should be made of Professor Herbert Parnes, professor Emeritus of Ohio State University, USA, and Mr Sylvain Lourié, Director, IIEP, who both took great pains in critically reviewing the draft and suggesting a large number of changes. I appreciated the assistance of Mr Lahcéne Yaici, Mr S. Kejariwal and Mrs Krystyna Koutcher in updating some of the statistics.

Finally, thanks are due to Mr Desmond Avery for editing this volume and to Ms Kay Brownrigg, the project secretary, for her contribution to the different stages of the work. Needless to say, I, as the author, am personally responsible for any errors or omissions which still remain.

Bikas C. Sanyal

1 *Introduction: The Situation, the Project and the Countries involved*

Whatever the political ideology of a government, the employment of graduates from institutions of higher education is considered an essential element of national development. This is not only because the employment market is at the core of social and economic development, determining the productive life of an active citizen, but also because every citizen is entitled to have a social role to play, and today gainful employment is the means of playing that role. In this chapter we describe the global situation of higher education and employment, analysing the conceptual relationship between these two realities, and presenting the rationale of the research undertaken by the IIEP.

The problem of graduate unemployment

As a result of economic stagnation, the employment intake slowed down in the 1970s. We have attempted to examine the situation around the world on the basis of statistics available at the International Labour Organization (ILO).[1] The unemployment statistics are available for 40 countries: 6 in Africa, 11 in North and South America, 12 in Asia and 11 in Europe (including Yugoslavia, but excluding other Eastern European countries). In most cases the period referred to was 1972–1981 and the exceptions also fall within this period.

General unemployment has increased in all the European countries except Finland, in all the African countries except Sierra Leone, in all the American countries except Trinidad and Tobago, and in all the Asian countries except Japan and Malaysia. This generalized growth in unemployment is not always due to the economic recession alone, as political changes have sometimes added their impact to that of economic forces. For example, the political independence of Angola and Mozambique brought many Portuguese people back to Portugal, adding to its unemployment problems in the mid 1970s.

Statistics on the level of unemployment in relation to the educational level of the citizens concerned are not available for most countries. The ILO publishes statistics on unemployment by different categories of occupation for the countries in which those figures are available. The two occupational categories defined as 'professional, technical and related workers' and 'administrative, executive and managerial workers' consist mostly of graduates, that is, people who have successfully completed any third-level education. The unemployment situation in these two categories thus refers mainly to graduates. According to the ILO, the number of unemployed people with previous employment experience in these two categories has increased in all the industrialized free-market countries and most of the developing countries during the last decade. In the Federal Republic of Germany, unemployment figures for the professional category alone rose from 10,897 in 1970 to 205,200 in 1982; in the United States for the same category they rose from 339,000 in 1970 to 579,000 in 1982; in India, for the professional and managerial categories combined, unemployment rose from 452,000 in 1954 to 846,000 in 1981; in Sri Lanka for the same categories the figures rose from 93,228 in 1970 to 110,644 in 1977; in Uruguay for the same categories they rose from 600 in 1970 to 1,400 in 1981.[2]

Particularly striking is the faster growth rate in unemployment among high-level professionals, both at the administrative and managerial level and at the professional/technical and related level. The growth rate of general unemployment during the given periods was less than that of graduate unemployment in 25 out of the 31 countries where general unemployment increased during the given periods. In addition to the individual and social problems involved, unemployed graduates represent an investment on which no return is being made.

Definition of unemployment and underemployment

The figures given above are based on the general definition used by the ILO for unemployment, which is as follows:

Persons in unemployment consist of all persons above a specified age who, on the specified day or for a specified week, were in the following categories:

(a) workers available for employment whose contract of employment had been terminated or temporarily suspended and who were without a job and seeking work for pay or profit;

(b) persons who were available for work (except for minor illness) during the specified period and were seeking work for pay or profit, who were never previously employed or whose most recent status was other than that of employee (i.e. former employers, etc.), or who had been in retirement;

(c) persons without a job and currently available for work who had made arrangements to start a new job at a date subsequent to the specified period;

(d) persons on temporary or indefinite lay-off without pay.

The following categories of persons are not considered to be unemployed:

(a) persons intending to establish their own business or farm, but who had not yet arranged to do so, who were not seeking work for pay or profit;

(b) former unpaid family workers not at work and not seeking work for pay or profit.

This definition of unemployment shows only the tip of the iceberg, because it does not include the enormous amount of underemployment which takes place in non-voluntary part-time work and the under-utilization of skills and capabilities on the job. The ILO therefore has categorized two types of underemployment: 'visible underemployment' involving shorter than normal periods of work, and 'invisible underemployment' which applies to persons whose earnings are abnormally low, whose jobs do not permit full use of their capacities or skills, or who are employed in establishments or economic units where productivity is abnormally low.

In most developing countries, underemployment of graduates is a more serious problem than their open unemployment. In the Philippines, where open graduate unemployment did not seem to exist during the last few years, one out of four employed persons was a non-voluntary part-time worker. This is an example of visible underemployment.

In Sri Lanka, it is estimated that from 1,000 to 2,000 university graduates in arts-based disciplines work in the clerical service, which requires only second-level education. This is an example of invisible underemployment. In Bangladesh, according to a Planning Commission estimate, out of 610,000 educated job-seekers employed (with secondary education or higher qualifications), 189,000 were inappropriately placed, being unable to utilize their training.

The industrialized countries also suffer from underemployment. According to one estimate, in the United States the under-utilization of college graduates ranges between a quarter and half of the graduate labour force.[3]

In countries where graduates are guaranteed employment, there is no open unemployment, but underemployment, particularly of the invisible type, is a common phenomenon. This is to be found in most of the socialist countries. Underemployment in the form of inappropriate placement of graduates is also widespread in the African countries.

Incidence and duration of unemployment

In addition to the different types of unemployment, one can make an important distinction between two different aspects of it: its incidence and its duration. Unemployment incidence is the percentage of unemployed people in a given population group. It is the 'unemployment rate'. Unemployment duration, on the other hand, has a calendar time attached to it. It is usually expressed as 'absorption rates × years after graduation', or simply as mean years or months spent unemployed since graduation.

One can observe some relationship between unemployment incidence and the level of education. In many cases it is the graduates of middle-level education who are most hard hit by unemployment, but there are exceptions. For example, in Italy in 1978, unemployment rates for people under 30 years old were positively related to education: graduates of secondary or higher education had about two and a half times the unemployment rate of those with an intermediate school certificate. On the other hand, in the United States in the same year, the unemployment rate of 16 to 24-year-olds not enrolled in school was 6.3 per cent for university graduates, but 18.6 per cent for high school drop-outs.[4] Similar are the cases of Kenya and Colombia.[5] The inverse relation between unemployment and educational attainment supports the 'labour queue' theory, according to which education is a critical background factor used by employers in ranking potential workers on the basis of their training costs. The increased social demand for higher education stems partly from this reasoning.

As for the duration of graduate unemployment, it appears to be a sharply declining function of age, i.e. it is principally a youth problem, nearly every graduate finding a job after some time.

The education-employment relationship and the context of IIEP research

The above description of the problem of graduate unemployment leads us to suppose that there is a relationship between higher education and graduate unemployment which could be studied within the overall framework of the relation between education and employment. This relationship has recently attracted the attention of researchers in the field of both education and economics. As is to be expected, they differ in their points of view.

One view is that education provides people with the skills to develop and manage the economy and related services, and therefore investment in education is an investment in human capital, that is, in the productive capacity of the people. This is known as the 'human capital theory'. A second view is that education not only provides skills for performing vocational tasks but also promotes social values by encouraging upward mobility in the society, and thus acts as a screening device to select the ablest people for the best jobs. A third view is that productivity is an attribute of jobs, not of people; people are matched to jobs by criteria which may be associated with education, but education is not a determinant of productivity. This approach has been called the 'labour market segment-ation theory'. There is also a fourth view, related to the third, according to which the idea of correspondence between education and employment is an illusion existing only in the minds of graduates and has little to do with their performance in active life. The usual practice of recruiting graduates for certain jobs on the basis of their educational qualifications leads new job-seekers to believe that they are entitled to such jobs.

These four points of view on graduate education and employment may be divided as follows: The first two accept the idea of education's contribution to the social and economic development of people, whereas the second two raise doubts about the role of education in this develop-ment. It is worth noting that in the 1960s expansion in higher education in both industrialized and developing countries was mostly supported by the first two points of view. It is only in recent years that the role of employment, and that of the employers in manipulating the labour market, have been recognized, mainly in the industrialized countries. However, there is not enough empirical evidence yet to support the segmentation theory or the illusory nature of the correspondence between education and employment, and the role of education in social and economic develop-ment, particularly for the developing world, cannot be ignored.

Most of the developing countries had an essentially subsistence agrarian economy before the advent of the Western commercial and industrial civilization. The primary task of the community was to produce food, which was the most important basic need. Other crafts and occupa-tions supported this primary function. The various kinds of services needed for subsistence were provided by different social groups. The socialization of the individual through training in a given skill and in the value system of the society was an inseparable element of a single learning system. The family, the workplace, the formal centres of learning, and the religious institutions, all provided education on how to live, work and follow the rules of the society into which one was born. The social leaders, elders, expert craftsmen and religious teachers set the standards and provided the learning. The world of work could hardly be separated from the world of education.

Even during the period when many of the developing countries were under colonial domination, the same system prevailed in most of these countries, particularly in the rural areas, where most people lived, and which remained unaffected by the Western civilization brought by the foreigners. However, in the urban areas and in the tiny modern part of the economy, namely the government and commercial sector, the colonial rulers needed local manpower at the subordinate level, and accordingly trained them in institutions set up to meet their own needs. The formal education system which produced these new executives was elitist, and generally the language of instruction was that of the colonizers. Higher education was restricted in quantity and type to meet the needs of the rulers.

At the same time, the modern organized sector started requiring the completion of an educational programme as a condition for employment, graded, perhaps arbitrarily, according to the type and duration of studies. Education and employment now had a correspondence, but the inherent interrelationship was lost; the world of education had been separated from the world of work.

When they became independent, many of the developing countries had to expand their educational systems. Development efforts and the departure of expatriates holding high-level decision-making positions created a heavy demand for higher education in quantitative terms. With demand exceeding supply and attention focused on types of higher education in which graduates were in short supply, little thought was given to unemployment. The distribution of income and employment were implicitly thought to be problems that would be solved by rapid economic expansion and by the upward mobility of the poor through increased educational opportunities. At the same time, industrial development was given precedence over agricultural development because agriculture appeared to be able to survive with unskilled labour, and because the planners and politicians thought that only dynamic industrial growth could absorb the masses of underemployed and lead the economy into 'take-off'. It was also believed that this would sustain economic growth, increase consumption and improve the overall economic condition of the people.

Economists were quick to argue that investment in human resources was a powerful factor for economic growth. The rates of return on such investments, although calculated very approximately and sometimes arbitrarily, were shown to be as high as, if not higher than, those on other kinds of investment. Thus more and more money was invested in education, with the institutions of higher education receiving a large share of it, which was thought to be justified by salary differentials, though those in their turn were based on educational differentials.

There were also social and various other reasons for expansion. For example, in many of these countries education has now come to be considered as a basic human right. Also, with improved communication systems, the benefits of higher education were more readily perceived. Once children had received some education, they saw the advantages of it and demanded more. Most institutions of higher education charged very low fees, while the special economic incentives, and prestige and power attached to the job supposed to be waiting for graduates of higher education, attracted more and more students.

Similarly, political factors contributed to the expansion in higher education: for all the countries, and for all the regions within a country, an institution of higher education was a symbol of national or regional prestige. Economic criteria received little attention in the establishment of many of the institutions of higher education, and the question of how employable the graduates would be often received none at all.

The rapid expansion of higher education has created as many problems as it has solved. Chief among the former are the following: (1) the lack of relevance in the content and structure of the system of higher education with respect to national needs, since in most of these countries the expansion was not combined with any real consideration of changed needs following political independence; (2) lack of confidence on the part of the key production sectors of the economy in the institutions of higher education. owing to the absence of any interaction between them; (3) rural exodus caused by the location of these institutions in urban areas; (4) the students' increased expectations, which could not be met; (5) deterioration in the quality of management of higher education; and (6) most important, the mismatch in both quantitative and qualitative terms between the output of the system and the capacity of the labour market to absorb it. The latter has come to the fore in problems of unemployment and underemployment among most university graduates, especially those qualified in the liberal arts. Conversely, in the professional fields fewer graduates have been produced than were needed.

To be fair, we should note that the authorities of higher education have been partly handicapped by the erratic behaviour of the employment market. It has been difficult for them to assess the absorptive capacity of the economy, or forecast manpower needs. The principal difficulties are lack of information on (1) the resource potential of the country, (2) the changing technology and labour productivity, (3) educational needs for different kinds of jobs, (4) occupational mobility, (5) attitudes and expectations of potential employees and employers, and (6) the recruitment and promotion practices of the employers. Furthermore, even if such information were available, economic uncertainties would still prevail. These difficulties can only be tackled by making the system of higher education more flexible in order to respond to the changing economic priorities.

It is in this context that the International Institute for Educational Planning launched a research project to relate the development of higher education within a country to the changing needs of the employment market, in both quantitative and qualitative terms, so as to improve the basis for planning the development of higher education and reduce the mismatch between the type of training offered by the institutions and the types of skills needed by the labour market.

It was believed that all four schools of thought mentioned above had some justification but none of them exactly fitted the situation prevailing in a particular country at a particular time. The approach followed by the IIEP therefore, was not to apply any of these concepts where precise information about the actual operation of the socio-political structure in a given country was not available. The IIEP approach follows neither the capitalist concept of social operation as the basis of the human capital theory, nor the Neo-Marxian theory which is behind the segmentation approach, nor the 'diploma disease' theory, according to which school-leavers are incapable of finding the real correspondence between education and a job. Instead, it has put the actual operation of the education system and the labour market to the test. It appears to us that all these theories are constantly under review and it is extremely difficult to identify a country's social system precisely on the basis of whether it follows a particular model of development. Whatever models for development a country uses, it has to adapt them to its own particular socio-economic and cultural environment. Bearing these considerations in mind, the IIEP project on higher education and employment had the medium-term objective of providing a knowledge base for use in formulating educational policy oriented towards the employment needs of the country concerned. The short-term objectives were as follows:

1 To identify the role played by the education system in general, and the higher education system in particular, in the overall socio-economic development of the country, and conversely, the influence of social, cultural and economic factors on the development of the education system;
2 To identify the imbalances, both quantitative and qualitative, that have developed in the education system and suggest measures to rectify them;
3 To shed light on the main variables to be considered in formulating policies of intake to different disciplines and institutions;
4 To identify the factors which hinder the implementation of such policies and suggest ways to minimize their effect;
5 To develop a system of indicators to be used by the national policy-makers, the university administrators, the potential employers and the students themselves, for decision-making;
6 To create a data base for researchers in educational planning, particularly in the area of employment.

To attain these objectives, an analysis of the quantitative aspects is not enough, and the investigation has to consider qualitative aspects, such as the expectations of students, graduates and employers, as well as quantitative ones, such as manpower needs, trends of output of the educational system, their intakes, or the structure of the labour force.

Framework of the project

The interdependence between educational development and the overall socio-economic development of a country calls for an analysis of the resource potential in natural, physical and human categories. To develop each region consistently, the development strategy of a country should take into account natural resource potential, as this partly determines the process of exploitation and the choice of technology. The exploitation of these resources needs skills which must be provided by the education system. The way in which natural resources are exploited, therefore, has a bearing on the structure and content of the educational development strategy. This also depends on the availability of other physical resources such as building, equipment, transportation and communication facilities. But at the same time the development of these physical resources depends on the development of education. Thus an analysis of physical resource potential becomes an important task in ascertaining the role of education, as well as in the overall development strategy of a country.

In the analysis of human resource development, traditions, customs and beliefs cherished by the people cannot be ignored. Demographic changes influence the human resource potential as well. Education at every level has to be planned in such a way as to develop this human resource potential so that it can respond to the needs of the social and economic development of the country, while taking into consideration the expectations and attitudes of the people. An analysis of human resource development therefore becomes indispensable to the overall analysis of the relationship between higher education and employment.

Conditions of work, recruitment and promotion policy influence the type of qualification that an employee may have. The full employment policy has to guarantee a job for every individual, but in countries where this policy does not prevail, employment is primarily an objective of the individual. Therefore, the development of human resources becomes dependent on the operation of the labour market and the prevailing employment policy. The policy of human resource development for economic and social needs calls for an analysis of the skills required to make the various parts of the economy function. At the same time the output of the education system, in terms of the skills taught, has to be known if proper use is to be made of the human resources it generates. Before the education system can be planned with respect to intake, content and structure, it is only logical that the demand for skills in quantitative terms should be estimated to whatever extent possible. These estimates of demand, which traditionally have been called manpower demand, but in our conception are broader than that, because they should include qualitative factors, are susceptible to inaccuracy owing to economic uncertainties and the changing nature of perceptions, attitudes and expectations of the various segments of the society. However, some guidance is needed as to the direction that the development of education, particularly higher education, should take in quantitative terms, so as to meet the future needs for skills and avoid unemployment or underemployment.

Estimates of this kind, if properly prepared, can provide such guidance. The quantitative estimates of needs for skills can be checked some years later against actual values, so as to identify their inaccuracies and form a checklist of missing parameters and variables. They are also useful for forming a strategy for the development of the structure and organization of the education system.

In the case of higher education the estimates are easier to make, because there is more correspondence here than at the other levels of education between the skills imparted and the skills needed on the job. With regard to the problem of estimating future needs for highly qualified manpower, an analysis of the match between the quantity of trained people and the types of training demanded by the economy, thus showing the responsiveness of the institutions of higher education, becomes particularly useful. This analysis of matching brings out the shortcomings of the education system, not only quantitatively but also qualitatively. A careful diagnosis of these problems should form the basis of any future strategy for the higher education system and provide a yardstick for achievements in restructuring the social system through change in the educational system. Furthermore, such a diagnosis illuminates the problems encountered in pursuing the goals of socialization and equality of opportunities in the world of work. These problems may be seen in the various education 'paths' of different population groups, which result in the different working opportunities in the labour market.

Identifying the factors obstructing socialization and equality of opportunities requires an analysis of the population, showing their perceptions, attitudes and expectations with regard to the education system and the labour market.

An analysis of the problem of the unemployment and under-utilization of graduates in terms of the training received and the skills needed by the job can provide useful information for decision-making aimed at improving the relationship between higher education and the world of work. Such an analysis also involves a study of the process of employment and its effectiveness as perceived by the graduates and the employers.

An institutional mechanism for interaction among the students, their parents, the institutions of higher education, the graduates, the employers and the planners and decision-makers could also assist in improving such a relationship. A better match between the expectations (of the students) and the admission policies of the institutions of higher education could result in better academic performance and better socialization. This could be achieved through the design of more rational selection criteria and a better counselling system.

Likewise, a better match between the expectations and qualifications of graduates and the expectations and requirements of the employers could result in higher productivity, more job satisfaction and less structural imbalance in highly qualified manpower, with the adoption of better employment procedures and selection criteria.

For the employers, some of the variables to be considered would be the size of the enterprise, the type of production or services offered, the location, the employment process, the selection criteria, and the salaries and other benefits including accommodation, etc. A compatible system for the different segments of society could be a useful tool in developing a 'fine tuning' procedure for constant revision of the higher education system and the labour market, which would be able to respond to changes in technology, developmental priorities and the structure of the education system, as well as the perceptions, attitudes and expectations of the different segments of society.

An attempt has been made in this project to go into as much detail as possible, following the conceptual framework step by step as we have described it. Such research is necessarily interdisciplinary, involving economists, psychologists, sociologists, educationists and computer scientists. It also calls for an extensive data base, which will be discussed at a later stage.

It should, however, be noted that the problem of economic uncertainties, which stem not only from factors within the nation but from the international situation as well, cannot be resolved. Only the flexibility of the system of higher education can reduce the ill effects of such uncertainties. With these limitations in mind, the tasks involved in achieving the objectives of the project can be summarized as follows:

1 Analysis of the socio-economic framework of the country and the pattern of development of education in general and higher education in particular;

2 Analysis of the demand of the economy for skills and the supply of them from the higher education system in quantitative and qualitative terms by types of skill;

3 Analysis of substitution between occupation and education;

4 Analysis of expectations of the students for different kinds of higher education and the reasons for the difference in popularity between fields of study, the availability of career guidance facilities and their influence on the students' aspirations;

5 Analysis of expectations of the employers with regard to their job requirements, promotion and recruitment practices, job description mechanism and salary structure, and the expectations of the employed graduates with regard to the higher education system and jobs;

6 Establishing a set of indicators showing the interaction between the higher education system and the labour market, to facilitate

continuous adjustment in planning the development of higher education both quantitatively and qualitatively.

It is obvious that carrying out the above tasks cannot be the job of one specialist. It involves the co-operation of several agencies or research organizations. This brings us to the question of how the research was organized for the various countries, and the role the IIEP has played in carrying it out.

Organization of the research

The research was organized in two phases. The first phase involved the country case studies, which carried out the above tasks in a more general way, placing the emphasis on identification of issues, thereby generating some indications for educational planning and decision-making within the country and identifying crucial issues which would need further in-depth analysis using the same data base. Although the main focus was on developing countries, it was thought useful to include some industrialized countries as well, so as to make known to developing countries their methods of relating education to employment, the problems they encountered and the ways in which they proposed to tackle them. The object was not to transplant these methods in developing countries but to acquaint their researchers and planners with them, so that they could adapt them to their own needs if they found them useful. In the organization of the research, national researchers were involved not only in collecting data, but also in designing the research, its methodology, analysis and interpretation. The report writing task was also shared among the different national researchers and staff of the IIEP. Wherever possible, the data analysis was carried out in the country, to reinforce local research capabilities. In forming the national team, not only institutions of higher education and the Ministry of Education were involved, but also private research agencies and other government agencies, particularly the Ministries of Planning and Labour. In substantive terms, the priority areas of research were developed through discussion among the researchers, educational planners and administrators of the country. The methodology proposed by the IIEP also underwent an initial examination by the national team members. The instruments for data collection were not only adapted but in some cases reformulated and redesigned by the national team and the analysis techniques and methods were adjusted to the comprehensibility of the users of the research in the country. It was understood that although international comparability might be lost to some extent, the country's own system and its own views were more important than the study's academic needs, which could be met in another phase if the basic framework was the same. It was also understood that no one country's experience could be transferred to another without proper adaptation. It was important that the country should concern itself with dealing with the problem of relating education to employment and know how to do so in its own context, using its own research infrastructure.

In this phase of the research, case studies have been conducted in Bangladesh, Benin, Botswana, Egypt, Federal Republic of Germany, Malaysia, Pakistan, People's Democratic Republic (PDR) of Yemen, Philippines, Poland, Sri Lanka, Sudan, Tanzania, the USSR, Zambia, and the State of West Bengal (India). In addition, studies have been undertaken on specific issues in Mali (on the graduates of the National School of Administration), Nepal (on the general problem of education and employment), France (a socio-economic analysis of the university students), Indonesia (on higher education and employment of the non-teacher graduates in the Java region), and Peru (on the employment experience of higher professional school (ESEP) leavers). In India, owing to the vastness of the country and the complexity of the problems, the following studies were also undertaken:

1 Formal education and on-the-job training in the industrial sector;
2 The job market for college graduates in Maharashtra and Karnataka State;
3 Post-graduation experience of the weaker castes in India,
4 Education and employment of the blind in the State of West Bengal.

Before publication, all of them went through an institutional mechanism of review by both national researchers and decision-makers, as well as outside reviewers, and they have been discussed at national workshops organized by the national research teams in the countries concerned.

The second phase of the project deals with particular issues and hypotheses to be tested. A series of technical monographs is appearing. Some of these have been published, others are under preparation with outside researchers and organizations. In this phase, further analysis of the data base created by the research project was carried out, since it was not possible to deal in depth with all the issues in one report, and it was also necessary that analysis techniques applied to the research should comply with international norms.

Since its inception, the project has been under constant critical review with respect to methodology, usefulness for policy formulation and possible impact on decision-making within the countries concerned. Follow-up studies have also been organized in the countries, to be conducted mainly by the national researchers wherever possible.

The synthesis report and typology of the countries

As has been mentioned, each case study was oriented towards the particular problems and priorities of the country concerned. However, for a researcher, general methodological lessons are very important, and although international comparability has been lost to a certain extent in putting emphasis on the specific context of the country, the material collected in these studies does provide a rich data base for deriving general implications for the planning of higher education. These are of interest to the researcher as well as the policy-maker in the field of education. The present report attempts to synthesize the findings for the different countries in order to derive these implications.

Using the data base, this report attempts to identify the determinants of demand for higher education in the different countries, and to examine the operation of the system of higher education, the transition from higher education to work, and the operation of the world of work. In doing this it seeks to derive the implications of these data for practitioners, planners and researchers involved in higher education planning.

For this purpose we have grouped the 21 countries in which studies have been conducted according to the following criteria: (1) the level of unemployment, (2) the participation rate in higher education, (3) the amount contributed by manufacturing and agriculture respectively to the gross domestic product (GDP) of the country. We have assumed that the relationship between higher education and employment can be better understood through these criteria.

In the following table countries are rated 1 to 3 on each of these categories. The first number in parenthesis refers to unemployment; 1 = low, 2 = medium, 3 = high. The second number refers to participation in higher education; 1 = high, 2 = medium, 3 = low. The third number refers to the amount contributed by manufacturing to GDP; 1 = large (with small amount of agriculture), 2 = medium, 3 = small (with large amount of agriculture).

1.	Bangladesh	(3, 3, 3)	8.	Indonesia	(2, 2, 3)	15.	Poland	(1, 1, 1)
2.	Benin	(2, 3, 3)	9.	Malaysia	(1, 2, 2)	16.	Sri Lanka	(3, 3, 2)
3.	Botswana	(2, 3, 3)	10.	Mali	(2, 3, 3)	17.	Sudan	(2, 3, 3)
4.	Egypt	(3, 2, 1)	11.	Nepal	(2, 3, 3)	18.	Tanzania	(1, 3, 3)
5.	France	(2, 1, 1)	12.	Pakistan	(3, 2, 2)	19.	USSR	(1, 1, 1)
6.	FR Germany	(2, 1, 1)	13.	Peru	(3, 2, 1)	20.	PDR Yemen	(1, 3, 3)
7.	India	(3, 2, 2)	14.	Philippines	(3, 1, 1)	21.	Zambia	(2, 3, 2)

Thus Peru, for example (3, 2, 1), has a high degree of unemployment, a medium participation rate in higher education (8 per cent gross enrolment ratio), and a large part of the GDP (more than 25 per cent) provided by manufacturing.

Obviously a country with a low participation rate in higher education, a low share of manufacturing in the GDP, and a serious problem of unemployment is in the most disadvantaged group. A country with a high rate of participation in higher education, a high share of manufacturing in the GDP, and low unemployment is in the most advantageous situation.

This enables us to define three types of country:

1 Those enjoying a relatively favourable higher education and employment situation — Poland, USSR, France and Federal Republic of Germany, each with total scores of only 3 or 4;

2 Those enjoying a moderately favourable higher education and employment situation — Malaysia, Philippines, Egypt, Peru, India, Indonesia, Pakistan, PDR Yemen, Tanzania and Zambia, each with a total score of 5 to 7;

3 Those with the least favourable higher education and employment situation — Bangladesh, Benin, Botswana, Mali, Nepal, Sri Lanka and Sudan, each with a total score of 8 or 9.

In studying the issues outlined above, we have grouped the findings accordingly, to see whether this typology has any bearing on the relationship between higher education and employment. A socio-economic profile is provided in Annex I, giving more specific information on each of these countries.

Notes

1 SANYAL, B., 'Graduate unemployment and education', in *The International Encyclopedia of Education*, Oxford, Pergamon Press, 1985, pp. 2068–2074. The base year and the current year differ, but some reasonable comparison can be made with the data available. By taking the growth rate as an indicator, most of the problems of definitional variation can also be avoided.

2 ILO *Statistical Yearbook* (various years).

3 SANYAL, B., *op. cit.*

4 JALLADE, J.P. (ed.), *Employment and Unemployment in Europe*, Staffordshire, Trentham Books, 1981.

5 BLAUG, M., *Education and the Employment Problem in Developing Countries*, Geneva, International Labour Organization, 1973.

2 The Methodology Used

The issues

As we mentioned in the section on the organization of the research, the issues to be analysed were developed by the national team, which was made up of members of several different agencies. A typical list of issues used to form the basis of the methodology to be adopted in a particular country study is given below. Any attempt to tackle these issues calls for a better understanding of the mechanism of articulation between employment and the education system. Such an understanding is useful for the education system, the individual (student, then wage earner), and the employer (or firm). It was noted that it would be desirable to develop an integrated picture of the education-employment complex by combining all three of these points of view. The issues are grouped in five categories: (1) those related to economic characteristics, (2) those related to the characteristics of the education system, (3) those related to the characteristics, expectations and aspirations of students, (4) those related to the labour-market experiences of the graduates and their employers, and (5) those related to the planning of higher education in relation to employment needs of the country. The issues are listed below for each group.

Issues related to economic characteristics

1 What role have the resource potentials in the country played in the development of the different sectors of the economy?
2 How do the different economic sectors operate? What are their development prospects?
3 What role do population characteristics play in the formulation of the education and manpower policy? Is education practised as a basic human right? Should work also be considered as a basic right?

4   What are the implications of the overall development strategy of the country for the planning of education in general and higher education in particular?
5   What roles are played by the different levels and types of education in the overall socio-economic development of the country?

Issues related to the characteristics of the educational system

6   How efficient and rational has educational development been in the past, with regard to structure, content and cost of operation?
7   What are the prospects of educational development in the future? What role does employability play in this development?
8   What role does manpower planning play in educational planning?
9   How is the employability of graduates measured? What role do manpower forecasts play in this?
10   How are the manpower forecasts made? How are they matched with the supply? What factors affect the supply?
11   What are the selection criteria for higher education?

Issues related to the characteristics, expectations and aspirations of students

12   What factors influence the pursuit of higher education? How are individual expectations and attitudes reconciled to the national need for skills and the absorption capacity of the labour market?
13   What is the correspondence between expected and actual educational career?
14   To what extent are the content and method of instruction relevant to the needs of the job as perceived by students?
15   What role does career guidance play in the choice of an education and an occupation?
16   What are the occupational and career expectations of the students? How are they determined?

Issues related to the labour market experience of graduates and employers

17   What is the prevailing degree of substitution between education and occupation? What role do educational and socio-economic background play in this substitution and in the waiting period for employment? To what extent are the needs of the job met by the

content and structure of the higher education system, in the view of the graduates and employers?

18 What characteristics of the job are satisfying to the graduates according to the graduates themselves and the employers? What is the degree of discrepancy between career expectations and achievements among the graduates?

19 What are the recruitment methods and selection criteria for a job and how relevant are they as perceived by the employers and the employees?

20 What role does wage structure play in the selection of a job by a graduate? How are starting salaries fixed? What is the degree of correspondence between academic performance and job performance as perceived by the graduates and the employers?

Issues related to the planning of higher education in relation to employment

21 What are the alternatives to formal education for meeting the needs for skills to perform a job? How are they organized?

22 In what areas of training could the employers (i.e. the consumers of education) and the institutions of higher education (i.e. the producers of skills) co-operate to bridge the gap between the training needed for a job and the training offered by the institutes of higher education?

23 What conclusions for planning in the field of higher education and in the employment market could be drawn from the results of the above analysis?

To answer the above questions, one could adopt different methodological approaches within the same conceptual framework of the research project. The various possibilities are discussed below, together with the rationale for choosing the approach adopted.

The methodology

Three methods of tackling these problems were explored in the study:

(1) *Longitudinal studies of students, graduates and employers* This method assumes that a representative sample of each of the sections of the society involved in the system of higher education has been selected. Their personal, social, economic and educational characteristics are noted over a given time so as to show the relation between the system of higher education and employment during that period. In this analysis, the problem

areas listed above would naturally have to be considered. Essentially, longitudinal studies consider the cohorts of students, the graduates and the employers. Over time the samples should refer to the same populations of students, graduates and employers, so that the different characteristics of different cohorts are shown. This also makes it possible to identify the effects of the characteristics of particular individuals in analysing the interrelationship. The difficulties encountered in using this method are as follows:

(a) The decision-makers and planners have to wait for a long time for the results of the analysis if they are to be of any use to them;

(b) During the time needed, the researchers, decision-makers and planners in the group change their places of work, so that retaining the same conceptual framework of the research or even the list of problem areas becomes difficult. One of the researchers of the United States who adopted the longitudinal approach observes that the whole team of researchers, except for himself, changed during the project. It is very likely that even the leader of the team would change in a developing country within a five-year period, and in that case the whole research project could fall through.

(c) Although the main argument in favour of the longitudinal studies has been to retain the characteristics of the population group studied over time, the changes in the socio-economic and political characteristics of a country greatly influence the characteristics of the population groups and so, in fact, the studies are considering different population groups over time.

However, what is more interesting in longitudinal studies is that they reveal the changes that occur among the same groups of people over time, owing to changes in the economic, political and social characteristics of a country. Although perhaps not very useful for a decision-maker or planner at a given moment, the results may be useful for a researcher for theoretical purposes. For a developing country, the costs involved in tracing the same population group, plus the risk of changes in the team of researchers and the composition of the decision-makers and planners, make such an approach less acceptable.

(2) *Analysis of census data over time*   The advantage of using census data is that this avoids sampling error. Generally, such data are collected already by different national agencies for their own purposes. For example, the population characteristics of the labour force is available from the census of employment, and educational statistics from the educational censuses. So, what the researcher has to do is to design his study so that answers to the listed problem areas can be found by analysing the census data. This greatly reduces the cost of data collection.

The disadvantages are as follows:

(a) Not many developing countries have census data available on population, employment and education systems.

(b) The questions asked in censuses cannot give all the information needed for an analysis of the relation between education and employment. The modification of the research design needed for adaptation to the census statistics may involve sacrificing the analysis of important problem areas.

(c) Accuracy of census statistics has often been questioned. Although the degree of inaccuracy may not severely affect the conclusions needed for policies in the area for which the census was conducted, analysis of detailed issues such as those discussed in the conceptual framework could be seriously handicapped.

(d) Census data very rarely consider the attitudes and expectations of the different social groups, which, according to our framework, play an important part in linking the world of education to the world of work. This is not as yet sufficiently recognized by the planners of education and employment. If census data are available for a particular population group needed for the analysis of the relationship between education and work, they still have to be appropriately adapted.

(3) *Analysis of cross-sectional data over time: Tracer studies on the interaction between education and employment*   This approach identifies the most important population groups at a given point in time, takes representative samples of these groups, and analyses the relationships between them. It does this with reference to the list of problem areas to be tackled and assuming that the important variables and issues concerning the relation between education and employment have been considered at the time referred to, so as to provide tools for the decision-makers for adjusting the world of education and the world of work to each other's needs. Such exercises are repeated at regular intervals, in order to examine the role time plays in the mechanism of interaction between the different factors of education and work. The exercises require each unit of observation of the samples to reflect both its past and its possible future characteristics. This latter aspect and that of repetition of the exercise over time enable the researcher to trace the relationship between education and employment over time. In the analysis, consideration is given to whatever secondary information is available on any of the characteristics, such as census data, survey data or any descriptive analysis of the situation.

The disadvantages of this method are as follows:

(a) The individuality of the units of observation is lost.

(b) The scope for analysing generalized aspects of the relationship between education and work is limited, as too much emphasis is given to the list of problem areas concerning the researchers and the decision-makers of the country. Thus theoretical aspects of the relationship are not tackled very deeply.

(c) Too many issues are treated sometimes with techniques which are too crude, particularly those concerning attitudes and expectations.

(d) Possibilities of repeating the same exercise in the same way after a period of time are limited.

(e) The exercise is more costly than the analysis of census data.

However, since this approach can (i) provide quick answers to some questions, (ii) provide the decision-maker and planner with a diagnostic analysis of the current situation, (iii) develop a data base with indicators for future use by the planners and decision-makers and (iv) develop a team spirit of research work in different disciplines within a country with marginal assistance from the IIEP, it was the method chosen by the national teams of researchers. Furthermore, the practical nature of the study, the simplicity of the analysis, the possibility of considering a large number of issues at the same time and the possibility of following up the situation over time also made this approach more acceptable to the research teams. We give below details of the rationale of the data base needed for the study and the methods of analysis.

In the analysis of socio-economic frameworks, we tried to identify the resource potentials quantitatively. When data were not available we depended upon resource estimates and attempted to relate the resource potential to the actual role that resources play in the economic activities. For example, if the country had large resources of metallic ore, the extent to which the primary sector of the economy was represented by that resource and the extent to which it was processed indigenously could be estimated either in quantitative terms or described on an ordinal scale. This information, however crude, made it possible to see if skills provided in the formal system of education could contribute to matching resource potential to actual exploitation.

The importance of the different sectors could be identified by their percentage share in the gross domestic product. This makes it possible to assess the contribution higher education could make to the development of particular sectors or in diversifying the economy. Here as well, we use simple indicators, such as ratios, compound growth rates, etc. Similar indicators are used to analyse the characteristics of the population and their implication for education and manpower planning. Where primary education is considered as a basic right, demographic factors are to be considered in the development of educational facilities within the country. If second-level education is not oriented only towards manpower needs, social demand will have an influence on the development pattern of second-level education as well. This, in turn, would influence the development of higher education. It is in this way that population characteristics do affect education and manpower planning. The participation rates by age, sex, and home background would provide useful indications for formulating development policies of education.

If the country had a social and economic development strategy its effect on educational development could be identified by the share of the budget for education. The skills needed for the development of the country and its regions could also be identified from the development strategy, thus indicating new training needs. Estimates could be based, for instance, on regional potentials for development and the available infrastructure. From the description of the development policies one can identify the kind of training activities that would have to be provided by the education system.

From the inventory of training needs one can then go on to analyse the potential responsive capacity of the education system, showing its strengths and weaknesses. This diagnostic analysis can involve identifying the factors affecting past developments and comparing them to the objectives set in the development strategy mentioned above. The influence of the socio-economic characteristics of different groups of people on the development of education is also identified. Rates of wastage can be estimated and reasons identified, so as to reduce them. One can also compare the development of different facilities of the education system to the enrolment growth, in order to check for the quality of instruction. An analysis of the validity of the examination system can be made by checking the scores with the performance at work in the case of school-leavers. A correlation analysis can also be made, to find the relation between educational performance and performance on the job. However, such an analysis has to be broken down into the different socio-economic characteristics of the student population, because not only formal education but other characteristics influence performance as well.

Analysis of cost per student, both social and private, is important, not only to check the economic efficiency of an educational programme but also to find ways to reduce this cost where it is unreasonably high. The diagnostic analysis of the operation of the present education system provides the basis for outlining its future development pattern. The future development strategy has to take into account the employability of the graduates, which is calculated on the basis of estimates of needs for trained skills. Manpower forecasts alone are not reliable estimates, as one can only make rough guesses as to the kinds of abilities they will involve. However, an analysis of the effectiveness of the manpower plans does become useful at this stage, as it provides the analyst with data on their unreliability and the extent to which other measures are needed. To assess the employability of different types of graduates one has to analyse the structure of the existing labour force, the pattern of employment (including recruitment and promotion practices), the wage policy, labour productivity, and growth rates in the different economic sectors as well as the policy of employment and the participation rates of different social groups in the employment market. In the traditional manpower forecasting methods only the sectoral economic growth rates and labour productivity are considered. In our research we first estimate the demand by the traditional method and then estimate the supply of graduates, following the flow rates in the educational system. After that we identify in order of magnitude the influence of 'other' factors on the employability of the graduates and their supply.

These 'other' factors include the system of admission to the institutions of higher education, the socio-economic characteristics of the students, the role of career guidance, the mobility of the students within the education system, and their expectations regarding the world of work. Expectations would include such aspects of the job as salary, career prospects and the conditions of work.

To identify the influence of each factor on the supply of graduates by field of studies, a set of hypotheses is developed to indicate the degree of association between the factor in question and a socio-economic characteristic of the student so that the implications of this association for educational planning can be drawn. A questionnaire survey is conducted within a representative sample of students to collect the data necessary for testing the hypotheses. Statistical analysis method varies with the nature of the hypothesis and the availability of data, but wherever possible multivariate analysis was used. The analysis was repeated for the graduates to compare the expectations of the students to the perceptions of the graduates.

The expected mobility of the students from education to jobs can be compared to the actual mobility of the graduates. Using this data, we can compare the specialization the graduate had in the education system to the specialization needed by the job. This reflects the flexibility of the labour market in response to educational needs, and indicates the flexibility of a particular educational programme in response to the needs of the job.

One of the factors by which the employability of a graduate in a particular field of specialization can be measured is the waiting period. Where accurate information on the unemployment of graduates is lacking, this period is a useful indicator.

The employability of graduates depends on the relevance of their training to the needs of the job. Relevance is estimated in terms of usefulness as perceived by the graduates, and checked for concordance with the perceptions of the employers. This information can provide some guidelines for the programmes carried out in the institutions of higher education.

The employability of graduates is also influenced by their mobility within the job. This mobility can be estimated from the questionnaire surveys conducted among the graduates, and reasons for it can be identified. This provides information for employers on changes needed in the characteristics of the job and for educators on how to modify the structure of the education system in the case of mismatch. It is also useful to note the effects of socio-economic and educational characteristics on the earnings and success in the career of the graduates. This can show what role education plays in the redistribution of income among graduates, which is one of its important functions, according to the human capital theorists.

Most of the analysis has been based on simple cross-tabulations, frequency distributions and chi-square statistics to calculate the degree of association among different characteristics. For the earnings functions, one can carry out regression analysis. Once the list of hypotheses has been determined (based on the checklist of questions mentioned previously) and the method of analysis decided upon, the data on the graduates are collected by means of a questionnaire survey conducted with a representative sample of employed graduates. The details of the sampling technique and the organization of the survey are given in the next section.

The employability of graduates also depends on the relationship between the employers and the institutions of higher education, and the recruitment and promotion system practised by the employers. The importance of the different methods of recruitment is determined by surveying a sample of employers giving them a scale of reference for each method. The mechanisms which could improve the interaction between the employers and the institutions are identified with the help of a checklist of such mechanisms, asking the employers to give their score for each of them. The difference in the recruitment and selection criteria for different types of labour market (public, private, etc.) can be analysed with cross-tabulations and chi-square statistics. For different types of labour market, the mechanisms of interaction may be different. This can also be identified by the score each type of labour market assigns to the different mechanisms. The average score with the standard deviation may indicate the preferred mechanism for each type of labour market.

Differences in wage structure influence the choice of a job by the graduates. An analysis of the minimum starting salary of the different types of employer and the criteria for fixing the minimum salary provides useful information for analysing the relation between salaries offered and the level and type of education. This analysis is again done by simple cross-tabulations and chi-square statistics, and the computation of average and standard deviations. Finally, an analysis is made of the concordance of the perceptions of the employers and graduates regarding the characteristics of a job, to identify areas where the degree of mismatch is excessive so that the importance of better interaction among the employers and employees can be shown by empirical evidence, and methods of corrective action can be devised. This analysis is done by assigning scores to each one in a set of identified characteristics according to its importance in making the job satisfactory. Simple measures of association are used as statistics for this analysis. The data on the employers are collected in the same way as data on the students and graduates.

From this cross-sectional analysis one can identify the existing degree of mismatch between the system of higher education and the world of work, and thus provide measures for corrective action. When such analysis is conducted periodically the impact of such studies in correcting the situation can be estimated. The effectiveness of the instruments for analysis can also be determined and new instruments devised as necessary.

The most important use of such follow-up studies is that they provide information on the changes in the relationship between higher education and employment over time. If the students, graduates and employers surveyed are identified so as to be representative of these populations, the follow-up studies will make it possible to check the expectations and achievements of these categories of the population. One could then also isolate individual characteristics which influence success in the career and determine what effect such characteristics have on educational performance. This analysis will also provide information on changes in attitudes and expectations over time and help to identify the reasons for such changes. In short, if the students, graduates and employers are truly representative, some simple indicators and statistical analysis can furnish the decision-makers in higher education and the employment market with useful guidance for reducing the mismatch between the higher education system and the labour market.

The data needed for such an analysis are listed with their sources in Table 1, Appendix II. They are divided into five sets. In terms of the issues listed at the beginning of this chapter, the first set, covering the socio-economic framework of the country, relates to issues 1 to 4 and 9 to 10. The second set of data, covering the development of the education system, relates to issues 5 to 8 and 11. These two sets of data are normally already available in published form. The remaining sets of data relate mainly to the attitudes and opinions of the students, graduates and employers, though sometimes they also include some objective information. These data are collected by questionnaires (see Appendices II and III). Based on the research framework, each questionnaire starts with a set of questions on personal or individual characteristics of the sample, followed by questions on the economic and educational status of the student and graduate samples. The last set of questions is aimed at testing a series of hypotheses. For example, to analyse the reasons for pursuing higher education (issue 12) a list of reasons was first compiled from any printed information available, and discussions with students and graduates. Initially four reasons were observed to be common. Each of them was listed and the students were asked to score them on a three-point scale according to the degree of importance they attached to each of these reasons. If they felt that factors not listed were also responsible for their pursuit of higher education, they were asked to list them as well. So a multiple-response item was included to correct any error in identifying their reasons. The average score for each of the reasons for pursuing higher education compared with the standard error indicates the importance of each factor, which may also be rated as statistically not important. In each identified case, the null hypothesis was that the reason was not important. On a three-point scale, where 2 indicated 'very important', 1 indicated 'important', and 0 indicated 'not important', the null hypothesis would be to set the average score in the population at zero and test if the average score of the hypothesis is significantly different from zero. This can be done by applying the 't' statistic. From the simple cross-tabulations, an idea can be formed as to whether any one reason was more important for a particular group of students. This could later be tested statistically with a more sophisticated statistical analysis. In several cases, the same question was asked of the students, the graduates and the employers. For example, the importance of the various characteristics which would make a job satisfactory to an individual was tested for all three population groups.

The sampling

The sampling design varied from country to country depending on the complexity of the population of students, graduates and employers and the availability of a sampling frame. It was easier to identify the population of students because the list of institutions of higher education is much smaller than the list of employing units in a country. The sampling of graduates and employers was a more difficult task. Most difficult was the sampling of the unemployed graduates, because of problems in tracing them, and because it was expensive to survey them, owing to lack of information on their addresses. However, attempts were made to trace them for the studies in West Bengal, Bangladesh and Sri Lanka. Employed graduates were traced through their employers. This process was chosen instead of an independent survey of graduates in order to save time and money and provide an opportunity for identifying interaction between the graduates and employers.

The sampling design described below was used in the study in the Philippines.

The student survey and the sample Information on the characteristics, attitudes, aspirations, and expectations of the students in the country was gathered through a survey among the post-secondary student population in the school year of 1977/78. Of the total student population of 613,807, 1.48 per cent or 9,105 students responded to a fourteen-page paper-and-pencil questionnaire. Sampling was done using three major criteria: (1) the year level of the student, (2) the region of the school in which the student was currently enrolled, and (3) the field of specialization of the student. Only students in their third or fourth year of post-secondary education were sampled; they were the ones about to enter the labour market, and comprised 40 per cent of the total relevant population.

Since 75 per cent of the students were studying in schools located in six of the 13 regions in the Philippines, sample schools were randomly selected from among these regions only. These were designated I, IV, VI, VII, X and XIII, representing Manila Region, Western Visayas, Central Visayas, Northern Mindanao, and Southern Tagalog.

The fields of specialization of students were classified into twelve major types: Agriculture, Commerce and Business Administration, Engineering and Technology, Food, Nutrition and Dietetics, Law and Foreign Service, Humanities, Physical and Biological Sciences, Social Sciences, Medical Sciences, Music and Fine Arts, Teacher Training, and Liberal Arts. Students in all these fields of specialization were sampled, in accordance with the distribution at the national level. This was done by taking 40 per cent of each region's enrolment per field of study. A systematic sampling technique with a random start was adopted.

The sampling design of the employers A stratified systematic sampling technique with a random start was adopted.

The population considered included all establishments and government offices employing five or more workers. It was divided into two major parts: the private sector and the government sector. A list of establishments from the 1975 Economic Census of Establishments of the National Census and Statistics Office (NCSO) was used as the sampling frame for the private sector stratum. Since there was no available list of government offices, the sampling frame for the other stratum was derived from the following sources:

1 A list of existing positions in the government offices at the national and regional levels as classified by the Office of Compensation and Position Classification.
2 The National Census and Statistics Office survey of local employment.

A $4 \times 9 \times 10$ stratification scheme was constructed for the private sector stratum using main economic activity, region, and employment size as substrata, so that substrata within a column fall under an employment size and region, and substrata within a row fall under an economic activity (see Figure 1).

The graduate survey and the sample The sample of the employed graduates is closely tied with the sampling of the employers. Graduates were all employed by the sampled employers, and were selected at random from amongst employees who have completed either a post-secondary programme or a collegiate programme.

In firms with less than 200 employed graduates, a 10 per cent sample was taken and in firms with 200 or more, 5 per cent. A systematic sampling with a random start was used in drawing the sample respondents. The total number of valid filled-in questionnaires was 4,655. Invalid questionnaires were negligible, as energetic efforts were made on site, inside the company, to ensure the return of the questionnaires.

Figure 1. Stratification scheme — private sector

Industry division	E_1	E_2	E_3	E_4
	RI–X	RI–X	RI–X	RI–X
(1-digit code)				
1				
2				
3				
4				
5				
6				
7				
8				
9				

Employment size strata used were as follows:

E_1. 5–9 workers
E_2. 10–49 workers
E_3. 50–199 workers
E_4. 200 or more workers

The main economic activity classification was patterned after the 1977 Philippine Standard of Industrial Classification. These activities are:

1: Agriculture, Hunting, Forestry and Fishing
2: Mining and Quarrying
3: Manufacturing
4: Electricity, Gas and Water
5: Construction
6: Wholesale and Retail Trade
7: Transportation, Storage and Communication
8: Financing, Insurance, Real Estate and Business Services
9: Community, Social, Recreational and Personal Services

All 13 of the administrative regional offices of the country were covered. In this study, however, Regions I and II (Ilocos and Cagayan Valley) and Regions IV, IV-A and V (Metro Manila, Southern Tagalog and Bicol) were combined in the selection of sample respondents. The ten regional groupings were as follows:

Ilocos and Cagayan Valley (RI)
Central Luzon (RII)
Metro Manila, Southern Tagalog and Bicol (RIII)
Western Visayas (RIV)
Central Visayas (RV)
Eastern Visayas (RVI)
Western Mindanao (RVII)
Northern Mindanao (RVIII)
Southern Mindanao (RIX)
Central Mindanao (RX)

The substratum of an employment size had a sampling fraction of 1/300 for size 5–9, 1/100 for size 10–49, 1/30 for size 50–199 and 1/10 for size 200 and over.

Sample establishments in each substratum were then drawn systematically using a random start. In the sampling process, however, a stratum with insufficient establishments was not left empty and at least two sample establishments were extracted, except in the case of the stratum employment size 5–9 which constitutes the biggest bulk of the population, where cells with less than 100 establishments were left empty.

For the government sector, offices were divided into two substrata: national and local. The national government substratum was further stratified into orientation and level, while the local government stratum was stratified into three levels.

A sampling fraction of 1/10 was used to determine the number of sampled offices. Again, samples were selected systematically using a random start. Samples for the regional level were not taken in the stratum of national security because national defence statistics were highly centralized and confidential.

The questionnaires

All three subjects of enquiry had some common variables in the lists of the conceptual groups of students, and the graduate and employer variables. These had to be measured in order to examine the issues and questions listed at the beginning of this chapter. The common variables for all three subjects of enquiry are given in Table 2 in Appendix II; lists of variables for students, graduates and employers are given in Tables 3, 4 and 5 in Appendix II.

From the conceptual groups of variables, a quasi-causal ordering of the three groups could be made, according to (1) the aspects of the relationship to be explored, (2) the availability of information among the subjects of enquiry, and (3) their relevance in answering the questions. This ordering is presented in Tables 6, 7 and 8 (Appendix II) for the students, graduates and employers. It may be noted that some specific questions, such as minimum starting salary of the graduates, are not asked in the employers' question-naire. This was because such information was already available for the public and parastatal sectors, which employ most of the graduates, in published documents. It is obvious that detailed items of the questionnaire had to be changed in accordance with the socio-economic, educational and political characteristics of the country. For example, in the list of student variables for the personal characteristics, the ancestral origin of the student was found to be an important item for the study in the Philippines, but the Tanzanian team found it superfluous. The preferred types of educational programme were included in the Philippines study with five alternative structures within the instructional system, but this was omitted in the Tan-zania study so as to reduce the length and complexity of the questionnaire. Items for each question were developed after thorough discussion with the national researchers, on the assumption that they had a better idea than extranationals of the probable responses to each question. Most of the questions had an open item to check for 'identification error'. It should be noted that some of the questions ask for direct information, particularly in dealing with background characteristics such as personal, community, home, educational and current employment context, whereas others ask about attitudes, and the opinions of the subjects on the educational system or the system of employment. Questions in the second category deal, for example, with satisfaction from the course, relevance of the course, reasons for choosing work in rural areas, characteristics which make jobs satis-factory, and opinions on the adequacy of the criteria for selection to education and occupation. There are also some questions about expecta-tions on such matters as occupation, earnings, etc. The last two types of questions have to be handled with care, although data of this kind are used extensively in the social sciences today.

In most cases, the questionnaire surveys were reinforced by direct interviews with respondents to increase the reliability of the responses. In some cases, field testing was adopted. Even after pre-testing the question-naires, they sometimes needed further improvement. The questionnaires were usually administered personally by the investigators. To serve as an example, the questionnaires used for the Tanzania study are given in Appendix III.

Limitations of the surveys

Criticisms we received of the questionnaires used for this research seem to indicate the following problems:

1   Sometimes we asked the subject to recall his past, which presents the risk of 'recalling error'. This was not so serious with the

students who did not have to recall facts from the distant past, but with the graduates we could not be sure of the extent of error in relation to what they had wanted as an occupational career when they graduated from secondary school, which in some cases was at least ten years previously.

2 Although we had kept an 'open' item with the closed questions, we could hardly have any convergence on that response. Usually the respondent did not have any item which he or she could add to the list. Although identification of the items is done with extensive consultation among national researchers and sometimes with pre-testing of the questionnaires, the closeness of the questions could bias the respondent. We could not estimate the extent of such bias, so there could be 'identification error' in the responses.

3 The non-response rate for items like father's income was very high, which means that the results could be biased by 'non-response error'.

4 For some questions, better formulation could increase the precision of the responses. For example, to analyse the substitution between education and occupation we asked the graduates about their field of study in the school and the field of study they thought could describe their job more relevantly (see for example Q. 16, Graduate questionnaire, Tanzania study). It would have been better if we had asked for a description of the job as well, in order to cross-check which field matched the respondent's work. However, this would have made an even more lengthy questionnaire. Here we depended on the graduate's own judgement of the relevance of his training.

5 The most important problem faced is the validity of attitudinal surveys. Although the need for them can hardly be ignored, we have to find ways to take care of the following points, forwarded by some critics of the project:

- The attitudinal surveys used were either to obtain the opinions of the individuals or to identify motivating factors. The answers can vary according to the context of the survey, or even to the phrasing of the questions.
- The opinions expressed are sometimes so general that it is not easy to include them in a planning process, even if one is willing to oversimplify the real world considerably.
- Another difficulty stems from the fact that motivations are seldom single and that it is an oversimplification to present the results in terms of mutually exclusive, one-sided answers.
- There was a division of opinion among researchers as to the mode of framing the questions: some suggested that questions on attitudes and motivations to be responded to frankly should be

put in a conditional way. Others thought that answers to conditional questions were the most difficult to interpret because the respondents tend to answer them positively to satisfy the investigator (e.g., Q. 41, Student questionnaire, Tanzania study — 'What factors might induce you to work in rural areas?').

We do not agree with the critics on every point, but they are of course not entirely wrong, and while interpreting the results, the reader should be aware of these problems, to which there are no easy solutions.

In studying the synthesis results that follow, one should also note that some of the country studies were completed some time ago, and the situation might have changed by now. Although most statistics have been updated, survey data cannot be updated without fresh surveys and we have therefore used the data as they were collected. However, this should not affect the results in any drastic way, and until new surveys are conducted the results will remain valid.

3   *The Demand for Higher Education*

In Chapter 1 we discussed the increasing demand for higher education, and the explanation for this increase in terms of manpower and social demand.

The manpower and social demand for higher education is seen in the individual demand for places in higher education. 'Individual demand' has been used as a concept at the collective level by aggregating the decisions of a specified group of individuals for the pursuit of a particular kind of education: demand at the collective level consists of decisions taken at the individual level. These decisions vary according to interests, aspirations and choices of those concerned. The attitudes and expectations of individuals also depend on their traditions, customs and beliefs, which in their turn depend on individual, family, and community characteristics, and socio-economic status represented by parental education, income and occupational background.

The individual demand for higher education has a vertical and a horizontal dimension. The vertical dimension stands for level of education and the status of occupation that may follow from it. The horizontal dimension stands for the type of education. Both these dimensions are important from the point of view of educational planning. Why do young people after completing secondary education decide to go on to higher education? What factors do they take into consideration? To what extent are economic considerations important and to what extent do non-economic factors become important in the pursuit of higher education? The same questions can be asked in the choice of a particular field of study at the level of higher education (i.e. the horizontal dimension of the individual demand). It should not be forgotten, however, that educational choices are only intermediate decisions in a career development process, and to some extent they are dependent on occupational decisions. The latter will be the subject of discussion in Chapter 7. In the present chapter we discuss the different factors determining pursuit of higher education, considering the vertical and the horizontal dimension of the individual demand. Three items were identified as the principal factors determining the pursuit of higher education: (1) career and employment opportunities, (2) scholarship or grants availability, (3) study for its own sake, and (4) others. We shall discuss the importance of each of these items below.

The vertical dimension of the individual demand for higher education

Career and employment opportunities

The motivation for career advancement through the pursuit of higher education relates to the individual demand and the manpower demand. Even if there is a need for manpower, individuals might not choose to pursue higher education to obtain specific skills and employment. This would mean that there is no direct relationship between economic needs for skills and the demand for higher education. However, the societal system of rewarding higher education with extra monetary benefits in most cases motivates individuals to pursue higher education. This is usually the case in developing countries, particularly where employment opportunities for secondary graduates are few. But economic incentives and employment are not always the *only* factors responsible for the creation of individual demand for higher education, although it appears to be the most important factor in all the countries studied by us, regardless of the typology of the country. We shall examine the situation for each of the typologies of the countries described in the previous chapter.

First group of countries The countries enjoying a favourable 'match' between higher education and employment are the Federal Republic of Germany, France, Poland and the USSR. Two of these countries have centrally planned economies (USSR and Poland) and the other two have market economies (France and the Federal Republic of Germany). Although one might expect individual demand to play a minor role in centrally planned economies, our research shows that this is not so. In spite of the career information and pre-service training orientation built into the planning mechanism, and in spite of the heavy reliance on manpower demand for skills, it is strongly maintained by the authors of the Soviet study that the admission of a young man or woman to an institution of higher education is based on mutual obligation.[1] The students most often express their interest in the field of study they want to pursue for career advancement. The institutions match the individual demands with the national demands for skills. The latter provides the number of places available in the institutions, and thus serves as the controlling factor for meeting the individual demands. It is for this reason that a mismatch between the expectations and the achievements of the students occurs. Attempts are made to minimize this through career information and pre-service orientation in the enterprises. In the USSR employment differentials may not result in serious earning differentials, but do result in differences in social status. This 'social prestige' often determines the demand for higher education. Thus career and employment opportunities provide social prestige and become the reason for higher education. The case of Poland is similar, as this country has the same planning mechanism. As our study on Poland shows, the most important reason for the pursuit of higher education is to ensure a higher socio-professional status,[2] this being determined by income level and the type of responsibility in the workplace.

In market economies like the Federal Republic of Germany and France, it is principally the economic incentive that attracts students to higher education.[3] This becomes particularly obvious when one observes the demand for specific disciplines and the rate of private return on education, as the demand for places follows the same order as the rate of private return. This aspect will be discussed later in more detail when we come to the horizontal dimension of individual demand.

In the Federal Republic of Germany, the ratio of applicants to number of places available follows the economic benefits available for a discipline at a particular point in time, as we shall see later. Economic benefits through employment therefore play an important role in creating demand for higher education in the market economies. In the case of non-market economies like those of the USSR and Poland, where monetary benefits do not play such an important role, it is socio-professional status that becomes the inducing factor for higher education. The number of applicants for each place is highest in fine arts schools, followed by physical training and medical academies (see Table 1). It should be noted that in Poland the medical profession does not bring with it any distinctive monetary advantage, whereas "Fine Arts" as a profession allows for additional benefits both monetary and non-monetary (e.g. travel abroad).

Table 1:   Poland: Candidates for admission in 1981/1982

Type of institution	No. of candidates	Percentage of candidates	No. of applicants for each place
Universities	28,116	24	2.15
Polytechnics	30,630	26	2.10
Agricultural institutes	13,651	12	2.13
Economic institutes	6,487	6	1.73
Pedagogical colleges	9,079	8	2.09
Medical academies	15,814	14	3.01
Fine arts schools	3,852	3	3.60
Physical training academies	6,910	6	3.09
Naval college	1,795	1	2.87
Total	116,334	100	2.53

Source: Statistical Yearbook, 1982, Warszawa, G.U.S., 1982, p. 206. (Rocznik Statystyczny Szkolnictwa).

This overall importance of career opportunities varies again according to the socio-economic background of the individual. In the Federal Republic of Germany for example, the career prospects become more important for students who are male, urban and have parents with high income and high-level professional and educational background. Similarly, in France, the largest group of students in the faculty of medicine (42.7 per cent) came from a highly placed socio-professional group, 27.4 per cent of the entrants to university had high-level executive parents[6] and the majority of the students of psychology (67.3 per cent) and classical literature (86.7 per cent) were female. These figures indicate that employment and career are more important for high status students and males.

In the non-market economies like the USSR and Poland, there is some difference in the attitude towards higher education. Wards of peasants, industrial workers and white-collar cadres attach different degrees of importance to the socio-professional status achieved through higher education. As shown in Table 2 the white-collar families in Poland dominate the system of higher education whereas peasants' wards are the least numerous. Although education as a whole has the highest importance in raising social status, the attractiveness of different disciplines varies for boys and girls. Girls are less attracted to career-oriented courses than boys, which indicates that the sex of the individual influences the demand for the various types of higher education. This will be discussed further when we deal with the demand for specific disciplines.

Second group of countries Those of the countries studied which enjoy a somewhat less favourable relationship between higher education and employment are Egypt, India, Indonesia, Malaysia, Pakistan, PDR Yemen, Peru, Philippines, Tanzania, and Zambia. In this group of countries career and employment opportunities come out as the most dominant factor for determining demand for higher education (see Table 3). In Tanzania, 95 per cent of the students surveyed indicated that good employment opportunities and a wide choice of careers were the most important reasons for their pursuit of higher education.[4] For the other countries this figure varied from 57 per cent (Sri Lanka) to 86 per cent (Philippines) (see Table 3). A large majority of the individuals cite career opportunities as the determinant of demand for higher education. In Democratic Yemen, where employment is guaranteed even for a secondary school graduate, another important factor is the contribution of higher education to social prestige, which accounts for 22 per cent of the cases. Social prestige being the result of improved socio-professional status acquired through higher education, it becomes related to the career aspect of higher education. This phenomenon is very similar to that of an industrialized socialist country such as Poland or USSR.

One can also observe that differences in socio-economic status influence the demand for higher education. In the Philippines and India,

Table 2: First-year students and graduates according to the socio-professional status of their parents in Poland (1983/84)

| 1 | Total in thousands | Employers (%) | | | Member of agricultural co-operatives (%) | Self-employed (%) | | Others |
| | | Total | Blue-collar | White-collar | | Total | Farmers, peasants | |
	2	3	4	5	6	7	8	9
1 Students at first year	66.0	89.1	35.1	54.0	0.2	9.6	8.0	1.1
– day students (full time)	56.9	90.5	32.9	57.6	0.2	8.2	6.7	1.1
– evening	0.4	92.1	54.0	38.1	–	4.8	4.0	3.1
– extramural	8.7	79.8	48.8	31.0	0.2	18.8	16.5	1.2
2 Graduates of	64.7	84.3	37.3	47.0	0.2	14.1	11.6	1.4
– day studies	44.1	87.7	32.0	55.7	0.2	10.8	9.1	1.2
– evening	2.6	92.2	56.1	36.1	0.5	5.6	0.3	1.7
– extramural	18.0	74.8	47.7	27.1	0.4	23.0	19.4	1.8

Source: Statistical Yearbook, 1984, Warszawa, G.U.S., 1984, Table 30 (688), p. 463 (Rocznik Statystyczny).

Table 3:   *Reasons for pursuit of higher education (percentage of respondents)*

Country	Career prospects	Study for its own sake	Scholarship/ grants	Others	Total
India (W. Bengal)	63	21	11	5	100
Egypt (1)	2.1	2.0	1.4	1.2	–
Indonesia (2)	72	8	0.4	19.6	100
Philippines	86	–	–	–	–
Zambia	85	9	1	5	100
Tanzania	95	4	1	–	100
PDR Yemen (2)	69	9	–	22	100
Sudan (2)	70	23	–	7	100
(3)	[67]	[19]	[11]	[3]	[100]
Botswana (4)	95	5	–	–	100
Sri Lanka	56.5	–	–	–	–

(1)   The value is the rank order on a three-point scale, 1 denoting unimportant, 3 denoting very important.

(2)   Preference for urban life has been included. The figures for Indonesia, PDR Yemen, and Sudan were respectively 13.2, 17.6 and 3.3.

(3)   The figures in parentheses relate to graduate survey.

(4)   Relate to graduate survey.

–   Not available.

Source: IIEP case studies.

females are at least as career-oriented as males. In Zambia males are more career-oriented than females (72 per cent as against 26 per cent) but in Tanzania female students gave employment-related factors greater importance than male students. Here too the higher the income of the guardian, the greater the importance of employment-related factors.

Third group of countries   For the countries with the least favourable relationship between higher education and employment, namely, Bangladesh, Benin, Botswana, Mali, Nepal, Sri Lanka and Sudan, the determinant for higher education demand is also career possibilities. For example, in Botswana 95 per cent of the graduates indicated that they pursued higher education because they wanted a specific professional qualification or better employment opportunities. In Sri Lanka the same reasons were cited by 56.5 per cent of students[5] and in the Sudan the corresponding figure was 70 per cent. Male students (72 per cent) and wards of government employees (73 per cent) in the Sudan give more importance to employment-related factors in the pursuit of higher education. Another striking feature in the Sudan is that the higher the income of the guardian, the less motivation there is to study for career reasons. In Sri Lanka male students also attach more importance to employment-related factors.

From the above it can be seen that in all the countries of our sample, career and employment opportunities came out as the dominant factors in motivating individuals for higher education. Monetary rewards derived from employment vary between market and non-market economies, but employment remains an important factor in non-market economies as a determinant of demand for higher education, because it provides socio-professional status. In the market economies monetary rewards received through employment become the motivating factor.

The above findings also show that although socio-economic characteristics influence the demand for higher education, this does not follow the same pattern in all the countries.

Under certain circumstances, monetary incentives available during higher education also generate demand for higher education. Developing countries often used this as a way to attract students, particularly in the areas where high-level manpower was needed by the economy. Also, to provide equality of opportunities in higher education, many countries have used monetary incentives, in the form of bursaries or grants. Thus one of the reasons for increased demand in higher education is that the opportunity cost is very little in many developing countries because of scholarship incentives, which make the private rate of return very high. We shall discuss below the importance individuals attach to bursary incentives as a factor for generating demand for higher education. Identification of the degree of this importance may help decision-makers to check on the usefulness of the scholarship system in attracting students to the fields necessary for the development of the economy.

Scholarship or grants availability

In the non-market economies like the USSR and Poland scholarships play an important role in attracting individuals to higher education. Between 85 and 90 per cent of the students have scholarships and those few who study at their own expense come from high-status families. The amount of the scholarship varies according to the academic performance of the students. Those who have higher academic scores receive 25 per cent more than the ordinary scholarship. For exceptional students the scholarship is still higher. In these economies the State uses scholarships as instruments for influencing the demand for higher education. In market economies like the Federal Republic of Germany, scholarships also influence this demand. During the late 1970s scholarships were not increased to keep up with the rising living costs, and it is believed that this presented a financial problem which discouraged some prospective students.[7] In France scholarships for university education are awarded only to economically underprivileged students. Behind this system is the objective of democratization of education.

In most of the developing countries, higher education is almost free.

Among the countries we studied, only very nominal fees are charged by institutions of higher education, except in the case of the Philippines, but even here it is only private higher education institutions which charge fees. However, the pursuit of higher education rarely depends entirely on scholarship incentives. In countries like Egypt scholarship incentive as a generator of demand for higher education has a score of only 1.4 on a three-point scale, where a score of 1 denotes 'unimportant' and a score of 3 denotes 'very important'.[8] In India, one out of ten students gave scholarship incentive as the reason for their pursuit of higher education. In the Philippines, a scholarship or grant 'was of no importance to most of the respondents of our sample'.[9] In Tanzania, bursary incentive was responsible for the pursuit of higher education did not exceed 1 per cent of the student population. In Zambia only 1.27 per cent of the students cited 'bursary incentive' as the reason for pursuit of higher education. These results show that 'bursary incentive' as such plays a very insignificant role in creating demand for higher education. Even in the least favoured countries the situation is not much different. In the Sudan, for example, about 10 per cent of the graduates gave financial assistance as the reason for pursuit of higher education.

Scholarships in one form or another being easily available in developing countries, one may ask how many of the students could have pursued higher education if there had been no grants? As the experience of some developed market economies shows, the demand for higher education would have definitely fallen. On the other hand, if bursaries are introduced to attract students to specific disciplines where manpower is needed, the result may not be satisfactory, as was seen in Zambia in the case of teacher education. It is the career and employment prospects inherent in the discipline that are the principal motivating factor in the pursuit of higher education, though scholarship and grants do influence the overall demand.

'Study for its own sake'

Complexities involved in the development of higher education stem mainly from the dualistic goals on which its guiding principles are based. The dominant goals are economic, education being seen as a production system to provide the manpower for various categories of jobs. This involves, on the one hand, matching the development of education to the qualifications called for by the national economy, and on the other, matching the career and employment expectations of individuals with the actual allocation of social roles. Thus education appears, a priori, to be based on the economic structure and potential of the country.

Another set of goals of education is socio-cultural, where education is seen as a consumption system preparing human beings with a variety of experiences on which to base their values and outlook on life. The accomplishment of the social and cultural goals of a society requires public education not only to develop skills, knowledge and technological information but also to provide character formation and opportunity for self-emancipation. There are thus two main sets of educational goals, one concerned with providing a wide range of up-to-date qualifications so that people can earn their living, while the other is not directly tied to employment but concerned basically with developing the personality. In the latter view, children and youth are not units of 'supply' for a level of 'demand', but individual human beings, and the principal task of the education system is to prepare them to live their lives, not just to earn their living. It is in this context that we sought to identify the role of 'study for its own sake' in determining the demand for higher education.

In the industrialized market economies, like the Federal Republic of Germany and France, 'study for its own sake' has been a less important factor in the demand for higher education in recent years. In the 1970s in particular, career and employment considerations have dominated. An increased participation rate of married women in the labour force in order to increase the family income has decreased the statistical importance of study for its own sake, which was more common in the past, and whatever study an individual undertakes has a career aspect built into it. When the career aspect can be combined with the cultural aspect, demand can increase, as is noted in France, particularly in the fields of law and economic sciences. In the early seventies demand for these two subjects was higher because career interests can be more easily combined with cultural interests[10] in the case of these subjects. In the non-market economies, the cultural aspects of higher education are supposed to be built into the programmes. As we have seen, potential earning differentials between levels of education being less important, the non-material benefits of higher education appear to be more important here than in market economies. This can be seen in the choice of subjects like literature, philosophy, psychology and sociology.

In the developing countries of our second type, study for its own sake appears to have a slightly more significant role in creating demand for higher education. In Egypt, it was rated on average as 'important' by a sample of 1,778 students. In West Bengal, India, 21 per cent out of a sample of 1,928 students gave this as a reason for pursuing higher education. It was also deemed important by the students in the Philippines. In Zambia, 9 per cent of the students gave this as the reason for pursuing higher education, and in Tanzania the corresponding figure was 4 per cent.

It has been mentioned that in the East education used to be considered primarily as a cultural good. This was true in many places until Western education with its bias towards materialism and skill formation spread to these countries, although the traditional cultural view was not entirely lost. In many developing countries the idea of relating education to employment has been regarded with mixed feelings. This comes out strongly in the significant proportion of individuals who claim that they pursue higher education for its own sake. This attitude is also related to the background of the individual in each country. The female students and the somewhat older students in India cite study for its own sake more frequently as the reason for pursuing higher education than do other students (see Table 4). In Zambia, this reason is cited more frequently by younger students (Table 5) and in Tanzania by older students (Table 6).

In the countries which have the least favourable relationship between higher education and employment, study for its own sake plays an important role in creating demand for higher education. In the Sudan 23 per cent of the students pursued higher education for its own sake. In Botswana, the figure is much lower at 5 per cent (see Table 3). In the Sudan, those with guardians in the high income bracket, and female students, gave study for its own sake more importance in creating their demand for higher education than did other students (see Table 7).

In summary, it is observed that study for its own sake, although less important in creating demand for higher education than career and employment prospects, does play a role in creating such a demand, especially among certain social groups in the developing countries. Among the three factors identified as determinants of demand for higher education, the career and employment aspect is the most important, followed by study for its own sake. The scholarship and grant incentives have the least overall importance. Differences in the socio-economic status of the individuals produce differences in the importance of each of the factors. The importance of each determinant also varies in degree according to the country concerned.

Other determinants

In addition to the factors identified above, others also seem to have played a role in creating a demand for higher education, especially in the developing countries. Preference for urban life came out as a distinct factor in Indonesia, PDR Yemen and the Sudan, with significant proportions of the students citing this as their reason for pursuing higher education (see Table 3). This could be true in other developing countries as well, where most of the higher education institutions are located in urban areas and eagerness to get away from the boredom of village life becomes a motivating factor to pursue higher education.

The horizontal dimension of the individual demand for higher education

So far, we have discussed the vertical dimension of the pursuit of higher education in general. This analysis becomes clearer when we consider the

Table 4: Distribution of respondents according to age and sex and reason for pursuing higher education in West Bengal, India

Age (years)	Reasons for pursuing higher education				
	Specific career needs	Bursary incentives	Study for its own sake	Employment opportunity	Others
A. Students					
15–19	642 (32.0)	207 (10.3)	428 (21.3)	642 (32.0)	87 (4.3)
20–24	796 (31.0)	290 (11.3)	533 (20.8)	801 (31.2)	145 (5.6)
25–29	117 (31.1)	45 (12.0)	72 (19.1)	123 (32.7)	19 (5.0)
30–34	17 (29.8)	6 (10.5)	15 (26.3)	18 (31.6)	1 (1.7)
35 and above	3 (23.1)	1 (7.7)	4 (30.8)	4 (30.8)	1 (7.7)
Total	1,575 (31.4)	549 (10.9)	1,052 (21.0)	1,588 (31.6)	253 (5.0)
B. Unemployed graduates					
20–24	62 (31.3)	26 (13.1)	32 (16.2)	65 (32.8)	13 (6.6)
25–29	162 (29.4)	78 (14.2)	105 (19.1)	163 (29.6)	42 (7.6)
30–39	72 (30.0)	29 (12.1)	51 (21.2)	77 (32.1)	11 (4.6)
Total	296 (29.9)	133 (13.5)	188 (19.0)	305 (30.9)	66 (6.7)
C. Employed graduates					
20–24	28 (26.9)	11 (10.6)	26 (25.0)	33 (31.7)	6 (5.8)
25–29	270 (30.3)	100 (11.2)	196 (22.0)	278 (31.2)	47 (5.3)
30–39	450 (30.6)	157 (10.7)	289 (19.6)	491 (33.4)	83 (5.6)
40–49	275 (30.4)	90 (9.9)	178 (19.7)	307 (34.0)	54 (6.0)
50 and above	58 (28.3)	14 (6.8)	46 (22.4)	75 (36.6)	12 (5.8)
Total	1,081 (30.5)	372 (10.4)	735 (20.6)	1,184 (33.1)	202 (5.6)
A. Students					
Male	1,173 (31.1)	451 (12.0)	734 (19.4)	1,201 (31.9)	208 (5.5)
Female	428 (32.2)	106 (8.0)	337 (25.4)	410 (30.9)	48 (3.6)
Total	1,601 (31.4)	557 (10.9)	1,071 (21.0)	1,611 (31.6)	256 (5.0)
B. Unemployed graduates					
Male	234 (30.1)	109 (14.0)	148 (19.0)	240 (30.8)	47 (6.0)
Female	65 (29.8)	26 (11.9)	42 (19.3)	66 (30.3)	19 (8.7)
Total	299 (30.0)	134 (13.5)	190 (19.1)	306 (30.7)	66 (6.6)
C. Employed graduates					
Male	104 (30.3)	362 (10.5)	697 (20.3)	1,144 (33.3)	192 (5.6)
Female	60 (28.8)	18 (8.6)	54 (26.0)	64 (30.8)	12 (5.8)
Total	1,101 (30.2)	380 (10.4)	751 (20.6)	1,208 (33.1)	204 (5.6)

Source: Bose, P.K., *et al.*, *Graduate Employment and Higher Education in West Bengal*, Paris, Unesco, and New Delhi, Wiley Eastern, 1983.

demand for specific disciplines. While higher education in general increases the probability of employment, as we have seen, this employability varies according to the discipline, which is reflected in the demand for places in the different disciplines. Table 8 shows that in 1976 in the Federal Republic of Germany the competition rate was highest in dentistry (8.15) and lowest

Table 5: Distribution of respondents according to age and reasons for pursuing higher education in Zambia (absolute numbers and percentages)

Age		Unknown	Professional qualification	Bursary incentive	Study for its own sake	Better employment Grand opportunities	total
						Why post-secondary training was undertaken	
16–	No.	81	879	22	130	171	1283
19	Row	6.31	68.51	1.71	10.13	13.33	100.00
	Col.	43.09	31.37	42.30	38.46	34.00	33.04
	Total	2.09	22.64	0.57	3.35	4.40	33.04
20	No.	31	465	11	64	79	650
	Row	4.77	71.54	1.69	9.85	12.15	100.00
	Col.	16.49	16.60	21.15	18.93	15.71	16.74
	Total	0.80	11.98	0.28	1.65	2.03	16.74
21	No.	20	412	3	45	73	553
	Row	3.62	74.50	0.54	8.14	13.20	100.00
	Col.	10.64	14.70	5.77	13.31	14.51	14.24
	Total	0.52	10.61	0.08	1.16	1.88	14.24
22	No.	27	357	4	36	68	492
	Row	5.49	72.56	0.81	7.32	13.82	100.00
	Col.	14.36	12.74	7.69	10.65	13.57	12.67
	Total	0.70	9.19	0.10	0.93	1.75	12.67
23	No.	7	216	5	22	36	286
	Row	2.45	75.52	1.75	7.69	12.59	100.00
	Col.	3.72	7.71	9.62	6.51	7.16	7.37
	Total	0.18	5.56	0.13	0.57	0.93	7.37
24	No.	8	179	1	19	32	239
	Row	3.35	74.90	0.42	7.95	13.39	100.00
	Col.	4.26	6.39	1.92	5.62	6.36	6.16
	Total	0.21	4.61	0.03	0.49	0.82	6.16
25	No.	3	101	4	9	20	137
	Row	2.19	73.72	2.92	6.57	14.60	100.00
	Col.	1.60	3.60	7.69	2.66	3.98	3.53
	Total	0.08	2.60	0.10	0.23	0.52	3.53
26–	No.	11	193	2	13	24	243
30	Row	4.53	79.42	0.82	5.35	9.88	100.00
	Col.	5.85	6.89	3.85	3.85	4.77	6.26
	Total	0.28	4.97	0.05	0.33	0.62	6.26

Source: SANYAL, B., and CASE, J. *Higher Education and the Labour Market in Zambia,* Paris Unesco, and Lusaka, UNZA, 1976, p. 264.

in mechanical engineering (1.64). This was because at that time, owing to the economic recession, engineering graduates were having difficulty in finding jobs and this problem of unemployment is reflected in the low demand for places in this field. There may also be another reason for the low competition rate: the number of places available for mechanical

Table 6: Distribution of respondents according to age and reasons for pursuing higher education in Tanzania (absolute numbers and percentages)

Age		Professional qualification	Bursary incentive	Study for its own sake	Better employment opportunities	Manpower needs[1]	Grand total
Up to 20	No.	6	0	0	0	5	11
	Row	3.1	0.0	0.0	0.0	2.3	
	Col.	54.5	0.0	0.0	0.0	45.5	
	Total	1.2	0.0	0.0	0.0	1.0	
20–25	No.	142	2	12	72	192	420
	Row	74.3	66.7	57.1	85.7	86.9	
	Col.	33.8	0.5	2.9	17.1	45.7	
	Total	27.3	0.4	2.3	13.8	36.9	
26–30	No.	0	1	5	9	16	64
	Row	17.3	33.3	23.8	10.7	7.2	
	Col.	51.6	1.6	7.8	14.1	25.0	
	Total	60.3	0.2	1.0	1.7	3.1	
Over 30	No.	0	0	4	3	8	25
	Row	5.2	0.0	19.0	3.6	3.6	
	Col.	40.0	0.0	16.0	12.0	32.0	
	Total	1.9	0.0	0.8	0.6	1.5	
							520

Heading: *Why post-secondary training was undertaken*

[1] To make oneself available for manpower needs.
Source: SANYAL, B., and KINUNDA, M., *Higher Education for Self-reliance: The Tanzanian Experience*, IIEP, 1978, p. 340.

engineering was higher than for the fields where the competition rate was higher.

In the case of France we have indicated before that the higher the private rate of return the higher the demand for the discipline. The private rates of return for selected fields of study are as follows:[11] medicine: 22 per cent; economics and law: 16 per cent; science: 12 per cent.

In the non-market economies, namely Poland and the USSR, the popularity of the different disciplines fluctuates over time. In the academic year 1975/76, for instance, the fine arts schools were the most popular in Poland, as was seen earlier in Table 1, showing the competition rate. However, the choice of a field of study in Poland is determined most of all by the interest in the subject as such, rather than by economic rewards.

It is also striking that interest in the subject was responsible for the choice of field of study in Egypt, as shown in Table 9. In India, on the other hand, engineering and management students cite career and employment opportunities as the most important reason for choosing these fields. In

Table 7: Scores of different reasons for continuing higher education in Sudan (absolute numbers and percentages)

Reasons		Need for particular professional qualification	Need for higher degree for career reasons	Desire for more study for its own sake	Lack of employment opportunities for secondary graduates	Preference for town life	Others	Non-response	Total
Overall sample		181	167	127	30	18	10	8	541
	%	33.46	30.87	23.47	5.54	3.33	1.85	1.48	100
By guardian's occupation									
Peasant		60	52	34	9	4	5	3	167
	%	35.93	31.14	20.36	5.39	2.39	2.99	1.80	100
Nomad		4	2	1	1	0	0	1	9
	%	44.45	22.22	11.11	11.11	0.0	0.0	11.11	100
Merchant		22	16	19	5	4	1	2	69
	%	31.88	23.19	27.54	7.24	5.80	1.45	2.90	100
Government employee		48	40	28	4	4	1	0	125
	%	38.40	32.00	22.40	3.20	3.20	0.80	0.0	100
Skilled worker		16	22	16	0	3	1	1	59
	%	27.12	37.29	27.12	0.0	5.09	1.69	1.69	100
Unskilled worker		10	10	11	6	0	0	0	37
	%	27.03	27.03	29.73	16.21	0.0	0.0	0.0	
Others		3	10	4	0	0	0	0	17
	%	17.65	58.82	23.53	0.0	0.0	0.0	0.0	100
Non-response		18	15	14	5	3	2	1	58
	%	31.04	25.86	24.14	8.62	5.17	3.45	1.72	100

By guardian's income								
Less than £S 250	90	85	60	16	6	4	6	267
%	33.71	31.83	22.47	5.99	2.25	1.50	2.25	100
£S 250–£S 500	45	39	29	7	6	5	0	131
%	34.35	29.77	22.14	5.34	4.58	3.82	0.0	100
£S 501–£S 1000	23	22	13	3	2	0	1	64
%	35.94	34.38	20.31	4.69	3.12	0.0	1.56	100
More than £S 1000	8	8	13	1	2	1	1	34
%	23.53	23.53	38.24	2.94	5.88	2.94	2.94	100
Non-response	15	13	12	3	2	0	0	45
%	33.33	28.89	26.67	6.67	4.44	0.0	0.0	100
By sex								
Male	152	155	97	29	17	10	8	468
%	32.49	33.12	20.73	6.19	3.63	2.13	1.71	100
Female	24	9	26	1	1	0	0	61
%	39.35	14.75	42.62	1.64	1.64	0.0	0	100
Non-response	5	3	4	0	0	0	0	12
%	41.67	25.00	33.33	0.0	0.0	0.0	0.0	100

Source: SANYAL, B., and YAKOUB, E., *Higher Education and Employment in the Sudan*, IIEP, 1975.

Table 8:   Competition rate in selected fields[1] of study at universities in the Federal Republic of Germany (winter 1976/77)

Field of study	Competition rate[2]
1 Dentistry	8.15
2 Veterinary medicine	6.61
3 Medicine	5.70
4 Pharmacy	5.29
5 Psychology	4.17
6 Sports	3.85
7 Nutrition	3.54
8 Surveying	2.70
9 Biology	2.38
10 Agriculture	2.25
11 Architecture	2.18
12 Education	1.94
13 Commerce	1.93
14 Vocational education	1.80
15 Mechanical engineering	1.64

Notes: 1.   Included are those fields of studies at universities administered by the Central Admissions Agency in which the competition rate exceeded 1.5.
2.   Competition rate = number of applicants/number of study places for beginner students.

Source: TEICHLER, U., and SANYAL. B., *Higher Education and the Labour Market in the Federal Republic of Germany*, Unesco, 1982, p. 72.

Zambia, students of health and medicine, engineering and technology, and agriculture, in that order, give more weight than students in other fields to career prospects as an incentive. In Tanzania career and employment opportunities are the dominant factors in the choice of all disciplines. In the Sudan, engineering and administration graduates gave highest importance to career prospects in determining demand for higher education.

The demand for specific disciplines is different for male and female students. In the Federal Republic of Germany in 1980 the demand for engineering, social and behavioural sciences, and natural sciences was higher among male students, whereas the demand for medical and health-related sciences, humanities, religion and theology was higher among females.

In France likewise, males dominate some fields, such as engineering and agriculture, and females dominate others such as literature and philosophy. In the centrally planned economies similar preferences are found. In Poland, more females than males seek higher education, and their demand is highest for commercial and business studies (22 per cent) followed by educational sciences and teacher training (20 per cent), and medical and health-related studies (15 per cent). Engineering and agriculture are mostly preferred by male students. In the USSR, economics, medicine and pedagogy are preferred by women, while agriculture and engineering are preferred by men. In the USSR also there is more demand for higher education from females than from males.

In the second group of countries the demand for higher education is greater among boys than girls in Tanzania, Zambia, India, Egypt, Indonesia, Malaysia and PDR Yemen, in that order, but in the Philippines the demand is greater among girls than boys. Subject preferences vary from country to country. Although engineering is chosen by boys more than girls in every case, social and commercial studies are chosen more by girls in some countries and by boys in others. The preference for education is high among girls in every country, though it is also high among boys in PDR Yemen and Zambia. Medical studies are in high demand among girls in several countries, and among boys in Pakistan. Preference for agricultural studies is noted in several cases among boys, but not among girls. Education and humanities are more popular among girls in general, but the number of girls choosing the scientific disciplines is increasing.

Table 9: *Reasons for seeking higher education by faculty in Egypt*

	Degree of importance		
Faculty	Scholarship incentives	Study for its own sake	Employment opportunity
Social Science and humanities	1.3	2.2	2.3
Science and medicine	1.4	2.3	2.3
Engineering	1.6	2.5	2.3
Arts education	1.3	2.6	2.0
Technology	1.6	2.5	2.3
Agriculture	1.4	2.2	2.4
Other	1.1	2.4	2.1
Total	1.3	2.3	2.3

Note: Calculated as mean using code 'unimportant' = 1, 'important' = 2, 'very important' = 3.

Source: SANYAL, B., *et al.*, *University Education and the Labour Market in the Arab Republic of Egypt*, Oxford, Pergamon Press, 1982, p. 130.

In the third group of countries the pattern is different again. The demand for higher education is far greater among boys than girls, varying from nearly three times as high in the Sudan to eight times as high in Mali. Engineering and agriculture are still preferred in general by boys, but in Mali the preference for agriculture is higher among girls than boys. In the Sudan the preference for law studies is higher among girls than boys, and among boys the preference for humanities is high in the Sudan, Nepal and Benin.

The demand for specific disciplines also varies according to the socio-professional background of the students. For example, in France those with fathers in agriculture are most likely to demand psychology, economics, science and the university institutes of technology (IUT) in that order, whereas those with fathers in senior managerial positions demand medicine most. What is striking here is that those with fathers as salaried workers choose philosophy and classical literature most frequently (see Table 10).

In Poland the popularity of any particular course could not be analysed, for lack of data, but this parental influence is reflected by the type of education selected. The regular full-time studies which offer the highest career prospects in education and employment have the largest proportion of children of white-collar workers, as shown in Table 2. One could argue then that these disciplines which have the highest career possibilities attract people from the higher rungs of the social ladder. It has also been observed in Poland that students who attach higher priority to these careers usually take courses in the polytechnics, whereas medicine, providing both career and knowledge motivation, attracts individuals of the highest social background.[12] It can therefore be argued that the most rewarding disciplines attract students from the highest socio-professional background in countries which enjoy a favourable relationship between higher education and employment. In the less favoured countries, like India, parental background influences demand for specific disciplines as well. Those with parents who are accountants tend to be more career oriented.[13] The choice of a particular field of study was also influenced by the socio-professional background of the student in the Philippines.[14] In the Sudan 48 per cent of the students seeking a course in agriculture came from peasant families and they constitute 35 per cent of the sample studied, giving a desirability coefficient of 1.37 for agriculture. The coefficient for engineering is 1.18; for medicine it is 1.06, whereas the coefficient for humanistic studies is only 0.41 and for business studies is 0.35. For the wards of government employees the pattern of popularity changes. Engineering has a desirability coefficient of 0.58, whereas for medicine it is 1.06, for social science it is 1.26 and for law it is 1.78.[15] On the other hand for the wards of skilled workers the desirability coefficient for engineering is 1.22, for medicine 0.79 and for social sciences 1.02.

In Bangladesh, for engineering, medicine and arts the desirability coefficients of the students belonging to upper income groups are 1.44, 0.63 and 1.08 respectively.[16] This shows that the pattern of demand for specific disciplines changes with the socio-economic background of the students, and the pattern varies from country to country.

Conclusion

The above discussion shows that individual determinants of educational choice play an important role in defining the demand for higher education.

Table 10: Desirability coefficient[1] of disciplines by father's occupation in France

	Discipline								
Father's profession	Economics	Medicine	Science[2]	Psychology	Philosophy	IUT[3]	Classical literature	Modern literature	Total
Agriculturist	1.53	0.57	1.21	1.69	0.30	1.09	–	0.49	1.0
Artisan, commercial	0.86	1.14	0.70	0.69	0.77	1.55	1.08	1.17	1.0
High-level and liberal professions	0.99	1.56	0.83	0.76	0.88	0.47	1.04	0.67	1.0
Middle management	1.01	0.95	1.25	0.72	1.27	0.96	0.75	1.20	1.0
Salaried workers	0.79	0.67	1.09	0.92	2.42	1.3	2.14	1.19	1.0
Workers	0.60	0.57	1.04	1.48	0.72	1.20	1.13	1.35	1
Total	1	1	1	1	1	1	1	1	1

1 A coefficient of the magnitude 1 means that the socio-professional background is evenly represented in a discipline, a value greater than 1 means the representation of that background in the discipline is more than its overall representation.

2 Science includes mathematics, physics and chemistry.

3 IUT: University institutes of technology — a short-cycle professional course.

Source: MINGAT, A., *Les Premières Inscriptions*, University of Dijon, IREDU, France, 1976.

The individual, family and community characteristics, and parental background influence these individual determinants. Manpower forecasts based on macro-economic analysis can only provide broad directions in relating higher education to employment in a mechanistic way. The effect of the micro-characteristics of individuals in determining demand for higher education also varies from country to country. A mechanical model cannot serve the purpose of balancing the supply of education with the demand for it. The achievement of a better match between supply and demand calls for the inclusion of individual socio-economic characteristics in the context of a particular country in the analysis of the relationship between higher education and employment.

Notes

1   CHUPRUNOV, D., *et al.*, *Enseignement Supérieur, Emploi et Progrès Technique en URSS*, Paris, Unesco, 1982, p. 141.

2   SANYAL, B., and JOZEFOWICZ, A. (ed.), *Graduate Employment and Planning of Higher Education in Poland*, IIEP, 1978, p. 163.

3   ORIVEL, F., *Une Analyse Socio-économique de l'Université Française*, IIEP, 1980, p. 32. See also MILLOT, B., and ORIVEL, F., *L'Economie de L'Enseignement Supérieur*, p. 124.

4   SANYAL, B., *et al.*, *Higher Education and the Labour Market in the Philippines*, Paris, Unesco and New Delhi, Wiley Eastern, 1981, p. 205.

5   SANYAL, B., *et al.*, *University Education and Graduate Employment in Sri Lanka*, Paris, Unesco and Colombo, Marga Institute, 1983, p. 209.

6   MINGAT, A., *op. cit.*, p. 20 (1976).

7   TEICHLER, U., and SANYAL, B., *Higher Education and the Labour Market in the Federal Republic of Germany*, Unesco, 1982, p. 125.

8   SANYAL, B., *et al.*, *University Education and the Labour Market in the Arab Republic of Egypt*, Oxford, Pergamon Press, 1982, p. 129.

9   See Philippines study, *op. cit.*, p. 183.

10 ORIVEL, F., *op. cit.*, p. 33.

11 ORIVEL, F., *op. cit.*, p. 32.

12 SANYAL, B., and JOZEFOWICZ, A. (ed.), *op. cit.*, p. 166.

13 BOSE, P. K., *et al.*, *Graduate Employment and Higher Education in West Bengal*, *op. cit.*, p. 109.

14 See Philippines study, *op. cit.*, p. 184.

15 SANYAL, B., and YACOUB, E., *Higher Education and Employment in the Sudan*, IIEP, 1975, p. 193.

16 HUQ, M., *et al.*, *Higher Education and Employment in Bangladesh*, IIEP, 1983, p. 146.

4   *Organization and Access to Higher Education*

To meet the demand for higher education described in the previous chapter, different countries have responded in different ways in developing their higher education systems, through their structures, planning mechanisms, programmes and delivery systems. The determinants of demand for higher education reconcile the individual objectives to the national ones and we have seen that these are different in different countries, if not in nature at least in degree. However, there are some legitimating traditions which are common to all systems of higher education. For instance, all the systems have a built-in agreement on democratization and the role of education in national development, and some vision of a tradition that is broader than the concept of a national community. In establishing the aims, objectives and priorities of the programmes in higher education, there is divergence because of the differences in economic, social and political markets, as has been noted in the International Conference of Education: 'What governments are prepared to try and implement as educational aims, objectives and priorities immediately increases a sense of confusion. What governments are prepared to try and do is always specific and complex and always, in some of its detail, unique. At first glance, the divergences of governments over educational aims, objectives and priorities are greater than the similarities. Each nation is, indeed, in important ways unique in its educational configuration.'[1] When these aims and objectives are to be related to the individual objectives of the citizens they become even more complex, as will be seen from the three types of countries of our sample.

The organizational structure of higher education

First group of countries

There is some similarity between the organizational structure of higher education in France, the Federal Republic of Germany, Poland and the

USSR. The systems of higher education in all these countries consist of three types of institution:

(1) *Traditional universities* offer courses in a large variety of general subjects. For example, the universities in France offer courses in the humanities, social sciences, law, economics, politics, exact and applied sciences, pharmacy, medicine and in some cases theology. The universities are divided into 'Units of Teaching and Research' (UER). In the Federal Republic of Germany, there are 37 traditional universities which offer instruction in disciplines ranging from theology to veterinary medicine. There are close connections between teaching and research in the universities. In Poland there are 10 universities which offer courses ranging from theology to technology and architecture. The majority of the institutions are divided into faculties or institutes of related specialities, and their main function is teaching. The USSR also has traditional universities, but a special feature of higher education in this country is that universities normally offer courses only in theoretical and human sciences and not in engineering, medical and other applied sciences.

(2) *Specialized institutes or universities* exist in all four countries in this group, and offer courses mainly in technical and other specialized professional subjects. In France, there are some specialized institutes such as the Institutes of Politics (IEP), the Higher School of Engineering (ENSI) and the University Technological Institute (IUT), all of which form part of the French university system. There are other public and private specialized institutes, which are independent of the universities. These offer courses in engineering, business and management, certain specific courses in civil services and fine arts. In this category there are Advanced Teacher Training Colleges (ENS), the National Institute of Applied Sciences (INSA), the National Schools of Arts and Crafts (ENAM), the Practical Schools of Higher Studies (EPHE), the School of Higher Studies in Social Sciences (EHESS), etc. In the Federal Republic of Germany specialized institutes include 7 technological universities, 9 colleges of theology, 17 schools of education, and 26 colleges of fine arts and music. Poland also has specialized institutes, consisting of 18 technical universities, 11 higher teacher training institutes, 17 higher schools of fine arts, 9 academies of agriculture, 10 of medicine, 6 of economics and 2 of theology, 6 academies and higher schools of physical training and 2 higher maritime schools. The Soviet Union also has specialized and polytechnic institutes, which are devoted to the fields of professional training, engineering, medical and other applied sciences.

(3) *Various non-traditional institutions* exist in these four countries. In France, there are the elitist 'Grandes Ecoles' which award diplomas recognized by the State. Access to these 'écoles' is controlled by a highly

competitive examination. In addition there is the College of France. In the Federal Republic of Germany, there are new and non-traditional institutions known as the comprehensive universities. These were established according to recommendations made in 1970, to train students for professional qualifications. The special feature of these universities is that they offer courses of short duration which have a practical orientation, and include compulsory periods of work experience. In Poland, there are several hundred post-secondary institutions offering short-cycle higher education in specific vocations, and awarding technical diplomas. Short courses are also offered to graduates who wish to be brought up to date with new developments in their fields or with areas of modern technology, such as automation, management, space science, etc. There is a highly developed system of correspondence and evening courses for workers. Evening courses are of the same standard as the regular daytime courses and admission is based not only on an entrance examination but also on proof of two years of work experience. A special certificate is also necessary, from the enterprise or employer, who then assumes partial financial responsibility for the student's study programme and agrees to provide leave or time off to attend courses. In the USSR the non-traditional system of higher education consists of part-time study and evening and correspondence courses for workers. These courses are organized during vacation periods. The enterprises must provide their staff with the necessary facilities for the pursuit of higher education.

In France, the Federal Republic of Germany, Poland and the USSR the State plays an important role in almost all matters such as the financing, organization, regulation and co-ordination of higher education. In France for example, most of the institutes of higher education (both the universities and the other public institutions) are financed by the State. The Ministry of Education regulates the national diplomas awarded by the universities. The organizational structure of French higher education is highly centralized but in recent years universities have acquired a reasonable degree of autonomy. Ministries other than the Ministry of Education also play substantial roles in the organization and control of higher education. For example, the Ministry of Defence, the Ministry of Industrial and Scientific Development, the Ministry of Post and Telecommunications, the Ministry of Agriculture and others have specialized institutes in their respective fields.

In the Federal Republic of Germany, the Länder (states) have the overall responsibility for higher education, including that of meeting all their financial needs, controlling their budget and overseeing the application of regulations. The Federal Government exercises only a limited control over the institutes of higher education. The institutes have a larger degree of autonomy than those of France, in terms of their internal structure, teaching methods, research and teaching programmes.

In Poland, the State is responsible for financing and organizing all the institutions and universities of higher education with the exception of the Catholic University at Lublin, which is under the private authority of the Polish episcopate. The Ministry of Education plays the most important role in higher education, but the other ministries such as Health and Welfare, Culture and Art, Foreign Trade and Maritime Economy, and the Central Committee of Physical Culture and Sports all have institutions in their specialized fields.

In the USSR all the institutions of higher education are State institutions. The Ministry of Higher and Specialized Secondary Education has the overall responsibility for them. Throughout the USSR admission requirements, courses, programmes of study, teaching and learning strategies, academic organization and credentialization are the same.

The administrative system of higher education   In France, the universities are administered by a Council and an elected President who controls the budget. There is a National Council for Higher Education which is consulted by the Minister of Education on all matters relating to higher education. This Council consists of representatives of teachers, researchers and students, as well as people from outside the university. A Conference of University Presidents and a General Assembly of Directors of Schools and Establishments of Engineering (AGREEPDDI), chaired by the Minister of Education, helps in the co-ordination of activities and programmes.

In the Federal Republic of Germany, at the federal level, there is the Standing Conference of the Ministers of Education and Culture which co-ordinates in a limited and normative way educational policies. There is also the Conference of West German Rectors which ensures a certain degree of harmonization in the fields of admissions, examinations, international exchange, etc.

In Poland, the Ministry of Science, Higher Education and Technology ensures the co-ordination between the various academic institutes and international exchange. The Minister of Education is assisted by the General Council for Science, Higher Education and Technology. This Council consists of representatives of all types of institutions of higher education.

In the USSR there are Councils of Rectors of Universities and other institutions of higher education, which co-ordinate academic activities. These councils are also responsible for studying the particular problems of higher education and for formulating proposals for further development of the centres and establishments of higher education.

To summarize, it is observed that the organization and structure of higher education differs somewhat in the market economies like France and the Federal Republic of Germany, the former having a more centralized system of operation than the latter. However, in the Federal Republic of Germany the Ministry of Education and Culture is responsible, with a limited authority, for all institutions of higher education, whereas in France, other ministries have their own institutions of higher education. In the non-market economies higher education is centralized, linked to national development planning, State controlled (except for one institution in Poland), and like France, has institutions belonging to ministries other then education.

In these countries part-time studies, correspondence courses and evening courses are more significant than in the market economies. Admission criteria, teaching programmes and the credential system are such that the graduates are given similar status to that of traditional full-time day scholars.

Second group of countries

The countries in this group (Egypt, India, Indonesia, Malaysia, Pakistan, Peru, Philippines, Tanzania, People's Democratic Republic of Yemen and Zambia) have much in common but also some important differences in the organizational structure of their systems of higher education. In all these countries the State plays a predominant role in financing, organizing and regulating the systems of higher education. The institutes of higher education are largely financed from public funds, but in some countries, for example Egypt, India, Malaysia, Peru and the Philippines, the private sector also plays a significant role and there are private institutions of higher education. They are privately financed but receive a substantial subsidy from the State. In Egypt there are twelve State universities and one private university. In India, besides the State universities there is a large number of private institutions of higher education offering their own diplomas. In Peru there are private universities. The Philippines has a very important private sector, with 707 private institutions and only 291 public ones, as of 1981. The private institutions consist of 46 universities, 490 colleges and 171 technical and professional institutions. They meet the educational needs of almost 85 per cent of all students enrolled in higher education in the Philippines.

In spite of the predominance of the State in the financing and organization of most higher education, the universities and institutes have academic and administrative freedom in almost all these countries. They enjoy a large degree of autonomy in academic matters, internal administration and staff recruitment. In Malaysia, however, higher education is more controlled by the State and more centralized.

There are special councils or other academic bodies which take care of the administration and co-ordination of the institutes of higher education. In Egypt, this role is played by the Supreme Council of Universities, chaired by the Minister of Education and consisting of the President and the Vice-President of each university, a Dean and five external members who are competent in university matters. It also has no less than sixteen committees, each responsible for a particular discipline, as well as committees on equivalence and cultural relations.

In India, there is the University Grants Commission, which was set up by an Act of Parliament as an autonomous body. It has the central responsibility at the national level for promoting and co-ordinating university education, maintaining academic standards and allocating and disbursing government grants to the universities. The universities are autonomous. The Executive Council or Syndicate and the Academic Council of each university are responsible for academic and other internal matters. The Association of Indian Universities provides liaison between universities, the central government, and other organizations.

In Indonesia, the Directorate General of Higher Education has the authority to co-ordinate both State and private institutions. There are eleven consortia which draw up a minimum curriculum in each field of study.

In Pakistan, the activities of the universities are co-ordinated by the University Grants Commission. This body examines the financial needs of the universities, prepares five-year development programmes, grants credits to the universities, monitors the use of funds, collects information on all questions concerning higher education, and makes recommendations to the universities concerning necessary measures for the improvement of higher education in Pakistan. The Syndicate and the Academic Council of each university are responsible for internal administrative and academic matters.

In Peru, the National Council of the Peruvian University is the governing body which co-ordinates national activities. There are also councils for co-ordination at the regional level. The universities are autonomous in academic, financial and staff recruitment matters.

In the Philippines, all the institutions are under the direct control of the State and must have the approval of the Ministry of Education and Culture. The control of private higher education is exercised by a Board of Trustees, the members of which are elected or appointed by the stockholders in stock corporations and foundations or by a Bishop of a congregation for religious institutions. The Board is responsible for formulating the general policies of the institution, the management, the approval of academic programmes and the awarding of degrees.

In Tanzania, the University of Dar es Salaam is governed by a council which includes members appointed by the government, representatives of the graduates and academic staff, and the political party. The university is funded mainly by government grants but is autonomous in its operation.

In PDR Yemen, the University is run by the Council of Higher Education, which consists of representatives of various economic sectors, the party, the students and the teachers. This council is responsible for executing the educational policy of the party and also for planning educational programmes.

In Zambia, the highest administrative body is a council which consists of representatives of the governement, graduates, teachers and outside agencies. The highest academic body is the Senate, which is comprised of deans and directors of schools, departments and institutes, and the representatives of teachers and students.

Countries in this group in general have both universities and specialized institutions for professional and technical training, and they award degrees and diplomas of higher education. Some countries have developed non-traditional institutions such as open universities, vocational courses, short-cycle programmes of study, or evening and correspondence courses.

In Egypt, as we have seen, there are 12 State universities and one private university. In addition to these, there are institutions of professional and technical training, of which some are affiliated to universities and others are private. They offer diplomas equivalent to those obtained at the universities. There is also a system of short-cycle higher education offered in various training centres affiliated to the higher technical institutes. These offer professional training in the industrial, commercial and agricultural fields. Specialized institutes such as the Institute of National Planning, the Higher Institute of Public Health and the Institute of Higher Arabic Studies offer instruction to students already holding university or higher education diplomas. Teachers of secondary schools are trained in the faculties of education in the universities and higher teacher-training colleges, while teachers for the preparatory and secondary industrial and technical schools are trained in the Higher Institute of Industrial Education. The Higher Institutes of Physical Education, Art, Music and Domestic Sciences offer programmes leading to diplomas in these fields. Egyptian universities are divided into faculties offering courses for diplomas in higher education, which in their turn often have affiliated institutes in which teaching is more specialized.

In India, higher education is offered in universities, polytechnic colleges, private institutions and various other institutions established under the authority of different government agencies. The universities are generally established by Acts of State Legislature, except in the case of the central universities, which are established by an Act of Parliament. Besides the universities, there are (a) institutions 'of national importance', declared as such by an Act of Parliament and (b) other institutes 'deemed to be universities', which provide instruction at a specialized level. The universities in India are of three categories: (1) affiliated, where some teaching work, especially at the post-graduate level, is undertaken by the university; (2) unitary, where all teaching and research is provided by the university itself; and (3) federal, where they are normally situated in major cities and have a number of university or constituent colleges associated with their work. Most of the teaching in the affiliated type of universities is done at the colleges affiliated to them, and the universities serve as the examining bodies. Some of the institutions offer correspondence and part-time courses for students who are employed. The Polytechnic Colleges offer professional courses of short duration. Teacher training is provided by some of the universities. Many universities are adopting regional languages as the medium of teaching, in order to promote greater participation in higher education.

In Indonesia, higher education is provided by both private and State institutions, consisting of universities, institutes, academies, and higher teacher-training institutes (IKIPS). The Institute of Technology in Bandung and Surabaya, the Agricultural Institute of Bogor and the IKIPS are State institutions of university status.

In Malaysia, the universities work under the faculty structure and provide instruction in most major disciplines in the arts, the sciences and the professional categories. The National University emphasizes arts-based programmes and medicine. The Malaysian University of Science in Penang is science-based but also offers courses in education, the humanities, and social sciences. The University of Agriculture provides courses mainly in agriculture but also in business studies and education. The University of Technology is engineering-based. In addition there are a large number of teacher-training institutions, polytechnics, and the Mara Institute of Technology.

In Pakistan, higher education is offered in universities, technical universities and their constituent or affiliated colleges. The university structure is one of faculties and departments. Some of them specialize in engineering or agriculture. There is also an open university, offering courses by means of long-distance learning systems; these are open to individuals who are employed.

In Peru, higher education is offered in both public and private universities which comprise academic departments (*departamentos académicos*) and academic programmes (*programas académicos*). The academic departments constitute operational modules of research, teaching and preparation for the professions. Academic programmes consist of functional courses offered by various departments which are co-ordinated to achieve specific goals in the academic, professional or training fields. Some universities specialize in technical and agricultural fields, as well as training teachers for all levels of education. The General Law of Education of 1972 established vocational higher education institutions (ESEPS) offering courses for six to eight semesters leading to professional qualifications.

In the Philippines since 1981, higher education has been offered, as we have seen, by 291 public institutions and 707 private institutions. Among the public institutions, there are 48 universities and chartered colleges, 108 technical institutions and 96 professional and technical institutions. The 707 private institutions consist of 46 universities, 490 colleges and 171 technical and professional institutions.

In Tanzania, higher education is provided by the University of Dar es Salaam and various institutes and colleges. There are five agricultural colleges and one technical college, as well as institutes offering courses in development management, financial management, estate management, urban and regional planning, fisheries, forestry, civil engineering and other subjects. The professional institutes offer post-secondary education, most of them awarding their own diplomas, and they operate in close co-operation with the relevant ministries of the government in developing their academic programmes.

In PDR Yemen, higher education is offered mainly through the University of Aden, which is administered through a faculty structure. Since 1982 the university has had six faculties: education, economy, agriculture, technology, medicine and law. The country has not yet developed its post-graduate and scientific research base.

In Zambia, higher education is provided by the University of Zambia and other specialized institutes. The university is divided into schools for agricultural sciences, education, engineering, the humanities and social sciences, law, medicine and natural sciences. At the university, there are also schools of extra-mural studies and correspondence studies, as well as an Institute for African Studies, a Rural Development and Studies Bureau, an Educational Research Bureau and an Institute for Human Relations. The specialized institutions are the College of Applied Art and Commercial Studies, the Technical College, the College for the Development of National Resources, the Institute of Public Administration, the Institute of Technology, and an Institute of Art Science Training. The University of Zambia also offers training for teachers at secondary levels. Its Ndola campus has two schools, one for business and industrial studies, the other for environmental studies. In addition, several research institutes under the auspices of different ministries carry out scientific research in agriculture and mining. There is also a national council for scientific research under the chairmanship of the Prime Minister.

To summarize, it is observed that countries having moderately favourable relationships between higher education and employment have widely varied organizational structures of higher education which are linked in varying degrees to the overall planning strategy of the country. At one extreme are countries like India and the Philippines where the linkage is minimal; on the other, there are countries like PDR Yemen and Tanzania, where the development of higher education is strictly related to the overall development strategy of the country, particularly in manpower development.

The control of higher education varies accordingly. One important characteristic is that ministries other than education are increasing their role in the development of higher education, particularly in programmes oriented towards the development of natural resources. Post-graduate and research programmes are also increasing. More and more countries are providing higher education through distance-learning systems and continuing education programmes. Except in the case of the Philippines, the government is the most important source of funding for higher education. The private control of higher education varies from a very high degree in the Philippines, to almost none in Tanzania and PDR Yemen. Another factor to note is the larger number of short-cycle programmes, particularly in technical fields. With the exception of Tanzania, higher education in these countries has not made use of the enterprises to relate itself to the world of work to any significant degree. Finally, an increasing participation of students and outside agencies is observed in the decision-making process of higher education.

Third group of countries

The higher education systems of the seven countries in this group (Bangladesh, Benin, Botswana, Mali, Nepal, Sri Lanka and the Sudan) are in the process of developing. Higher education is offered in universities and specialized institutes, and the State plays an important role in the organization and financing of it.

In the People's Republic of Bangladesh, higher education is provided by six universities which have a faculty structure and, in some cases, a number of institutes. Three of the universities are of affiliating nature, determining the courses of study and conducting examinations at the undergraduate level and offering teaching courses at the post-graduate level. The remaining three concentrate on teaching. In addition to the universities, there are several institutes of higher education, namely, the Bangladesh Agricultural Institute, the Chittagong Polytechnic Institute, the Dhaka Polytechnic Institute, the Institute of Leather Technology, and the Institute of Post-Graduate Medicine and Research.

In the People's Republic of Benin there is one university, the National University of Benin, one Higher Polytechnic College, and the national institutes of physical education and sport, law, administration, economy and agronomy, and the National School of Social Workers.

In Botswana higher education is provided by the University of Botswana and in institutes associated with it, such as the National Institute of Development and Cultural Research. In addition, there is the Botswana Agricultural College. The university has faculties of economic and social studies, education, humanities and science. The faculty of education provides in-service and pre-service training for secondary school teachers.

In Mali, there is as yet no university, but higher education is offered in five national schools and two institutes. These are as follows: the School of Practical Higher Studies; the National Schools of Administration, Engineering, Medicine and Dentistry, and Higher Teacher Training (including the

Centre of Higher Pedagogical Studies); the Institute of Productivity, Management and Forecasts; and the Rural Polytechnic Institute of Katiboryon. In addition, there are research institutes in the fields of agriculture, health, forestry and mines.

In Nepal, higher education is available on 71 campuses, all under the direction of the Tribhuvan University. The university consists of ten institutes and four research centres.

In Sri Lanka, higher education is offered at the universities of Colombo, Jaffna, Kelaniya, Moratuwa, Paradeniya, and Sri Jaye Wardenpura and the university colleges of Batticaloa and Ruhuna. There is also an open university and some specialized institutions which provide technical and professional education, and teacher training.

In the Sudan, higher education is offered in five universities and eight institutions of professional education. Attached to the universities are the faculties, graduate colleges and institutes. One of the institutions of professional education is for women only and is run on a private basis.

The systems of administration and finance of higher education   In all seven countries, the universities and other institutes of higher education are mostly financed by the governments. In Botswana and the Sudan, students receive an 'out-of-pocket' allowance, irrespective of their economic background. In Bangladesh, private colleges are partially financed by the government.

In the countries of this group, the government plays an important role in the administration of the universities.

In Bangladesh, administrative matters are controlled by the government or the local bodies. All the universities are autonomous but the statutes are subject to the sanction of the government. A University Grants Commission, constituted by the government, allocates the financial resources to the universities. The Association of the Universities of Bangladesh co-ordinates the activities of the different universities in academic and administrative fields. There is a standing Committee of Vice-Chancellors which maintains the liaison between the government and the University Grants Committee.

In Benin, all institutes of higher education are under State control and are overseen by the Directorate General of Higher Education, in the Ministry of Higher Education.

In Botswana, although the university is controlled by the State, officially it enjoys the status of intellectual autonomy. There is a University Council, in which the government is represented by the permanent secretaries of the Ministries of Education, Finance and Development Planning, but the university has its own Senate (the academic authority of the university) which is controlled by the University Council.

In Mali, higher education is controlled by the State.

In Nepal, the university is financed by the State but enjoys an autonomous status. It is run by a Vice-Chancellor with the help of a Senate and an Academic Council. Research centres and other institutes also have a large degree of autonomy.

In Sri Lanka, the University Grants Commission co-ordinates the activities of the different universities, maintains academic standards and allocates resources to the universities, each of which is run by a Vice-Chancellor. The university colleges are administered by Directors. Some of the specialized institutes are autonomous, others are dependent entirely on the State. The programmes of the institutes are co-ordinated by the relevant ministries.

In the Sudan, the State universities and some of the institutes are co-ordinated by the National Council for Higher Education, which formulates the national policies for education, academic studies and staff recruitment. A Higher Education Grants Committee is responsible for the allocation of resources to the universities. In the Sudan, higher education is the responsibility of the Ministry of Education and other ministries.

To summarize, higher education in this category of countries is still expanding. Some countries like Mali do not yet have universities. The planning mechanism is often poor, owing either to the absence of national development planning or to the lack of institutional infrastructure with an information base. Higher education is often heavily financed by the State (including provision of out-of-pocket allowances in some countries); it is also controlled by the State (except in Bangladesh, Sri Lanka and the Sudan). We should add that, except in the case of Bangladesh and Sri Lanka, it also depends heavily on foreign institutions.

Certain new trends are to be noted, especially the regionalization of higher education, the diversification of programmes towards natural resource development and scientific and technological development, and the distribution of responsibilities among different ministries (with a co-ordination mechanism). Another significant trend is the increasing number of programmes in non-traditional forms, such as the open university, and education and training closely related to practical applications, with courses organized under the sponsorship of ministries other than education, and of public and private enterprises. These courses are open to people who missed the chance of pursuing traditional higher education, and they often lead to degrees or diplomas which are recognized on the employment market.

The access policy, duration of studies and credentials

First group of countries

Access policy In this group of countries, access to higher education is based on performance at the secondary school level and entrance examinations.

The duration of secondary school education varies from ten to thirteen years. In the USSR, secondary school education is generally of ten years duration except in certain fields of study where the completion of twelve years of specialized secondary education with some work experience is required. In Poland, it is of twelve to thirteen years duration, in France and the Federal Republic of Germany, twelve and thirteen years respectively.

In France, Poland and the Federal Republic of Germany an additional prerequisite for entrance into higher education may be a competitive entrance examination. In France, examinations are essential for entry into the elitest 'Grandes Ecoles' and for professional studies such as medicine, pharmacy and dentistry.

In Poland and the USSR, the socio-economic background of the student plays an important role in admission policy: in both these countries precedence is given to students who belong to the families of workers and peasants or who come from small towns and villages.

Practical training or work experience of varying duration may also be a requirement for entrance into higher education. This is the case in some subjects of a technical nature in countries like the Federal Republic of Germany, the USSR and Poland.

Duration and credit system　Higher education has been divided into three stages in France, the Federal Republic of Germany and the USSR. In Poland, however, there are only two stages.

In France, the first stage (cycle) lasts for two years and leads to the award of the *Diplôme d'études universitaires générales* (DEUG). French universities also offer short courses in technology at the University Technological Institutes (IUT), which lead to a variety of diplomas such as the *Diplôme universitaire de technologie* or the *Brevet de technicien supérieur* (BTS). They also offer certain other professionally oriented short courses. The second stage or cycle aims at providing advanced scientific training and leads to the *licence* after one year and the *maîtrise* after two years. In certain fields, such as architecture, fine arts, engineering, medical sciences and agriculture, the duration of studies has no bearing on the awarding of diplomas. Training for secondary school teaching requires a competitive examination after the *maîtrise*. The third stage or cycle involves a higher degree of specialization, with training in the techniques of research. This stage leads to various diplomas which can take from one to five or more years to obtain. After one year, the *Diplôme d'études supérieures specialisées* (DESS) or a *Diplôme d'études approfondies* (DEA) are obtainable. These diplomas are generally prerequisites for the *Docteur ingénieur* and *Doctorat de troisième cycle*, and are awarded after the submission and public defence of a thesis, which requires two to three years of research work. The *Doctorat d'Etat* is awarded for scientific research of a higher order which may take five or more years, depending on the topic. University teaching appointments are subject to a competitive examination, the *aggrégation*, which takes place after the *Doctorat d'Etat*. The studies at the third stage have been restructured. In the new system, which came into effect in 1984, the duration of preparations for the *Diplôme d'études approfondies* (DEA) is still one year and there is only one type of doctoral degree (*diplôme de doctorat*), awarded for a thesis based on research of a higher order which may take two to four years.

In the Federal Republic of Germany, there are also three stages in the higher education system. The first is devoted to the study of general subjects for a period of four or five semesters. This stage leads to an intermediate examination called the *Vorprüfung* or *Vordiplom* in most subjects, or the *Zwischenprüfung* in the arts. In medicine, this stage corresponds to the first cycle of practical studies. The second stage leads to a terminal examination, called the *Staatsexamen* (State Examination), or to a university examination offering a diploma (*diplom*), *Magister Artium*, or a qualification awarded by the State. The duration of the course is from four to six years (even in the case of medicine). The State examinations are compulsory for professions such as medicine, pharmacy, law and teaching at both primary and secondary levels. The third stage is of varying duration and it leads to a doctorate degree after a thesis is presented and an examination, the *Rigorosum*, is passed. This can lead to a further qualification called the *Habilitation*, which is a requirement for teachers of higher education and is awarded to candidates who have a doctorate, pass a special examination and submit a thesis.

In Poland, there are two stages in higher education. The main stage varies according to the discipline but normally lasts for four or five years, and six years in the case of medical sciences, fine arts, drama and music. The first two or three years are devoted to general studies and the next two or three to specialization leading to the qualification of 'Magister'. The students of engineering and technology obtain the qualification *Inzynier* after four years and that of *Magister Inzynier* after five years. In the medical sciences the corresponding qualification is the *lekarz*. In some cases, training for medical graduates is supplemented by hospital practice or by apprenticeship in the case of legal students. The second stage offers doctoral study programmes which last three to five years. The degree is awarded to candidates who submit a thesis based on original research and pass two *doktorat* examinations. The highest qualification is the *Doktor Habibitowany*, which requires a further three or four years research.

In the USSR, higher education in most disciplines is of five years duration, but in the case of medicine it is six years plus one year of internship. This programme leads to the diploma of higher education in the related field of study. The next stage, known as the *aspirantura* requires at least three years of post-diploma study and research, and leads to the higher degree of *Kandidat nauk* (Candidate of the Sciences), after the presentation and defence of a thesis. The final stage leads to the highest academic qualification awarded in the USSR, called the *Doktor Nauk*

(Doctor of Sciences), requiring at least two years further research (in most cases it takes longer) and awarded for a valuable contribution to knowledge or its application, and presentation and defence of a thesis.

In summary, access to higher education in this group of countries is based primarily on academic performance at the secondary school level, which is of twelve or thirteen years, duration, except in the case of the USSR, where it is usually ten years. In Poland and the USSR, socio-economic factors play a role in admission policy, and admission is based on a competitive entrance examination. The number of students admitted is determined by the manpower development plan.

There are three stages of higher education in each of these countries, except Poland which has only two stages. The first stage is of intermediate level in France and the Federal Republic of Germany, giving a general background, whereas in Poland and the USSR this stage leads to a profession. Duration of this stage is normally two years in France and in the Federal Republic of Germany, but in Poland and the USSR it is from four to five years. The second stage is most important in France and the FRG, leading to a professional degree, whereas in Poland and the USSR it leads to further specialization, oriented towards research. The third stage in all these countries involves research. The duration of studies in medicine is longest in all these countries and is normally seven years.

Second group of countries

Access policy   In the countries of this group, access to higher education is mainly based on completion of secondary education. The duration of secondary schooling is eleven or twelve years in most of these countries, except in Peru, where it is nine years, the Philippines where it is ten years, Tanzania, where it is thirteen years, and PDR Yemen, where it is normally twelve years but thirteen in technical, commercial and agricultural subjects. Generally there is no entrance examination, but in Egypt, Indonesia and India a competitive entrance examination is required in some cases. In the Philippines, some institutes have their own entrance examinations, and some require interviews and letters of recommendation. In Egypt, some students may register themselves as external students, in which case the regular academic conditions are waived. In India, precedence may be given on the basis of socio-economic background, as in the case of some Indian universities, for example, in which a number of seats are reserved for women and people of lower social strata. In Zambia, the university follows a quota system established jointly by the government and the university for the admissions to the different fields of study. In Zambia and Tanzania, work experience is often an advantage.

Duration and credit system   In this group of countries, the system of higher education is divided into three stages. The first stage normally provides multi-disciplinary and general education. The second stage is somewhat specialized and generally limited to one subject. The third stage is highly specialized and involves research work. There are, however, some differences amongst these countries in the duration of each stage and the diploma or degree awarded at the end of it. In PDR Yemen, higher education has only one stage at present, as post-graduate studies and research are not yet available.

In Egypt, India, Tanzania and Pakistan, the first stage of higher education normally lasts for three years. However, in India and Tanzania, it takes five years to obtain a technical education and only two years to obtain a 'pass degree' in the arts and sciences. In Pakistan, an honours degree is offered after three years. In Indonesia, PDR Yemen, Zambia, the Philippines and Peru, this stage normally lasts for four years, but in the Philippines architecture, engineering, pharmacy and agriculture require five years of study. In Peru, technical subjects such as engineering also require five years of study. In Malaysia, three or four years are required for the humanities, social and natural sciences, and five or six years for medicine, dentistry, etc.

In Egypt the first stage leads to the *baccalauréos* or, for the students of technology, the 'diploma of technicians'.

In India, it leads to a 'bachelor's degree' or a professional diploma in technology and agriculture. The bachelor's degree with honours is also awarded in specific subjects. In law and education, bachelor's degree studies are available only to those who already have a bachelor's degree in science, the humanities or commerce, or a master's degree.

In Indonesia, the first stage leads to a *Sarjana* degree in most studies, except the medical sciences, engineering and teacher training. For teacher training, there are different diplomas requiring one to five years of study.

In Malaysia, the first stage leads either to a diploma (at the university of technology or the university of agriculture) or to a bachelor's degree. Both honours and pass degree courses are offered in the humanities, social sciences and natural sciences.

In Pakistan, the first stage of higher education leads to a bachelor's degree or a professional qualification. In social and natural sciences the bachelor's degree is offered with honours and at pass levels. In engineering a bachelor's degree is offered after four years, and in medicine and architecture after five years. A bachelor's degree in education requires one year's additional study after a bachelor's degree in arts and science. In law a bachelor's degree requires two additional years of study after a first degree. Some professional studies lead to a certificate or a diploma after one or two years.

In the Philippines, the first stage offers an associate's degree in fine arts, commercial studies and agricultural studies, or a bachelor's degree in education, letters, fine arts, law, business management, natural sciences, medicine and similar subjects. Law and medical students must hold a bachelor's degree before going on with studies of the subjects. In medicine the first stage leads to the title of 'doctor' after eight years of study.

In Peru, the first phase of university education, which is considered to be the second stage of higher education, leads to professional qualifications awarded by specialized professional schools and polytechnical institutes or by universities (*licenciaturas* in sociology, engineering, medicine, law and architecture). The title of *licenciado* covers those of *sociólogo* (sociologist), *ingeniero* (engineer), *abogado* (lawyer), *médico* (doctor), etc. Further professional or interdisciplinary studies lead to specialized certificates and diplomas. Another academic degree, which is a university prerogative awarded at this stage of higher education, is the *bachiller académico*.

In Tanzania, the first stage of higher education leads to the bachelor's degree. In shorter courses, a post-secondary certificate or diploma is offered after one, two or three years of study.

In the People's Democratic Republic of Yemen, bachelor of arts and science degrees are offered by the university. In addition, the higher college of education offers two-year diploma courses in education. Professional diplomas are awarded after completion of two-year courses offered by the Aviation Institute, the Irrigation and Mechanical Institute and the Co-operation Institute.

In Zambia, the first stage leads to the award of a bachelor of arts degree or a bachelor of science degree, for studies in social and natural sciences. There are also several diploma and certificate programmes in social work, library studies, teacher training and adult education. In addition, some diploma courses are offered by different ministries, varying from two to four years in duration.

The duration of the second stage of higher education varies in the countries of this group. In most of these countries, including Egypt, India, Malaysia, Indonesia, the Philippines and Zambia, it lasts two years. In Pakistan, it lasts for one year for those who already have a bachelor's degree with honours or for two years for those with a pass degree. In Tanzania, it takes one to three years of study.

The second stage of higher education leads to the awarding of a variety of degrees and diplomas. In Egypt, it leads to the 'magister' degree; in India, either to a master's degree in arts, sciences, commerce, engineering, agriculture, pharmacy, etc. or to a Doctor of Medicine (M.D.) degree or a Master of Surgery (M.S.) Degree. In Malaysia, this stage leads to a master's degree in education, letters, economics, commercial and natural sciences, engineering, agriculture and medicine. In Pakistan, the second stage of higher education leads to a master's degree or to a professional qualification. Some universities offer a Master of Philosophy (M.Phil.) degree, which is between a Master's Degree and a Doctor's Degree and requires one to four years of study and the submission of a thesis. In the Philippines, it may lead to a certificate after one or two years of study or to a master's degree after two years of study with submission of a thesis. In Tanzania, the second stage leads to the master's degree in arts, science, law, engineering and agriculture. Studies for this comprise either the preparation of a dissertation alone or course work as well as a dissertation, depending on the field of study. In Zambia this stage has study programmes offering master's degrees. In Indonesia, it leads to the degree of *Pasca Sarjana* or to a professional qualification in medicine, engineering and pharmacy.

In this group of countries, the third stage of higher education lasts two to four years and normally leads to the awarding of a doctor's degree such as the Ph.D. In PDR Yemen, there is no provision for education at the third stage. In Zambia, a Ph.D. programme is about to be implemented. In all these countries doctor's degrees are awarded on the basis of the presentation and defence of a thesis. In India and Pakistan, there are the degrees of Doctor of Science (D.Sc.) and Doctor of Literature (D.Lit.) for those who carry out further original research specializing in any scientific or arts-based discipline. In Pakistan, there is also the Doctor of Law degree. In Peru, the third stage of higher education is comprised of studies for the *maestría* and the *doctorado*.

In summary, access to higher education in the countries of this group depends mainly on one's performance at the secondary school level. In some cases, entrance examinations, interviews, recommendations, socio-economic background and work experience may also play a role. The duration of studies at the secondary level and the degrees awarded vary widely, but there is less variation in the duration of studies at the higher level, particularly at the second and the third stages. Generally the duration of medical and other scientific studies is longer than that of non-technical subjects. In countries like Tanzania, and to a certain extent PDR Yemen and Zambia, manpower demand plays a role in deciding on the number of places to be made available in particular fields.

Third group of countries

Access policy   In this group of countries access to higher education is based on completion of secondary school or its equivalent. The duration of secondary education, however, varies from country to country. Duration is normally twelve years in Bangladesh, Benin, Botswana, Mali and Sudan, but it is only ten years in Nepal (3 years of primary and 4 years of lower secondary and 3 years of secondary education) and thirteen years in Sri Lanka. At the end of secondary education the 'baccalaureat' is awarded in Benin and Mali. In Botswana the Cambridge Overseas School Certificate is awarded after the passing of an examination prepared in the United Kingdom. In Nepal, Sudan and Bangladesh school-leaving certificates are awarded. In Bangladesh, in some polytechnics a ten-year secondary school certificate also allows students to follow some post-secondary education in certain vocations.

Generally, there are no entrance examinations except in Mali, where a number of institutions require candidates to take a competitive entrance examination. In Sri Lanka, special consideration is given to students coming from educationally disadvantaged groups and districts.

Duration and credit system In the countries of this group, the system of higher education is broadly divided into three stages. However, in Botswana and Mali, the third stage of higher education, i.e., post-graduate studies and research, has yet to be developed, and in Sudan and Nepal doctoral research is not yet developed.

At the end of the first stage, a variety of degrees or diplomas are awarded in these countries. For example, in Bangladesh there are two types of bachelor's degrees: a 'pass degree' after two years and an 'honours degree' after three years. For a bachelor's degree in engineering and agriculture, four years of study are required, whereas in medicine, fine arts and pharmacy five years are required. The Bachelor of Education (B.Ed.) degree is offered after two years of studies after obtaining a B.A. or a B.Sc. degree. There are also B.A. degree courses in education.

In Benin, the first stage of higher education varies in length according to whether it constitutes a terminal phase leading to a professional qualification, or whether it constitutes the first phase of long-term studies. In the first case, a three-year training course is offered; in the second, two years of studies lead to the *Diplôme universitaire d'études littéraires* (DUEL), the *Diplôme universitaire d'études scientifiques* (DUES), the *Diplôme d'études juridiques générales*, or the *Diplôme d'études economiques générales*. During this stage, students acquire basic knowledge.

In Botswana, the first stage of higher education leads to the awarding of the bachelor's degree (B.A. or B.Sc.), which requires four years' study. There are also shorter higher education courses of one or two years' duration which lead to professional qualifications (the Certificate of Business Studies or the Certificate of Statistics).

In Mali, the first stage of studies comprises a three- or four-year course which entails both in-depth study and practical experience. This stage leads to a diploma or a professional qualification as administrator, engineer, secondary teacher, doctor or pharmacist, after five and a half years of study.

In Nepal, the first phase is the certificate level, a two-year programme (except in medicine which takes two and a half to three years).

In Sri Lanka, the first stage leads to a Bachelor's Degree (general) after three years, and a Bachelor's Degree (special) after four years. In medicine it takes five years. For most of the faculties, the Bachelor's Degree may be taken at pass or honours levels. The professional certificates or diplomas are normally awarded after three or four years, but sometimes after only one year. Study is normally full-time, but there is a provision for part-time studies also.

In Sudan, the first stage leads to a Bachelor's Degree, which normally takes four years, except in medicine, where it takes six years, and in architecture, pharmacy and veterinary medicine, where it takes five years. The more specialized bachelor's degree with honours normally requires an additional year of study.

The second stage of higher education in this group of countries leads to a master's degree in Bangladesh, Botswana, Sudan and Sri Lanka, or to a *maîtrise* in Benin. In Bangladesh, this stage offers a master's degree after one year of additional study after an honours degree or two years of additional study after a pass degree. The Master's Degree in Education (M.Ed.) takes one more year after a B.Ed. or two years after a pass or master's degree. The Bachelor's Degree of Law (LL.B.) is taken two years after a first degree. In Benin, this stage lasts usually for two years and leads to the *maîtrise* in science, letters, law and economics. Submission of a thesis is obligatory. The faculty of agricultural sciences offers a six-year course leading to the *Diplôme d'Ingénieur Agronome*. Medical studies last six years (instead of three as before) and lead to the title of *Docteur en Médecine*. In Botswana, the second stage leads, via examinations and the submission of a dissertation, to the Master of Arts Degree (M.A.) or a Master of Science Degree (M.Sc.). In Mali, at the second stage, some post-graduate training is provided at the Centre Pédagogique Supérieur in various fields of studies. In Nepal, the second stage is the 'diploma' level. Normally this lasts for two years, but in law and engineering it lasts for three years and in medicine four. In Sri Lanka, the second stage leads, after one or two years of study (depending on the subject), to a master's degree. Studies are completed with the submission of a dissertation and the taking of written or oral examinations. A higher certificate may be awarded for a period of specialized or continuing studies between the bachelor's degree (or professional qualification) and the master's degree. In Sudan, the second stage leads, after two or three years of study, to the master's degree.

The third stage of higher education is developed only in some of these countries. In Bangladesh it leads to the Doctoral Degree (Ph.D.) and requires at least two years of specialization and individual research presented as a thesis. In Benin, the third stage does not lead to the normal doctoral degree, but to a professional degree in fields such as administration, management, diplomacy or social work. It prepares the students for managerial posts in public and private administration. In Botswana, the third stage of higher education or post-graduate studies and research is yet to be developed. In Mali, this stage leads to a *Doctorat* or to a *Diplôme de docteur ingénieur ès sciences*. These courses are offered at specialized institutes. In Mali, there is no university yet. In Nepal, the third stage does not lead to the normal research-based doctoral degree, but offers a three-year programme of which two years involve course-work and one is spent in the National Development Service (NDS). This programme offers degree-level courses. The NDS programme is an integral part of the degree programme, during which students must stay at an assigned location in the country and perform a particular job. In Sri Lanka, the third stage leads, after a minimum of two years of research work and the submission of a thesis, to the Doctor of Philosophy degree (Ph.D.) or to the Doctor of Medicine degree (M.D.). The doctorate may be started, in some exceptional cases, immediately after obtaining a bachelor's degree with honours. Further research and publication of a work constituting an original and high-level contribution to knowledge may lead to a higher doctor's degree in arts (D.Litt.) or in science (D.Sc.). In Sudan, this stage lasts three years, during which a student does research work and presents a thesis. It leads to the Doctor of Philosophy degree (Ph.D.).

In summary, in the countries of this group, access basically depends on academic performance, except in Sri Lanka where some privilege is given to students coming from disadvantaged areas. In some cases, e.g. Benin and Sri Lanka, special entrance examinations may waive the requirement of high performance in secondary examinations. In most cases, the required period of secondary education is twelve years, except in Nepal where it is ten years and in Sir Landa where it is thirteen years but in the process of being reduced to eleven years.

The duration of studies for a post-secondary certificate varies from one to two years, for a diploma from two to three years, and for a degree from three to four years. In some countries, like Bangladesh, Sri Lanka and Sudan, the bachelor's degree has two levels, pass and honours. In Nepal, the degree programme includes obligatory national development service. In Mali, higher education is offered in non-university institutions. Except in the case of Bangladesh and Sri Lanka, post-graduate studies have yet to be developed in the countries of this group.

Note

1 *International Yearbook of Education*, Volume XXXIV, Paris, Unesco, 1982.

5   The Quantitative Development of Higher Education

In the last chapter we discussed the organizational structure, planning mechanism and admission policy of the higher education system in the countries selected for our study. These features provide the basic framework within which the country concerned attempts to respond to the demand for higher education discussed in Chapter 3. These attempts in their turn have led to the expansion of higher education — a phenomenon which was discussed, together with its consequences, in Chapter 2. In this chapter we discuss the expansion of higher education in more concrete terms. The analysis of this expansion for the selected countries will follow the analysis of the world situation of higher education. First we shall look into the resources available for education.

Allocation of public expenditure on education

Though the growth of the world economy has slowed down, public expenditure on education as a percentage of gross national product has increased in all continents during the period 1970–1980, as is noted in the following table.

Table 1:   Public expenditure on education as percentage of GNP

	1970	1980
World total	5.4	5.7
Africa	4.1	4.6
America	6.3	6.5
Asia	3.5	5.0
Europe	5.2	5.6
Oceania	4.4	5.9

Source: Statistical Yearbook, Paris, Unesco, 1983.

Although the growth of the percentage slowed down in the later part of the seventies, all continents except for Europe and Oceania registered an increase in the percentage of gross national product spent on education. This shows that the economic crisis has not reduced the importance of education in the world as a whole. The most important increase in noted for Asia and Oceania (1.5 per cent in each case). The Arab States as a group, however, registered a decrease in the share of educational expenditure in their gross national product during this period, from 5 per cent to 4.7 per cent. This is a striking fact, in view of the economic boom many countries in this region experienced during the period. The growth rate of the GNP must have been too high for allocations to education to keep pace with it. This suggests another characteristic of resource allocations to education: neither economic boom nor recession has influenced the share of allocations in the gross national product significantly. Another striking fact is that allocations for education as a percentage of the gross national product of Africa still lag far behind the world average in the overall development of education.

The intercontinental comparison hides the actual situation of the countries studied. The share of the GNP allocated to public expenditure on education varies significantly from one country to another even in the same continent, as is shown in Table 2. One observes that the countries with a favourable higher education and employment situation devote a larger share of their GNP to public expenditure on education. This varies from 4 per cent in the Federal Republic of Germany to 5.9 per cent in the USSR (where GNP is measured as the net material product). The countries having a moderately favourable higher education and employment situation have a lower share on the whole, and the share is very disparate, ranging from 1.3 per cent in Pakistan to 5.2 per cent in Malaysia. In the countries having the least favourable higher education and employment situation the position is the same as in the second group, though with a wider variation, from 1.1 per cent in Bangladesh to 5.3 per cent in Benin.

Expenditure on higher education has also been widely disparate in the countries under consideration. The developed countries, except for Poland, allocate a smaller share of the education budget to higher education, whereas the developing countries on the whole allocate a larger share. Bangladesh and Nepal, with a very small share of GNP allocated to education, also have the largest percentage of the education budget devoted to higher education. Tanzania and Mali have the lowest level of participation in higher education and thus have good reason to allocate more to this level. Botswana, Sri Lanka, Benin and Zambia also have very low participation rates but their allocations to higher education have remained at less than 20 per cent of their total education budget. On the other hand Egypt, the Philippines and Poland already have strong participation in higher education but continue to allocate larger amounts of money to this level. The participation rate in higher education might lead to policy decisions on the allocation of resources. It is observed in several of the

Table 2: Public expenditure on education and participation rate in higher education

Country	Year	As percentage of GNP	Third level percentage of total	Gross enrolment ratio
Bangladesh	1980	1.1	23.0	3.0
Benin	1978	5.3	18.5	1.0
Botswana	1979	5.8	13.2	1.5
Egypt	1980	2.9	30.9	14.7
France	1980	4.6	16.3	25.5
FR Germany	1979	4.0	14.8	26.4
India	1980	3.0	13.3	8.0
Indonesia	1980	1.9	–	3.0
Malaysia	1980	5.2	12.4	4.1
Mali	1978	4.5	24.6	0.8
Nepal	1980	1.5	35.0	3.1
Pakistan	1980	1.3	19.7	2.5
Peru	1980	3.1	3.1[1]	19.0
Philippines	1980	1.5	22.1	26.1
Poland	1980	4.1	23.6	17.3
PDR Yemen	1980	5.9	11.6	2.0
Sri Lanka	1978	2.8	8.7	2.8
Sudan	1980	4.4	20.7	1.8
Tanzania	1979	4.8	26.7	0.3
Zambia	1980	5.0	18.0	1.5
USSR	1981	5.9	13.6	21.2

1   25.2 per cent of the expenditure is 'not distributed' by levels of education.
Source: Statistical Yearbook, Paris, Unesco, 1983, Tables 4.1 and 4.3.

Table 3: Sources of funds for education in Egypt (percentage of funding)

Source	None (1)	Less than 50% (2)	Less than 100% (3)	100% (4)
Government scholarship	95.0	3.8	1.0	0.2
Government loans	95.3	4.0	0.6	0.1
University scholarship	87.0	9.4	3.2	0.4
Family support	23.5	6.7	22.1	47.5
Personal financing	89.6	6.6	3.1	0.7
Non-government loans	97.9	1.9	0.3	0.0
Other	93.7	4.9	1.1	0.3

Notes: 1.   Funding categories are defined as follows: (1) 0.0 per cent, (2) More than 0.0 but less than 50.0 per cent, (3) 50.0 per cent or more, but less than 100.0 per cent, (4) 100.0 per cent.
    2.   Response irregularities suggest that the figures presented here underestimate the actual contribution of the respective sources of financing.
Source: Egypt study, *op. cit.*, student survey.

countries of our sample that such allocations have not been based on the principle of balanced development at all the levels, since countries with very low participation rates in higher education continue to allocate very small amounts of resources to this area. Similarly, some countries with a very high participation rate continue to allocate large amounts to higher education at the expense of other levels.

In this context, however, one has to remember that public expenditure on education is only a part of overall expenditures and very often these statistics do not include the resources allocated to training provided by other agencies and ministries. Also, in addition to public sector support, higher education is funded to a large extent by the individuals receiving it, especially through their families. To identify the importance of the different sources, we asked the individual students to state the sources of financing for their higher education. The results of these surveys for a few countries are shown in the tables here.

Sources of funds for higher education as indicated by the respondents of the surveys

The most important single source in Egypt was family support. Over 50 per cent of the students sampled depended entirely on family support, and nearly 70 per cent depended for at least half their expenses on family support (see Table 3).

In Zambia, although the largest single source of finance was government bursaries (55 per cent), non-government bursaries funded 25 per cent of the students surveyed. The primary sponsors of non-government bursaries are the mining companies, which funded approximately 14 per cent of the students (see Table 4).

In Botswana the role of the family in funding higher education is much smaller. The government finances more than 95 per cent of higher education. This includes annual tuition fees, accommodation fees, books, transport and even pocket money. The case of Sudan is similar.

The general observation is that for developing countries, non-government sources do play an important role in financing higher education, and the less favourable the relationship is between higher education and employment the greater is the role played by the government in funding higher education. For centrally planned economies, the State is the principal financing source for higher education.

We can conclude that the quantitative development of higher education has depended on the allocation of resources to it, principally by the government, although non-government and private sources played a part.

In the next section we examine the development of higher education around the world in general, and then observe this development in the countries of our sample.

Table 4: Major sources of finance for post-secondary education in Zambia for students of both sexes (absolute numbers and percentages)

Major source of finance		Unknown	Male	Female	Total
			Sex		
Unknown	Number	4	88	85	177
	Total	0.12	2.59	2.50	5.21
	Row	2.26	49.72	48.02	100.00
	Column	9.76	3.59	9.36	5.21
Government bursary	Number	21	1,328	529	1,878
	Total	0.62	39.07	15.56	55.25
	Row	1.12	70.71	28.17	100.00
	Column	51.22	54.20	58.26	55.25
Non-government bursary	Number	13	776	83	872
	Total	0.38	22.83	2.44	25.65
	Row	1.49	88.99	9.52	100.00
	Column	31.71	31.67	9.14	25.65
Family	Number	2	113	76	191
	Total	0.06	3.32	2.24	5.62
	Row	1.05	59.16	39.79	100.00
	Column	4.88	4.61	8.37	5.62
Own efforts	Number	1	145	135	281
	Total	0.03	4.27	3.97	8.27
	Row	0.36	51.60	48.04	100.00
	Column	2.44	5.92	14.87	8.27
Total	Number	41	2,450	908	3,399
	Total	1.21	72.08	26.71	100.00
	Row	1.21	72.08	26.71	100.00
	Column	100.00	100.00	100.00	100.00

Source: Zambia study, *op. cit.*, p. 297.

The development of enrolment in higher education around the world

The development of higher education around the world has followed three different patterns during the 22 years from 1960 to 1982; (1) a period of high growth from 1960 to 1970 (7.9 per cent per year on average), (2) a period of slightly diminishing growth from 1970 to 1975 (7.0 per cent per year on average) and (3) a period of reduced growth from 1975 to 1982 (3.3 per cent per year on average). These three patterns were produced by the different development processes in the developing and industrialized countries of the world (see Table 5). The industrialized countries responded quickly to the demand for higher education in the 1960s, with an average annual growth rate of 8.2 per cent. After 1970 this was sharply reduced, to 5.2 per cent per year from 1970 to 1975, and down to 1.2 per cent per year after 1975. The reason for this reduction in growth rate can be attributed to the following factors: (1) disillusionment about the benefits of higher education, caused by decreased employment opportunities; (2) demographic changes, the effects of the baby boom of the post-war period having diminished; (3) the control of formal higher education by governments in response to economic and employment problems. In developing countries the pattern has been slightly different. The 1960s saw a growth rate of 7 per cent per year, less than that of the developed countries. This was the period when these countries were building the infrastructure for higher education in response to the demand of their people. The period 1970–1975 saw the highest growth rate — 11.7 per cent per year — the result of the expansion of facilities which took place earlier. The development rate decreased during the period 1975–1982 to 7.2 per cent per year. This reduction may be partially explained as follows: (1) having achieved the minimum enrolment, these countries are emphasizing non-quantitative aspects of higher education development; (2) the disillusionment about the economic benefits of higher education, already perceived in industrialized countries, might also have affected the developing countries; (3) the control of formal higher education by governments in response to economic and employment problems.

In the industrialized countries the following trends are observed: in North America, enrolment in higher education has been decreasing in recent years, showing a negative growth rate of −0.2 per cent per year. In Europe, including the USSR, enrolment is still increasing in absolute numbers although at a diminishing rate. In Oceania, enrolment increases followed the same pattern as the developing countries: during the period 1960–1970, they grew at the rate of 7.6 per cent per year, and from 1970 to 1975 the rate of growth increased to 9.7 per cent per year, and then fell again to 2.6 per cent per year during the period 1975–1982. In the developing countries, although all major regions showed the same pattern of development, the Latin American countries had the largest growth in higher education, followed by Africa and Asia. Considered separately, the growth in enrolment in higher education in the Arab States was higher than that of Africa and Asia but lower than that of Latin America and the Caribbean. These continental growth rates are to be read with the state of development of higher education in the base years, which is reflected in the adjusted gross enrolment ratios[1] of the respective continents. It can be observed from Table 5 that the growth rate of the developing countries during the period 1960–1970 was too low in comparison with that of the industrialized countries in the same period, given the fact that the participation rate in higher education in the latter group was 12.8 per cent as against 2 per cent in the former in 1960. During the period 1960–1982, the participation rate increased at a higher rate in the industrialized countries, by 17 percentage points as against 4.3 in the developing countries. This shows that the efforts in the developing countries to expand higher education have been less successful than in the industrialized countries, which already had a substantial base. The small base in the developing countries would have had to have a very high growth rate in order to demonstrate any significant increase in participation.

Increase in the participation rate during the period 1960–1982 was largest in North America (23.1 percentage points) followed by Europe including USSR (13.1 percentage points) and Latin America and the Caribbean (12.7 percentage points). Although Africa had increased its participation rate by five times (from 0.7 per cent to 3.6 per cent) this continent still has the lowest participation rate in higher education. Asia more than doubled its participation rate during the same period, but still has a very low rate. The Arab States as a separate region also experienced a very high increase in participation (from 1.9 per cent to 8.9 per cent). A striking factor in the development of higher education around the world is that the differences in participation rates between developing and industrialized countries have increased over the years (from 10.8 percentage points in 1970 to 23.5 in 1982). Inter-regional differences have likewise increased over the years, as can be seen in Table 5.

One of the results expected from the expansion in higher education is the reduction of inequalities of opportunity in this field. Although the female share of enrolment increased from 32 per cent in 1960 to 41 per cent in 1982 in the world as a whole (see Table 5), this increase has stagnated in recent years. The developing countries have done as well as the industrialized countries in increasing the female share of total higher education enrolment: there are 11 percentage points of increase for both groups during the 1960–1982 period. This means that the difference between the female participation rate in developing and industrialized countries has remained the same during this period. The share has increased from 35 per cent in 1960 to 46 per cent in 1982 in the industrialized countries and from 24 to 35 per cent in the same years in the developing countries. Although the female share in enrolment is still less than the male share in all the regions, the differences have been reduced in all regions to less than 5 percentage points. Significant achievements have been made in the region of Latin America and the Caribbean and that of the Arab States, the latter having made an increase of 29 percentage points in the female share of enrolment over the 22 years. Progress in Asia has been slowest, with 8 percentage points (from 23 per cent in 1960 to 31 per cent in 1982). Africa, which still has the lowest female share of total enrolment (28 per cent), increased its score by 11 percentage points during this period. While the female participation rate measured by gross enrolment ratios (ratio of enrolment with respect to total female population in the relevant age group) increased nearly threefold in the world (from 3.3 percentage points in 1960 to 9.7 per cent in 1982), the

Table 5: *Adjusted gross enrolment ratio¹ at third level by sex and major regions*

Region	Year	Third level² standardized enrolment (thousands)	Enrolment ratio			Third level female enrolment as % of total third level enrolment
			Total	Male	Female	
World	1960	13,185.5	5.1	6.8	3.3	32
	1965	20,185.0	7.3	9.3	5.2	35
	1970	28,189.7	8.5	10.4	6.5	38
	1975	39,470.5	10.2	12.0	8.3	40
	1980	47,643.6	11.2	12.8	9.4	41
	1982	49,587.1	11.5	13.3	9.7	41
Growth rate (%)	1960–1970	7.9				
	1970–1975	7.0				
	1975–1982	3.3				
Developed countries	1960	9,598.6	12.8	16.5	9.1	35
	1965	14,915.5	19.6	24.1	14.9	38
	1970	21,104.9	23.4	27.4	19.3	41
	1975	27,154.0	28.3	31.2	25.4	44
	1980	29,718.8	30.0	31.7	28.2	46
	1982	29,533.0	29.8	31.7	27.9	46
Growth rate (%)	1960–1970	8.2				
	1970–1975	5.2				
	1975–1982	1.2				
Developing countries	1960	3,586.9	2.0	2.9	1.0	24
	1965	5,269.4	2.6	3.8	1.4	26
	1970	7,084.8	2.9	4.1	1.7	29
	1975	12,316.5	4.2	5.7	2.7	31
	1980	17,924.8	5.4	7.1	3.7	34
	1982	20,054.1	6.3	8.0	4.5	35

Africa					
1960	184.8	0.7	1.2	0.3	17
1965	310.5	1.1	1.8	0.4	20
1970	478.5	1.6	2.4	0.7	23
1975	901.5	2.5	3.7	1.2	25
1980	1,366.4	3.2	4.7	1.7	27
1982	1,616.3	3.6	5.1	2.0	28
Growth rate (%)					
1960–1970	7.0				
1970–1975	11.7				
1975–1982	7.2				
Latin America and Caribbean					
1960	572.6	3.0	4.2	1.8	30
1965	913.2	4.2	5.6	2.8	33
1970	1,638.3	6.3	8.0	4.5	35
1975	3,653.6	11.8	13.6	10.0	42
1980	5,156.4	14.3	16.0	12.6	44
1982	6,001.4	15.7	17.2	14.1	45
Growth rate (%)					
1960–1970	11.1				
1970–1975	17.4				
1975–1982	7.3				
North America					
1960	3,778.9	27.9	34.8	20.8	37
1965	5,890.4	34.0	41.2	26.8	39
1970	9,140.1	44.5	51.7	37.2	41
1975	12,003.0	52.5	57.0	47.9	45
1980	12,644.0	53.4	53.7	53.1	49
1982	11,806.1	51.0	52.1	49.9	48
Growth rate (%)					
1960–1970	9.2				
1970–1975	5.6				
1975–1982	−0.2				

Table 5: *Adjusted gross enrolment ratio[1] at third level by sex and major regions (continued)*

Region	Year	Third level[2] standardized enrolment (thousands)	Enrolment ratio			Third level female enrolment as % of total third level enrolment
			Total	Male	Female	
Asia	1960	3,677.2	2.5	3.7	1.2	23
	1965	5,321.8	3.2	4.7	1.7	25
	1970	6,922.2	3.5	4.9	1.9	27
	1975	10,187.9	4.3	6.0	2.5	31
	1980	14,090.6	5.4	7.4	3.4	31
	1982		5.7	7.7	3.6	31
Growth rate (%)	1960–1970	6.5				
	1970–1975	8.0				
	1975–1982	6.1				
Europe and USSR	1960	4,863.3	9.7	12.3	7.2	37
	1965	7,588.5	16.5	19.8	13.1	39
	1970	9,784.3	17.6	19.8	15.3	45
	1975	12,365.2	20.5	21.9	19.0	46
	1980	13,965.9	22.2	23.4	21.0	46
	1982	14,342.3	22.8	23.9	21.6	46
Growth rate (%)	1960–1970	7.2				
	1970–1975	4.8				
	1975–1982	2.1				

Oceania					
1960	108.7	9.9	14.0	5.6	28
1965	160.5	11.4	15.5	7.2	31
1970	226.3	13.9	17.9	9.7	34
1975	359.3	20.0	23.7	16.2	40
1980	420.3	21.1	23.1	18.9	44
1982	431.4	21.2	22.8	19.4	46
Growth rate (%) 1960–1970	7.6				
1970–1975	9.7				
1975–1982	2.6				
Arab States					
1960	163.4	1.9	3.1	0.7	17
1965	296.5	3.2	5.0	1.3	20
1970	443.6	4.2	6.4	2.0	24
1975	871.2	6.9	9.7	3.9	28
1980	1,265.5	8.2	11.2	5.1	44
1982	1,479.4	8.9	11.8	5.9	46
Growth rate (%) 1960–1970	10.5				
1970–1975	14.5				
1975–1982	7.9				

1 The term 'adjusted' indicates that the population groups used in deriving these ratios for a particular region have been obtained by taking into account the organizational structure of education of each country in that region.

2 Figures have been standardized to reflect the structure existing in 1982.

Source: UNESCO, *A Summary Statistical Review of Education in the World: 1960–82*, Paris, July 1984.

developing countries multiplied their score by 4.5 times as against indus-trialized countries which tripled theirs. The region of Latin America and the Caribbean scores highest in this respect in relative terms, having increased female gross enrolment ratio from 1.8 per cent to 14.1 per cent (Table 5). North America has almost equalized the participation rate by bringing the male-female difference down to 2.2 percentage points. Europe including USSR, whose overall participation rate in higher education has been half that in North America has also reduced the gap to 2.3 percentage points. The largest difference is in the Arab States (5.9 percentage points) followed by Asia (4.1 percentage points). It should be noted, however, that the Arab States have increased their female participation rate more than eight times (next is Latin America) while the male participation rate has increased by four times, and the female participant rate in 1982 was higher than in Africa and Asia. In 1960 only 0.7 per cent of the relevant age group was obtaining higher education, and in 1982 this figure had increased to 5.9 per cent.

The development of higher education in the selected countries

It is observed that in the groups of countries with a favourable higher education and employment situation the enrolment growth rate was higher for countries which started with a lower participation rate in the base year (1970). In the USSR, which had the highest participation rate in 1970, there was a decrease during the period 1970–1980, from 25.4 per cent to 21.2 per cent. In the Federal Republic of Germany, which had the lowest participa-tion rate in 1970, the increase was highest during the same period, rising from 13.4 per cent to 27.6 per cent (see Table 6).

In the second group, the phenomenon is different. Although in two countries (Peru and the Philippines) participation rate in the base year was quite high, enrolment continued to grow rapidly. Pakistan and Tanzania, which had low participation rates, still have a very low growth rate in enrolment. Spectacular advances in higher education have been made by PDR Yemen, Zambia and Malaysia, with average annual growth rates of 44 per cent, 20 per cent and 15.2 per cent respectively. PDR Yemen had very little higher education infrastructure (only 91 students) in 1970. The enrolment had increased to 3,500 by 1980.

In the third group of countries enrolment increased more rapidly than in the second group. Except for the Sudan and Bangladesh, all countries experienced an enrolment growth rate of over 10 per cent per year. In this group one can also observe the phenomenon of higher growth in countries which began with a lower base (namely, Mali, Benin and Botswana). The analysis brings out the following interesting findings: (1) Countries which had very little higher education in 1970 made a strong effort to expand their programme. (2) The USSR reduced its participation rate in higher educa-tion. (3) Some of the developing countries continued to allow their higher education programme to expand although they had already achieved a very

Table 6: Growth rate in third-level enrolment and participation rate in higher education in the base year and the current year

Country	Annual growth rate (per cent)	Participation rate	
		1970	1980
France	3	19.5	25.5
FRG	9.3	13.4	27.6
Poland	4	14.0	17.3
USSR	1.3	25.4	21.2
Egypt	8.5	8.0	14.7
India	5.5	6.2	7.5
Indonesia	6.2	2.8	3.3
Malaysia	15.2	1.6	4.1
Pakistan	2.9	2.3	2.0
Peru	9.3	11.0	19.0
Philippines	7.0	19.8	26.1
Tanzania	8.0	0.2	0.3
PDR Yemen	44	0.1	2.4
Zambia	20	0.4	1.5
Bangladesh	7.3	2.1	3.0
Benin	29	0.1	1.0
Botswana	17.9	0.8	1.8
Mali	25	0.2	0.9
Nepal	10.3	2.3	3.1
Sri Lanka	12.9	1.2	2.8
Sudan	7.3	1.2	1.8

Source: Statistical Yearbook, Paris, Unesco, 1983.

high participation rate. This may be due to social pressure. (4) A country like Sri Lanka can have a very high participation rate at primary and secondary level together with a very low participation rate at higher level. However, there has been significant expansion in recent years (13 per cent average annual growth rate from 1970 to 1980).

Another interesting feature of the development of higher education in these countries is that there has been a significant increase in female participation. This is a phenomenon common to all the groups of countries. In the Federal Republic of Germany female enrolment was as low as a quarter of the total enrolment in 1970, and by 1980 this had reached over 40 per cent. Poland had more females than males in higher education in 1980.

Everywhere except in the African countries as a whole and Nepal, female participation has reached more than a quarter of the total enrolment. In Botswana and the Arab States female enrolment has also reached more than a quarter of the total. This increase is phenomenal, given the low female participation that prevailed in 1970. In the other countries, as well, one can see a significant increase in female involvement. In Mali it increased from 77 to 600, in Benin from 23 to 534, in Tanzania from 300 to

700 and in Zambia from 200 to 1,700 during the period from 1970 to 1980. In Botswana, female enrolment is almost equal to male enrolment (though this parity is modified by the fact that a large number of male students go abroad for higher education).

Another characteristic of the development of higher education is the diversification of delivery systems. This phenomenon takes two forms: (1) structure and organization and (2) discipline and content. With regard to structure and organization one can observe an increased number of non-university institutions (including short-cycle, teacher-training and technical higher education) in countries of all types in our sample. Enrolment of this category has increased from 140,000 in France in 1970 to 207,000 in 1980, and in Poland from 67,000 to 135,000 during the same period. Increase in this type of enrolment has also been very significant in Malaysia, the Philippines, Peru and Zambia. In Zambia, for example, it increased from 200 in 1970 to 3,900 in 1980. Since Mali does not yet have any university, its entire higher education programme is undertaken by non-university institutions. Bangladesh has a large enrolment population in non-university institutions (nearly 86 per cent in 1970 and 85 per cent in 1980) most of which are undergraduate colleges. In Sri Lanka this type of higher education proliferated in the 1970s. In Nepal, on the other hand, all higher education is covered by the university.

With regard to discipline and content, one can observe an increasing variety in higher education, especially in the countries of Africa and Asia. For example, in 1970 Mali did not have any students in engineering, whereas in 1979 there were 539. In Botswana there were no students in science and engineering in 1970, and by 1980 there were 238 students in mathematical sciences and engineering, with science students constituting 20 per cent of the total. One can observe a similar phenomenon in Tanzania, which had no engineering students in 1970 whereas in 1980 30 per cent of the higher education student population were studying engineering. Likewise PDR Yemen and Nepal did not have any students in the engineering field in 1970, whereas in 1980 PDR Yemen had 734 students (21 per cent of total) enrolled for engineering and Nepal had 150.

In the developed countries of our sample, the number of specializations was also increasing very rapidly, especially in the area of electronics, bio-engineering, space sciences and communications. There is a notable difference in the development of new disciplines in the Eastern European and the Western industrialized countries: in the former most of the new specializations were being taught in the formal system of higher education (i.e. in the universities) whereas, in the latter, most of them were being developed in the research and development units of the enterprises, with collaboration from the universities.

An analysis of the distribution of enrolment by sex and fields of study supports the hypothesis that arts-based disciplines are more popular with women and science-based disciplines with men. For example, in Benin

Table 7: *Enrolment in third level (in thousands)*

Country	1970				1980			
	University[1]		Total		University[1]		Total	
	MF	F	MF	F	MF	F	MF	F
France	661	–	801	–	870	–	1,077	–
FR Germany	352	89	504	135	1,032	379	1,223	503
Poland	331	140	398	189	454	227	589	328
USSR	–	–	4,581	2,247	–	–	5,235	–
Egypt	213	56	233	62	529	168	–	–
India (2)	–	–	2,903	–	–	–	4,456	1,126
Indonesia (3)	–	–	248	62	–	–	481	–
Malaysia	8.2	2.4	14.0	3.8	26.3	9.1	57.7	22.2
Pakistan	115	25	115	25	154	40	154	40
Peru	109	33	126	43	247	84	306	108
Philippines	–	–	652	362	1,144	613	1,276	681
Tanzania (1)	1.8	0.3	2.0	0.3	3.2	0.6	4.0	0.7
PDR Yemen	0.091	0.025	0.091	0.025	3.5	1.5	3.5	1.5
Zambia (1)	1.2	0.2	1.4	0.2	3.4	0.7	7.3	1.7
Bangladesh	16.5	2.3	118	11	36.5	6.6	240	33
Benin (1)	0.311	0.023	0.311	0.023	2.704	0.490	3.003	0.534
Botswana (1) (4)	0.469	0.152	0.469	0.152	1.052	0.424	1.052	0.424
Mali (1)	0	0	0.731	0.077	0	0	5.281	0.600
Nepal (4)	23.5	–	23.5	–	38.4	7.4	38.4	7.4
Sri Lanka (1)	12.3	5.3	12.3	5.3	26.8	11.1	36.6	14.4
Sudan (4)	12.1	1.5	14.3	1.9	25.2	6.6	27.0	6.9

1 University and equivalent institutions.
(1) The terminal year is 1979 instead of 1980. (2) The terminal year is 1978 instead of 1980. (3) The terminal year is 1981 instead of 1980.
(4) The base year is 1975 instead of 1970.
Source: *Statistical Yearbook*, Paris, Unesco, 1983.

female students in science accounted for only 4 per cent of the total enrolment. In Egypt the corresponding figure was 10 per cent, in Mali 3 per cent, in the Sudan 5 per cent, and in India 6 per cent. The female enrolment in scientific disciplines constitutes only one quarter of the total female enrolment, and 30 per cent of total enrolment (both women and men) in science disciplines.

One can also observe the expansion in sub-Saharan Africa of post-graduate programmes, of which there were very few in the early 1970s. By 1980 Benin had 33 per cent of its third-level enrolment in post-graduate courses, while Egypt had 10 per cent and Tanzania had 12 per cent. The corresponding figures for Bangladesh, India, Malaysia and Nepal were 4 per cent, 7 per cent, 1.3 per cent and 5 per cent respectively. Mali and the Sudan did not yet have any students in post-graduate degree programmes. The industrialized countries have a very high proportion of enrolment at post-graduate level. In 1980, 17 per cent of the third-level enrolment in France was in post-graduate degree programmes. The corresponding figure for Poland was 64 per cent. Strikingly, it was only 1.3 per cent in the Federal Republic of Germany. However, that figure includes only doctoral students. Including the non-doctoral students it rises to 84 per cent.

Another interesting feature of the development of higher education is that the background of the students has become more diversified, which contributes to the democratization of higher education. Our surveys of students and graduates of the different countries demonstrate this. It is observed that the percentage of students from rural and lower socio-economic groups is higher than that found in graduates. For example, in the Sudan, 22 per cent of the graduates of our sample came from peasant families whereas in the case of students the figures was 32 per cent. In Zambia no less than 71 per cent of our student sample came from rural areas.

The graduates of higher education in the selected countries

The analysis of enrolment in higher education leads logically to the analysis of graduation. It is the graduates who figure more directly in the relationship between higher education and employment. This analysis indicates some trends in the development of the higher education system, its output and its effect on the labour market. It can be observed that on the whole the number of graduates increased at a higher rate than enrolment. This is due to the fact that the enrolment in the early 1970s had increased at a higher rate than in the late 1970s as indicated before. Only one country — Sri Lanka — shows a negative growth rate during the period 1971–1979 (see Table 8). It can also be observed that the countries with the least favourable relationship between higher education and employment had a very small number of graduates in the base year but a very high growth

Table 8:   *Number of graduates by fields of study (in thousands)*

Country	1970 Total	1970 Science-based	1980 Total	1980 Science-based	Average annual growth rate total	Science-based
France	102.0[1]	45.0	162.6[7]	77.5	9.7	11.5
FR Germany	63.3	22.3	185.9[5]	85.9[10]	12.7	16.2
Poland	88.8	44.4	117.3	67.0	2.8	4.2
USSR	672.0	341.0	831.2	490.0	2.1	3.7
Egypt	30.9	14.5	80.4	31.8	10.0	8.1
India	368.1[4]	115.0	1,095.7[8]	250.4	11.5	8.1
Indonesia	13.3[1]	4.3	26.7[7]	8.6	14.9	14.9
Malaysia	4.6	1.2	16.7	4.5	13.7	14.1
Pakistan	48.0	10.0	55.1[6]	8.5	2.0	− 2.7
Peru	5.8[1]	2.0	18.5	7.7	13.7	16.2
Philippines	83.0	15.5	189.1[5]	57.1[10]	9.6	15.6
Tanzania	0.529	0.070	0.853[5]	0.313	5.5	18.1
PDR Yemen	0.068[3]	0.0	0.539	0.244	41.0	−
Zambia	0.243	0.033	2.030	0.647	24.0	34.0
Bangladesh	16.3[9]	3.4	27.1	8.0	10.7	18.6
Benin	0.051	0.051	0.834[5]	0.195	36.0	16.0
Botswana	−	−	0.246[5]	0.049	−	−
Mali	0.13[2]	0.047	0.476[5]	0.306	13.8	21.0
Nepal	1.82	0.4	10.4[8]	2.4	21.0	22.0
Sri Lanka	4.11	0.8	3.6[5]	1.1	− 1.6	4.0
Sudan[1]	2.2	0.54	3.9[8]	1.5	8.5	15.9

1   Refers to 1971.
2   Refers to 1969.
3   Refers to 1974.
4   Refers to 1968.
5   Refers to 1979.
6   Refers to 1977.
7   Refers to 1976.
8   Refers to 1978.
9   Refers to 1975.
10   Trade and craft are excluded.
11   Excluding 'others and unspecified'.
Source: *Statistical Yearbook*, Paris, Unesco, various years.

rate, except in the case of Sri Lanka. This extra rapid growth has been a major source of employment problems. One may also note a relatively modest growth rate of graduates in the group of countries which enjoy a favourable relationship between higher education and employment. The growth rate varies from 2.1 per cent in USSR to 12.7 per cent in the Federal Republic of Germany.

The countries with centrally planned economies had the lowest growth rate of graduates. Among the countries with a moderately favourable relationship between higher education and employment, PDR Yemen and Zambia had the highest growth rates of graduates. This is because they had a very small higher education infrastructure in the early 1970s and had to turn out large numbers of graduates to meet high-level manpower needs. In this group Pakistan stands out with a very low growth rate in the number of graduates.

Another interesting characteristic of graduation patterns is the higher growth in science graduates than in the graduate population as a whole. Except for the countries where higher education had a long history (India, Pakistan and Egypt) they all had a higher growth rate of science graduates. Benin is another exception where there were no arts graduates at all in 1970 but some in 1979. Benin actually reduced its growth rate of science graduates. The generally increased growth rates of science graduates show that the countries concerned are oriented towards technological development and therefore trying to increase the share of science graduates in the labour market. Even so, the share of science graduates in the total graduate population is less than that of arts graduates except in the centrally planned economies. In most countries science graduates are less than 40 per cent of the total and in Pakistan they were 15 per cent in 1977 (the latest year for which such data for this country were available).

Summary of findings

The above analysis shows that public expenditure on education has been either increased or maintained at the same percentage of the gross national product in most of the countries around the world during the last decade, in spite of the economic recession. Higher education has taken a disproportionately large share of expenditures in developing countries, but public expenditure on education as a whole receives a smaller share of the GNP in these countries, particularly in Africa. It is also important to note that the private sector plays an important role in financing higher education, which further increases the disparity.

Enrolment in higher education is decreasing in North America in absolute terms. The growth rates in Africa, Asia, Latin America and the Caribbean, and Oceania were higher during the period 1970–1975 than during the period 1960–1970. The growth rates decreased between 1975 and 1982. In North America and Europe the growth rates decreased during all three of these periods consistently.

Female enrolment has almost reached parity with male enrolment in North America, Europe, Oceania and Latin America. The female share of enrolment is lowest in Africa. The Arab States as a group have overtaken the Asian countries in the female share of total enrolment.

The difference in the participation rate in higher education between developing and industrialized countries has increased over time. It rose from 10.8 per cent in 1960 to 23.5 per cent in 1982. Interregional differences have also increased. Of the countries in our study, it is noted that those which had a low participation rate in 1970 generally had a higher growth rate in enrolment during the 1970–1980 period. However, Peru and the Philippines continued to have higher growth rates despite the fact that they had a larger base in 1970.

The delivery of higher education has gone through many modifications during the last decade. An increasing number of countries are adopting new structures such as short-cycle higher education, open higher education, etc. The number of disciplines being taught in many African countries has increased significantly during the last decade. Programmes in science-based disciplines are on the increase, but the majority of female students enrol in liberal arts disciplines.

The higher education student population of the late 1970s and early 1980s has a more diversified socio-economic background. More rural youth than before are receiving higher education. The development of students graduating follows a different pattern from that of enrolment. During the period 1970–1980, the number of graduates grew faster than enrolment, which indicates a growth of enrolment prior to 1970. A striking feature is the higher growth rate among graduates in science-based fields in almost all the countries of our sample.

The above gives some idea of the quantitative development of higher education in the countries selected for our study, within the context of worldwide trends. What goes on within the system in these countries is the subject of the following chapter.

Note

1   Gross enrolment ratio is the ratio of students enrolled in higher education with respect to the total population in the relevant age group, expressed in percentages. See footnote for Table 5 for the term 'adjusted'.

6   The Operation of the Higher Education System

In the two preceding chapters we described the organizational mechanism of higher education and its quantitative development. The extent to which this infrastructure is effective in the context of a particular country is the subject of analysis in this chapter. We shall study the following aspects of the question: (i) the role of career guidance, (ii) mobility in education, and (iii) degree of satisfaction with the content and methods of higher education as perceived by students, graduates and employers, and the proposed delivery system of education.

The role of career guidance

The two main approaches to educational planning are based respectively on social demand and manpower demand, and have often been seen by the educational planners as conflicting. The social demand approach is said to be the one which emphasizes the individual demand for higher education and the manpower demand approach is said to be the one which meets the economic needs of the society. It is usually thought that a free-market economy emphasizes the first and a controlled economy emphasizes the second. We believe, however, that the two approaches are complementary, in that economic needs are, or can be, dictated by individual demands for goods and services, which would include comfort, leisure and security. We also believe that individual demands for higher education are, or can be, based on the social and economic needs of the country, and that these needs are reflected in the return that one would obtain from such an education. For these realities to take effect, however, a good information mechanism is necessary. This mechanism would inform students about the different kinds of education needed for the social and economic development of the country and the return they could expect from following a particular kind of education. This return need not always be expressed in monetary terms but can indicate other values, such as job satisfaction, job security, prestige, and the service a job renders to the country. This information mechanism can go a little further and inform students, through an analysis of their mental and physical characteristics, which type of education and subsequent career would suit them best. This mechanism is an essential component of the career guidance programme prevailing in many education systems.

This approach involves the accumulation, display and utilization of educational and vocational information for the purpose of assisting students to make the right decision in their choice of an educational career. Wahib I. Samaan lists the objectives of a career information system as follows:[1]

1   Developing student interests in the world of work and in the many activities used by people for living.
2   Stimulating students to give careful consideration to the many educational and vocational possibilities open to them.
3   Providing experiences and a wholesome atmosphere by which healthy attitudes of respect for all kinds of useful work are developed.
4   Helping students make wise choices in educational experiences, by which personal development may be enhanced and adequate preparation realized for future experience.
5   Providing information about the many opportunities open to young people in various colleges and universities among which choices may be made.
6   Providing a continuous programme of experience which is well integrated with the university programme, and which provides strength and continuity for the total educational process.
7   Keeping to a minimum frustration and indecisiveness, and eliminating wasteful trial-and-error approaches to decision-making.
8   Improving the self-understanding of young people, from which a greater appreciation for other people may emerge.

The information service is thus an essential part of the overall career guidance programme which, if properly organized, should include an appraisal of individual students, a counselling service to provide the student with the best opportunity for self-study, decision-making, planning and dealing with any personal problems, and a placement and follow-up service.

To examine the choice of post-secondary institutions in the different countries of our sample, the following questions are asked: (i) What are the available sources of career information for students with different backgrounds? (ii) How helpful has this information been in choosing a field of study for different types of students? (iii) If the service was not satisfactory, could it be organized better, so as to lead the student to a different course of study?

The sources of career information were identified as follows: (1) the staff of educational institutions at the next level down, including career counsellors, where they existed; (2) friends, parents and relatives; (3) peer groups; (4) previous employment, if any; (5) other general information sources, such as books, newspapers, or radio.

The importance of each of these sources varies from country to country. In the countries of the first group of our study, however, it was difficult to identify this difference. All these sources played an important role, except of course No. 4, for those who did not have previous employment experience and took advantage of other sources. The students of rural origin and poorer home background depend more heavily on the staff of educational institutions and other general information sources. In Poland and the USSR one can observe attempts to orient the students towards areas where there are needs for manpower. In France and the Federal Republic of Germany, an organized career information system is generally lacking. In the Federal Republic, however, secondary school students receive a monthly magazine, free of charge, informing them about educational career possibilities, but it has been observed that official information on the labour market has not been used to direct individual decisions on educational careers.[2]

In the countries with a moderately favourable higher education and employment situation (Group 2), career information facilities are worse. Although countries like Zambia and India have the services of career masters in the schools their performance has been unsatisfactory because their preoccupation was with teaching rather than counselling. In these countries, sources of career information varied substantially with the socio-economic background of the students. Parents and relatives were the most important source for students of higher socio-economic status, whereas school staff were an important source of information for all types of students. For students of lower socio-economic status, school staff were the most important source of information, followed by general information sources.

In the least favoured countries (Group 3) career information systems are virtually non-existent. Informal sources like parents, friends and relations are the most important source, followed by general information and school staff.

The degree of satisfaction with career advice also varied from country to country. In general, students of the most favoured countries, including those with planned economies, expect more from the State in the way of career information. In the second category of countries, although career information is less organized, the degree of satisfaction with what is available seems to be high. In the Philippines and Zambia, the percentages of students who are satisfied with their career information are 95 per cent and 59 per cent respectively. This high degree of satisfaction may reflect lack of knowledge about the potential benefits of organized career information.

Among the least favoured countries, Botswana stands out with the highest degree of dissatisfaction among students with the availability of career information: three out of four students there are not satisfied with the available information on courses. One can observe the same phenomenon in countries like Mali, Nepal, Bangladesh and Sri Lanka.

Several interesting findings emerge from our analysis of the adequacy of career information. These are as follows:

1 Where they are available, parents, friends and relatives are the best source of career information with regard to the quality of the information they supply.

2 The satisfaction with the course of study followed by the student is positively correlated with the degree of satisfaction with the career information received.

3 Willingness to change the field of study is inversely associated with the degree of satisfaction with career information. In Zambia, for example, only 1 per cent of students who had access to career information would have changed their fields of study if better information had been available. The corresponding figure for those who did not receive information was 39 per cent.[3]

4 Irrespective of the development status of a country, career information deserves a lot more attention, if students are to make better educational decisions.

Mobility in education

A certain amount of change takes place during the course of a student's education. It can occur either in the transition between secondary and higher education or during the period of higher education itself. In measuring these changes aggregation is a problem. For example, if a secondary school student wants to become a medical doctor, fails to get a place and is admitted to veterinary medicine instead, there is a difference between expectation and achievement unless medicine and veterinary medicine are aggregated in one category covering all medical professions. But if they are aggregated no mobility can be measured. In our analysis, mobility is measured by the shifts made from one aggregate field of study to another.

First group of countries

In the first category of countries mobility has not been measured, owing to lack of data, but one can see from the determinants of demand for higher education, discussed above, that a certain amount of mobility did occur.

It was due to academic performance, proximity of institutions offering different courses, and financial factors. For example in Poland, a large number of students wished to study fine arts but only one out of three could do so.[4] In France the 'Grandes Ecoles' are the most sought after institutions but very few can gain admission to them. In the Soviet Union likewise, a large number of male students wishing to study engineering had to move to other fields because of lack of places, and a large number of female students had to change from medicine.[5] In the Federal Republic of Germany in the year 1976/77 a large number of students desiring to study dentistry had to move to other fields.[6]

Second group of countries

The data on mobility for the countries of the second category were collected through surveys. Mobility was slight in the Philippines where 82 per cent of the students were pursuing the courses of their choice. In Egypt, on the other hand, more than 50 per cent of the sampled students were studying in a field different from the one they had wanted at the completion of the secondary school. These changes varied greatly from field to field. Slightly less than 50 per cent of the students studying social sciences and the humanities were in fields different from their choice, and more than 70 per cent of those studying technology had chosen different fields. Women showed greater mobility than men. Women in social sciences and humanities were more likely than men to be studying in the field they desired, but women studying science and medicine were less likely than men to be studying in the field they had originally preferred.

The picture shown in Table 1 is put in sharper focus in Table 2, where mobility is reported for each of the 21 educational categories. It can be seen that some specific fields of study appear to represent second choice fields, in the sense that most students had desired a different field at the end of their secondary schooling. Examples are advanced health, archaeology, technology, and mining and petroleum, where more than 70 per cent of the students had originally wanted to study another subject. In arts, law, sciences, medicine, chemistry, and some other fields, fewer than 50 per cent of the students had wanted to study a different field. In some fields, there were great differences between men and women. For instance, more than 70 per cent of the men studying commerce had wanted to study a different field at the end of their secondary schooling, but of the women studying commerce, only 36 per cent had wanted to study a different field. Half of the men but 74 per cent of the women studying advanced health had desired a different field.

Reasons for these changes between the completion of secondary schooling and current studies are not easy to find. Although the question was asked, no clear picture emerged.

Table 1: *Difference between desired field of study and current field of study in Egypt (percentages)*

Field	Men	Women	Total
Social science and humanities	52.2	44.8	49.2
Science and medicine	48.0	55.1	50.7
Engineering	55.5	67.5	58.9
Technology	65.6	77.8	70.5
Agriculture	53.3	69.2	58.3
Other	66.0	69.0	67.4
Total	53.5	56.0	54.5

Note: Calculated as the percentage of persons in each field of study who had wanted to enter another field at the end of secondary school.

Source: Egypt study, *op. cit.*, p. 140.

Table 2: *Differences between desired field of study and current field of study for 21 fields in Egypt (percentages)[1,2]*

Field	Men	Women	Total
Arts	35.2	25.8	31.0
Law	39.3	56.7	45.1
Economy and political science	55.7	55.9	55.8
Commerce	71.4	36.0	56.7
Sciences	47.3	46.2	46.6
Medicine	45.1	50.0	46.4
Advanced health	50.0	74.3	73.0
Dentistry	70.6	60.0	64.9
Chemistry	54.5	33.3	45.9
Architecture	46.0	50.0	47.4
Agronomy	53.3	69.2	58.3
Veterinary medicine	38.9	66.7	42.9
Archaeology	73.7	82.4	77.8
Education	72.8	63.3	69.5
Technology	72.1	82.5	76.4
Fine arts	81.2	100.0	85.0
Applied arts	41.7	42.9	42.1
Social affairs	10.0	33.3	22.7
Cotton technology	37.5	25.0	35.0
Mining and petroleum	66.7	80.0	75.0
Other	70.5	77.8	73.8

Notes: 1.   Calculated as the percentages of persons in each field of study who had wanted to enter a different field at the completion of secondary schooling.
2.   Results not reported where the total number of cases in a field is less than 10.

Source: Egypt study, *op. cit.*, p. 141.

Striking differences also appear in India, as is seen in the West Bengal study. Of the 10.3 per cent of all students who had chosen the medical profession on completing their school education, only 2.6 per cent actually studied medicine. Similarly, more students wished to study engineering than could actually do so. On the other hand, 4.3 per cent of the students studied technology although originally only 3.2 per cent had intended to do so. Other contrasts include 117 law students, only 9 of whom had chosen this subject on leaving school, and 318 commerce students, only 222 of whom had chosen this subject.

Table 3: *Distribution of students according to course intended to follow after Class VIII examination and course currently being followed in West Bengal (numbers and percentages)*

Course being followed	Course intended after Class VIII		
	Identical	*Different*	*Total*
Natural science	115 (85.2)	20 (14.8)	135
Biological science	37 (69.8)	16 (30.2)	53
Social science	281 (68.0)	132 (32.0)	413
Medicine	47 (95.9)	2 (4.1)	49
Engineering	188 (92.6)	15 (7.4)	203
Technology	77 (95.1)	4 (4.9)	81
Agriculture	10 (90.9)	1 (9.1)	11
Management	37 (84.1)	7 (15.9)	44
Law	79 (68.1)	37 (31.9)	116
Commerce	233 (73.0)	86 (27.0)	319
Language	20 (80.0)	5 (20.0)	25
Arts	196 (76.6)	60 (23.4)	256
Science	130 (87.8)	18 (12.2)	148
Education	23 (71.9)	9 (28.1)	32
Total	1,473 (78.1)	412 (21.9)	1,885

Source: West Bengal study, *op. cit.*, p. 127.

In Tanzania, nearly one out of six students changed fields during their course of studies. The most frequently cited reasons for such changes were academic failure or lack of proper course information when it was needed. In the analysis of the data it was observed that one out of every five students who changed because of lack of proper information had cited 'career masters' as their source of information. This might reflect the ineffectiveness of the programme of 'career masters' in Tanzania.

In Zambia, one out of four students had changed fields during their educational career. Here also the reason for change was lack of proper career information. In this country the distribution by age of students who changed courses appears to be the product of two factors: (1) the amount of general information one has about a career, a course, or oneself increases with age, and (2) the opportunity to change one's career, and the range of alternative careers effectively available, decrease with age.

In Indonesia, about one tenth of the students changed their fields of study in our sample. Dislike of the course and lack of proper information in time are cited as the most important reasons for these changes.

Third group of countries

A striking example in this group is the Sudan, where 61 per cent of the students were studying a subject they had not chosen at the time of their admission to higher education. The amount was almost the same (59 per cent) in the case of the graduates. In this country academic requirements was the most frequently cited reason for such shifts, and financial reasons were cited as the next most important.

In Botswana, 20 per cent of the sampled students changed their field of study from their first choice. The most important reason for this change was academic inadequacy, followed by lack of proper career information in time.

It can be observed that mobility within the education system is quite significant in these countries, varying from 10 per cent in Indonesia to over 60 per cent in the Sudan. This is one of the least studied areas in any analysis of education and employment as yet, but its importance cannot be ignored in planning education for employment purposes, because of its direct relationship with the supply of high-level manpower. It should be remembered, however, that whatever the perfection of an education system may be, it is not possible to prevent changes of field during the course of a student's educational career. In fact, a certain amount of mobility among the different fields of studies is desirable, so that if a bad choice is made at the time of admission, corrective action can be applied later. If sufficient information is available, it is possible for the planner to take such mobility into account, so as to adjust intakes to different specializations.

Degree of satisfaction with education and the preferred arrangement for making education more responsive to the world of work

Educated individuals are never satisfied. They want to have things better and do them better. This discontent is essential if any system is to improve. No system is perfect. Therefore, it is useful to find the extent of this discontent and identify possible improvements as perceived by the social groups concerned — in our case, the students, the graduates and the employers.

First group of countries

In these countries the performance of the education system has been estimated for specific disciplines, but it also provides some indication of the overall quality of education offered by the country. Some concern in the Soviet Union is being caused by the small degree of satisfaction graduates were able to find in the system. It is observed in our survey that only 63 per cent of the engineering graduates were satisfied with the type of instruction they had received. Similarly, in industry as a whole 62.8 per cent of the respondents were satisfied with their work, as against 27.3 per cent who were downright dissatisfied and 9.9 per cent who were indifferent.[7]

In the Federal Republic of Germany the economics graduates felt the need for social skills to be taught in the training system, in addition to the emphasis on leadership qualities, planning, decision-making and computer skills. The engineering graduates estimated that they had acquired 75 per cent of the knowledge they needed of mathematics and science during their education, but only 50 per cent of the engineering knowledge they needed and 20 per cent of their non-technical skills.[8] The engineering curricula, according to this survey, should incorporate more elements of the social aspects of the role of engineers.

In Poland, in a more general survey, the majority of the students (54 per cent) assessed the quality of their instruction as good and a small number (8 per cent) as very good. Twenty per cent of the students, however, had an unfavourable opinion of their lecturers. Favourable opinions of academic staff are more often expressed in universities and medical academies than in polytechnics. The training organization as a whole (combination of lecturer, seminars, tutorials, laboratory work and workshop training), however, had a lower rate of appreciation. This report stressed that the task of higher education was not only to impart knowledge to students and turn out specialists for the country's economic development, but also to shape proper social and ethical foundations in the student community and prepare them for the part they would play in society, depending on the job they subsequently took. Professional efficiency is seen here not only as a matter of qualifications, but also as certain 'behavioural' abilities to deal effectively with concrete professional and social situations. According to various investigations,[9] effectiveness at work often depends less on specialized knowledge than on the 'behaviour' of graduates in their work, and the expectations of those with whom they come into contact. Lack of success in one's chosen profession, loss of self-confidence, and unsatisfactory relationships are usually caused by inability to apply one's acquired proficiencies, or by an unco-operative attitude towards others. Graduates are often unprepared, at first, to step into the required roles of subordinate, superior or partner in an employment community. They have no experience of making decisions, obeying orders or taking the initiative, and they are often unable to adopt a friendly approach without at the same time becoming disrespectful towards their superiors. This inability to fit into a work role is frequently connected with a lack of personal strengths, such as punctuality, self-discipline, perseverance, a sense of responsibility, etc.

The difficulty in preparing a graduate for a role in society stems from the fact that a school cannot foresee where and at what level his skills may be applied, or what his position will be in the social or job hierarchy. For instance, will a student studying engineering become a foreman, a director, a research worker or an office clerk? Will he work in a factory, a design office or a ministry? The narrow scope for individually shaped instructional processes together with the wide variety of future employment situations and, above all, the virtual impossibility of forecasting the individual student's job options, all help to explain why the university cannot adequately prepare its students for their future roles in life. This difficulty is aggravated by the students' own inability to grasp, both in professional and social terms, the character of the jobs they are hoping for.

In the opinion of J. Szczepanski, 'The internal conflict of school up-bringing is that in its desire to mould the pupil according to its own best standards and prepare him for future life, it creates an environment which is remote from real conditions, imparts an idealistic concept of life and working conditions; then, when the pupil goes out into the real world, he finds that what the school had taught him is of very limited application, and that he is even less prepared for fitting into community life.' [10]

In the search for a way out of this contradiction, while still giving students the best possible preparation for their future duties, it is planned to give them a chance to connect their studies directly to productive activities in addition to continually refining teaching methods, and linking school life more and more to the real developmental process. By taking part in productive work a student gains a direct and valuable foretaste of his future duties and of the environment he is likely to encounter. Short periods of work, even if they are unrelated to future employment positions, are worthwhile from this point of view. They dispel idealistic dreams of working life and thus lessen the danger of disillusionment. They help students form a more realistic view of life, and anticipate experiences and confrontations which they would otherwise encounter all at once on leaving school.

For these reasons productive work has been included in many higher education programmes and activities in Poland. During the last three decades it has assumed various structural reforms, and undergone a series of changes. In 1969, training activities of one month's duration were introduced for first-year students. At present, they take place before the beginning of the first year. This training has resulted in the growth of the importance of productive work in the teaching process of higher education. Apart from its other advantages, the students' working experience fulfils both an economic function, by involving young people in the economic development of the country, and an instructional objective, by enlarging their experience of community life.

At the present time, there are two parallel forms of students' work practice: professional and manual.[11] Although they are the most wide-spread, these are not the only ways in which students come into contact with practical work. A large part is also played by paid jobs undertaken by students, and voluntary social work of a productive nature performed within the framework of student organizations. Although each of these forms of practical training accustoms students to work, each plays a different part in their development and makes a different contribution to their character formation.

A new, non-traditional form of 'education through work' is shortly to be introduced, of which the first examples can already be observed in Polish academic institutions, and promises to be a great success in the future: commissioned research work, which provides an opportunity to enrich the teaching processes on the one hand, while at the same time giving the student some measure of career pre-orientation.

Second group of countries

The situation is somewhat different in our second group of countries, where the degree of satisfaction with courses is high. For example, in the Philippines 73 per cent of the students thought their course was satisfactory in meeting career objectives, and 70 per cent felt that it met their personal interests as well. However, only 49 per cent of the graduates surveyed felt that the content and method of instruction had been adequate. The graduates also observed that non-formal (on the job, out of school) training was essential to making education more responsive to the world of work, but as a supplement to formal education, not a substitute. They suggested that formal education programmes interspersed with work-related programmes would make education more responsive to the changing needs of the world of work.

In Egypt, 60 per cent of the employers indicated that the graduates lacked the training needed for the job they had been recruited to. One of the reasons they gave was the lack of co-ordination between the universities and the employing agencies. Some 15 per cent of the graduates indicated that the education they had received was neither necessary for the job nor useful for it (see Tables 4 and 5). As for the preferred arrangement, the most popular one among the students and graduates was 'Recurrent education', i.e. formal education with interludes of work experience. Nearly half of the employers preferred such an arrangement. Students also preferred having work experience as a requisite for studies, but graduates were somewhat less favourable and employers still less so. The most popular arrangement for employers was for teachers to provide

Table 4:   Problems faced in establishing compatibility between levels of studies and employment requirements in Egypt

Problem	Per cent who report problem
No links between university studies and employment prerequisites	38.2
Graduates lack required training	60.7
Good academic performance does not mean good job performance	44.4
Jobs are too complex for precise specification of educational requirements	12.4
Other	0.2

Source: Egypt study, *op. cit.,* p. 163.

Table 5:   Necessity and utility of education in the job in Egypt

Problem	Necessity (%)	Utility (%)
Not necessary/useful	15.7	14.13
Necessary/useful	16.2	21.9
Very necessary/useful	68.0	63.8
Total	100.0	100.0

Note: Owing to rounding off, totals do not equal exactly 100 per cent.
Source: Egypt study, *op. cit.,* p. 164.

Table 6:   Preference for arrangements for making education more responsive to the world of work in Egypt

Arrangement	Per cent preferring		
	Students	Graduates	Employers
Education and work separate	13.1	17.5	19.0
Recurrent education	61.6	48.9	47.3
Work experience as prerequisite	54.8	38.4	21.7
Teachers do practical work	52.1	40.1	63.1
Practical work for diploma	–	–	49.0

Note: The figures show the percentages of respondents ranking the given item first or second.
Source: Egypt study, *op. cit.,* p. 166.

practical experience, and the least popular one was having education and work separate (see Table 6).

In the State of West Bengal in India, only 14 per cent of the employed graduates felt that their training was irrelevant for their job, and 20 per cent thought that the education they had was not necessary for obtaining their job. This probably indicates that they were employed in jobs needing lower academic qualifications.[12] The graduates who suffered most were those of languages, bioscience, and natural science. With respect to the arrangement of education, the first choice of students was that of allowing teachers to refresh their knowledge with related field experience. They also preferred a system incorporating formal education programmes with related work experience. Among the employed graduates of different occupational categories, the sandwich course pattern was preferred by respondents employed as accountants, managers, medical workers, engineers and scientists. The teachers and clerks preferred the arrangement of allowing teachers to gain adequate field experience. Technologists preferred the arrangement by which work experience would be a requirement for certification, and agricultural workers preferred work experience to be a requirement for entry into higher education. Both students and graduates found the arrangement of educational programmes completely set apart from related work programmes to be the least satisfactory.[13]

In Indonesia, satisfaction with higher education was almost 100 per cent on the part of students and graduates. According to both groups, practical job experience during educational career would make education more responsive to the world of work.

In Tanzania also, the overall degree of satisfaction with the courses followed by the students was very high, at 93 per cent, though the degree of satisfaction in the faculty of arts of the University of Dar es Salaam was only 50 per cent. In this country it was noted that the degree of satisfaction with a course was associated positively with lack of choice of courses and with the adequacy of the secondary school education institution attended (the Forestry Institute was rated best, Iringa College of National Education worst). Satisfaction was also linked positively to adequacy of career advice received and to the higher age group of respondents.

In Tanzania 61 per cent of the graduates surveyed thought that their choice of career depended on their success in their studies. Ninety-three per cent of them found the training they had received necessary for getting their job and 96 per cent found the training useful for performing the tasks on the job. These figures seem to indicate the effectiveness of the education system. In this country work experience has already been introduced as a prerequisite for higher education. Moreover, each institution and faculty is making work experience a prerequisite for certification.

In Zambia the figures on relevance of education were almost the same as in Tanzania, with only 2 per cent of the graduates stating that the education they had received was not useful or necessary for their present job. However, the job performance of university graduates was ranked lowest by government and private employers but highest by the parastatal organizations, perhaps because the latter are very heavily manned by recent university graduates of the best quality. The employers in Zambia would like to see institutions of higher education develop new training programmes related to the changing needs of the country and carry out research projects related to employers' needs. The employers also feel the need for sandwich courses for the students and would be willing to co-operate in arranging them.

Third group of countries

The degree of satisfaction with the educational programmes and the preferred arrangement for education was also the subject of analysis in the countries with the least favourable relationship between higher education and employment. In the Sudan, 22 per cent of the students were dissatisfied with the courses they were following. Males, younger students and those in fields that were their second and third choice were more dissatisfied than the females and older students. Interestingly, adequacy of career information did not have any impact on the degree of satisfaction with courses in this case. Among the employed graduates, only 5 per cent thought that the education they had received was irrelevant to their jobs. Eleven per cent of those in the education sector found their training irrelevant to their job. Eight per cent of the graduates of less than 25 years of age also found their training irrelevant. It is thought that in the Sudan a better interaction among the educational institutions and employment agencies makes education more responsive to the world of work.

In Sri Lanka the majority of students thought that their university education had not been a waste of time, and only 14.9 per cent were not sure about this. However, 36.9 per cent were dissatisfied with what they had learnt, mainly because they felt they had not gained enough knowledge from their courses, but also because it had given them no job opportunities or practical skills. Inadequate knowledge of English and inadequate course content were also cited as causes of dissatisfaction.

Insufficient knowledge of the subject was the main cause of dissatisfaction among students of economics, general arts and education, but science students were mostly dissatisfied with the practical skills they had acquired at university. They also cited irrelevance to the needs of the country, insufficient knowledge of the subject or of English, 'does not promote creativity', 'is not intellectually challenging' and 'uninteresting'.

In terms of subjects, there was dissatisfaction with the Combined and General Arts course in all five of the universities, as well as with the general science courses. This is probably because of the poor employment opportunities and inadequate content these courses offer.

Only 69.3 per cent of the students answered the question on what improvements they would suggest for their courses. Of these, 44.3 per cent wanted more practical content and 23.3 per cent broader knowledge of the subject.

Revision of course content to meet national needs was recommended in all main subjects, as well as the need for practical experience, though the latter was not stressed in general and combined arts. The main suggestions for improvements in teaching involved the inclusion of techniques for increasing practical know-how, such as first-hand experience, use of audiovisual aids and research programmes.

For all courses combined, 32.5 per cent of the students felt that an exchange of academic and non-academic staff at the university would help supplement theoretical knowledge with practical experience and 21.9 per cent of the arts students felt that such exchanges would improve their knowledge of employment conditions. Those who disapproved of such an arrangement did so mainly because they felt it would cause confusion and burden the curriculum with inappropriate or irrelevant material.

In Botswana an examination of the students' responses on the preferred arrangement bring outs the following points:

- 80.9 per cent of the students felt that related field-work experience should be a requirement for teachers. In fact this always had been an important requirement in all higher education institutions concerned with teacher education.
- 51.8 per cent of the respondents felt it was very important that formal educational programmes should be interspersed with related work experience. An issue of crucial importance here was the amount of time that could profitably be devoted to this kind of work experience without lengthening the period of training.
- Formal educational programmes interspersed with related work experience (each year spent in an educational programme to be followed by an equivalent year of related work experience) was rated low by 63.8 per cent of the respondents. This is an indication of the students' unwillingness to spend what they consider to be an unduly long period in training. Quite clearly, over 50 per cent of the students regarded related work experience as an essential element of their training, but on the other hand, to implement this arrangement on an equal basis was not acceptable to them.
- The degree of importance of related work experience as a prerequisite for entrance into higher education was very low; 9.9 per cent of the students regarded such experience as 'very important', while 69.8 per cent considered it to be unimportant.
- It must be observed here that, in general, the students rated the need for relevant work experience highly, but any suggestion that such field-work experience should delay their graduation was unacceptable.
- 65.4 per cent of the students regarded related work experience as a requirement for graduation from a post-secondary institution as being unimportant while only 2.3 per cent considered it to be very

important. It is worth noting, however, that 85.3 per cent of those who rated this kind of work experience highly and would accept it as a prerequisite for graduation were pursuing studies of a professional nature, such as teaching, nursing, agriculture, law and engineering.

In summary then, it may be postulated that over 50 per cent of the students in Botswana regarded it as very important that educational programmes should be planned to provide related work experience during the period of training.

In Botswana, the degree of satisfaction among the students with their educational programmes was very high; 91 per cent of them thought that their training was meeting career objectives and 98 per cent thought that the training met with their personal interests. There was a difference in degree of satisfaction between students and graduates: 71.2 per cent of the graduates in education were happy with their training but 41 per cent of the scientists and 67 per cent of the humanities graduates felt that they had not had any specific training for their job. Twenty-five per cent of the graduates in Botswana thought that their qualification was not necessary for getting their job and the degree of correspondence between academic performance and performance on the job was observed to be lowest for those with a university first degree (47 per cent of the employers thought that there was no correspondence).

Some concluding remarks

The above analysis gives an idea of the functioning of the education system as perceived by the students, graduates and employers. It can be noted that the degree of the students' satisfaction with the course is higher in the least favoured countries, a paradoxical situation. It may be due to the fact that higher education is still in a developing stage and expectations are not yet high among the students. However, one can have a more realistic appreciation of its adequacy from the perception of the graduates and the reactions of the employers. It should be noted, however, that the question of satisfaction involves many factors. The major factors contributing to it may be subjective in nature, and hence cannot fully describe the state of affairs pertaining to the demands of the personnel specializing in different faculties, and other relevant aspects of the question. Satisfaction, being a state of mind, depends on the dimension of aspiration and the degree of disillusionment that follows. This helps to explain the differences in the degree of satisfaction among different groups.

Regarding the preferred arrangement of the educational delivery system, in every country of all three groups the alienation of education from practical work has been criticized. The incorporation of work experience in the formal training programme emerges as the most preferred arrangement. It has also been observed that out-of-school training cannot replace formal training but can supplement it. What was very interesting to note was the preference for teachers to be allowed time for practical field experience — a suggestion which has not been very much talked about in the literature.

Notes

1   SAMAAN, W., *Guidance and Counselling at the Higher Education Level in East Africa*, Paris, Unesco, 1974, p. 17. (Mimeo.)
2   FRG study, *op. cit.*, p. 112.
3   Zambia study, *op. cit.*, p. 165.
4   Poland study, *op. cit.*, p. 165.
5   USSR study, *op. cit.*, p. 102.
6   FRG study, *op. cit.*, p. 72.
7   CHUPRUNOV, D., *et al.*, *Enseignement Supérieur, Emploi et Progrès Technique en URSS*, Paris, Unesco, 1982, p. 112.
8   FRG study, *op. cit.*, p. 103.
9   Poland study, *op. cit.*, pp. 167–168.
10 SZCZEPANSKI, J., *Socjologiczne Zagadnienie Wyzszego Wyksztalcenia*, Warsaw, 1963, p. 187.
11 Manual practice consists of a month of general manual work by freshmen in industry and agriculture and has a stronger 'social' orientation; professional practice involves senior students in various industrial jobs directly connected with the type of education they have been pursuing.
12 West Bengal study, *op. cit.*, Tables 11.4 and 11.5.
13 West Bengal study, *op. cit.*, pp. 211–215.

7 Transition from the World of Higher Education to the World of Work

In the previous chapter we discussed the functioning of the higher education system as perceived by students, graduates and employers, with special reference to its responsiveness to the world of work. One objective of this research programme was to find ways and means of making a student's transition from the education system to the world of work easier. A diagnostic analysis of the system of higher education provides a basis on which to analyse this transition. We have already discussed the role of educational career guidance, which is in some ways related to occupational guidance, and therefore will only refer to it briefly here, in so far as it relates to the choice of an occupation. In this chapter we shall discuss the placement services available for the graduate job seekers, the methods of recruitment practised by the employers, the waiting period for first employment, and the gap between the type of education obtained and the type of education needed for the occupation actually held by the graduate.

Professional counselling and placement of graduates

In the first group of countries we had more detailed information on the Federal Republic of Germany and Poland on the transition of graduates in the world of work. We shall therefore look mainly at those two countries.

In the Federal Republic in the early 1970s, government and other official agencies made special efforts to establish an efficient system of information, counselling and placement in the area of higher education. The increasing numbers of students, the debate about possible future mismatches of demand and supply for highly qualified manpower, and the difficulties of students, especially those whose parents had not attended colleges, to cope with the existing informal information and placement system, necessitated far-reaching changes. A few years later the rising unemployment further emphasized the need for such efforts.

Until the 1960s there was little in the way of a systematic employment information service for students. Some information and advice was available from local employment offices but most students relied mainly on family, friends and teachers. Most secondary school leavers had a profession in mind before enrolling for higher education,[1] and placement was achieved through individual search on their part, and advertisement on the part of the employers. Although a Federal Employment Agency has existed in the Federal Republic since 1952, its regional and local employment offices expanded only gradually.

During the 1960s the counselling services for more academic students were improved, and in 1971 co-operation between schools and employment agencies was officially announced by the government. This arrangement stressed the responsibility of the schools to inform their students on working life, and of the employment agencies to find them places.[2]

The latter extended their activities to institutions of higher education,[3] and their services now include monthly and annual publications for students, as well as lectures and counselling. Career counselling and placement has become an important profession in itself in the Federal Republic. Virtually all secondary school leavers are now contacted by the public counselling and placement system. During the academic year of 1976/77, 129,000 secondary school leavers received individual counselling, and these represent only 16 per cent of the total number who received counselling during that year.[4]

A survey of fourth-year students shows that they are quite well informed on the labour market for graduates.[5] In the case of highly qualified manpower, however, the public employment system plays a much smaller role in placing them in jobs. The data in Table 1 show some of the factors involved. Probably not more than 10 per cent of the placement of highly qualified students in jobs is handled through the public employment services.

Table 1: Employment status and placement of highly qualified manpower as compared to total labour force, 1977 (in thousands)

	Higher qualified manpower	All levels of education
Labour force	c. 1,900	26,855
Persons newly registered as job searchers	43	4,241
Placement through employment offices	10	2,290
Recent school leavers/graduates	c. 100	c. 1,100
Unemployed (annual average)	40	911

Source: Estimates on labour force based on statistics of Statistisches Bundesamt; for the data on unemployment see Manfred Tessaring, 'Über den Beruf?' *UNI*, No. 7–8, 1979, p. 27; for job search and placement see Bundesanstalt für Arbeit, *Fachvermittlung: Arbeitsmarktbeobachtung im Bereich besonders qualifizierter Berufe im 2. Halbjahr 1977*, Nürnberg, 1978, p. 1; Bundesanstalt für Arbeit, *Daten Fakten 78*, Nürnberg, 1978, pp. 10–11.

In general, the guidance and placement services available at colleges are considered to be still far from sufficient. According to the Federal State Commission for Educational Planning and Research Promotion (BLK), there was only one guidance counsellor for every 1,500 students at colleges in 1975. The Commission called for a ratio of one to 500 by 1985. Furthermore, the ratio of college students to career counsellors in employment offices was about 5,000:1 in 1976, and was not expected to change significantly in the foreseeable future.[6]

There has been some discussion as to whether it was desirable to have a split between the personal counselling and study courses provided by the colleges on the one hand, and the career counselling and placement provided by the public employment system on the other, but there have been no moves to change this pattern. The Federal Employment Agency intends to improve the placement of graduates through more decentralization of its specialized personnel, and the use of a centralized computer-based information system on job openings and job seekers.

Career guidance, in principle, is a suitable instrument for adjusting expectations and choice of educational careers to the estimated manpower demand. As concern about the over-supply of graduates has become widespread in the Federal Republic of Germany, and as the Constitution guarantees the right of any qualified person to enrol at institutions of higher education, career guidance could be seen as the major tool for adjustment. However, the Federal Employment Agency does not discourage youth from choosing college education. Its publications, especially those written by members of the Institute for Labour Market and Occupational Research, have often been criticized for giving an over-optimistic view of career prospects for graduates and for encouraging youth to choose higher levels of education.[7]

Altogether, it seems fair to say that the official information on the labour market has not been used to influence individual choices on education and career with considerations of manpower planning. On the other hand, it fails to give a clear picture of the hardships in store for many young people. Caution seems to dominate guidance in higher education, aiming since recently to lower career expectations rather than to discourage enrolment at institutions of higher education. The official publications offer only limited information about the process of placement and recruitment itself and the criteria of the employers. Apart from some essays in the monthly magazines mentioned above, the students have to rely primarily on manuals sold by private publishers, statements made in the media, and rumours.

Employment policy in modern Poland has developed in four main phases: 1950–1956, 1956–1964, 1964–1980, and 1980 onwards.

In the first phase, 1950–1956, graduate courses were shortened to three years in response to the absolute shortage of qualified manpower, and an Act of Planned Employment was passed in 1950 to make the best use possible of graduates. This system was abandoned in 1956 because other methods, largely non-administrative, had begun to supersede it.

In 1956 an employment exchange system was adopted to help graduates find jobs. Incentives were introduced to ensure that important posts were filled, through study grants and other financial assistance from the State, local authorities, industries and banks. Firms offering scholarships 20 to 30 per cent higher than those provided by the State made them conditional on taking employment with them on graduation.

This incentive system did not adequately distribute the qualified personnel, however, and major geographical and occupational imbalances developed. In Warsaw, for instance, there were 94 graduates for every 1,000 employed people, while in some provinces there were only 20. Similarly, doctors and economists were relatively plentiful in Warsaw and in short supply or lacking altogether in the provinces. By 1964 education, science and culture had 31 per cent of the graduates and manufacturing had less than 20 per cent. Forestry, agriculture and housing all had less than 2 per cent each of the graduates.

The Act of 1964 was designed to correct these distortions through a 'planned graduate employment system'.[8] It obliged graduates of certain disciplines to take employment for a specified period (usually three years) in a State or co-operative enterprise. Polytechnical, medical and economic specializations, as well as most of the arts and science-based subjects, including, for instance, philology, law and geophysics, all came under the Act. Thus 80 per cent of Poland's graduates of daytime courses were subject to this arrangement, though exemptions were granted for disablement, military service and some teaching and research responsibilities.

The Act obliged employers to accept graduates with the required qualifications and graduates to accept employment in the prescribed post for the specified period. Employers who failed to comply could be fined, and graduates who failed to do so could be required to reimburse their education costs. In this system the distribution of graduates is mainly the responsibility of the Ministry of Employment, Salaries and Social Affairs. This body draws up five-year plans for the allocation of graduates, directing their placement annually and updating the lists of firms authorized to offer grants. The allocation of graduates from agricultural, medical and teacher-training establishments is the responsibility of the ministries concerned, though their plans must be approved by the State Planning Committee. Within the framework of the five-year plan, annual job placement programmes co-ordinate the supply of graduates with the employers' demand for them.

To implement the centrally formulated policy, the Ministry of Employment, Salaries and Social Affairs has delegates attached to each higher education institution. Their responsibilities include providing students with employment information, implementing graduate placement plans, directing graduates to suitable vacancies, and ensuring satisfactory co-operation with the enterprises. They also work with the provincial authorities to ensure that obligations are fulfilled. Within the teaching institutions the delegates are assisted by a consultative committee which consists of a head of the institution and appropriate faculties, plus a representative of the Socialist Union of Polish Students (SZSP). This committee provides advice and rules on decisions contested by the students.

The planned employment of graduates is organized through three main arrangements. The first of these is sponsored grants, which offer 20 to 30 per cent more than the regular State scholarship. The employer under this system is also obliged to provide the students concerned with housing assistance. The second is the pre-engagement agreement between students in their final or penultimate year and enterprises. The third is directed placement, by which placement orders are issued to students during their last three months of study. Although the second two measures were designed only to supplement the first, the proportion of graduates employed through sponsored grants has decreased considerably, while directed placement has increased correspondingly. Table 2 shows how this progressed from 1964 to 1974. The decline of sponsored grant placement was due partly to an increase in the value of State scholarships.

To evaluate the graduate employment system, two methods were proposed, one focused externally, on the macro-economic development of the country, the other internally, on the occupational mobility of the graduates. This second method should perhaps receive more attention than it does, as the extent to which a young graduate's needs and ambitions are fulfilled in employment has a direct bearing on the performance of the economy. In this context, a high turnover of graduates in certain enterprises represents a serious problem.

Between 1964 and 1975, 221,000 graduates were placed in jobs through the Ministry of Employment, Salaries and Social Affairs, which is 90 per cent of those who came under the provisions of the Act. The other 10 per cent were granted exemption or postponement.

Nearly half of Poland's graduate manpower increment from 1964 to 1975 was obtained through this planned employment system, but unforeseeable economic changes make it impossible to assess its success on the basis of the broad studies referred to. At all events, regional and provincial disparities have not yet been overcome.

The Act of 1964 gradually became obsolete as reforms were introduced to deal with particular crises. In 1982 a new Act abolished the directed placement system, converted sponsored grants into loans and made pre-engagement agreements more flexible. These measures were accompanied by the use of employment agencies and financial incentives similar to those of a market economy.

However, the 1964 Act is representative of the system still used in the Soviet Union and many of the planned economies. In the USSR, planned employment is implemented through a commission[9] which directs

Table 2: Percentage of graduates entering employment by the three methods in the period 1964–1974 (percentage of overall placement) in Poland

| Year | Type of first job placement | | |
	Sponsored grants	Pre-engagement agreements	Directed placement
1964	63	3	34
1965	62	14	24
1966	57	18	25
1967	51	18	31
1968	39	24	37
1969	33	29	38
1970	35	26	39
1971	49	16	35
1972	48	14	38
1973	47	13	40
1974	25	6	69

Source: BERNAT, S., *op. cit.*, p. 58.

graduates to orientation and internship programmes, and attempts to ensure adaptation through a series of testing procedures.

In France, according to a survey undertaken in 1982 by the Association for the Employment of Executives (APEC), the principal job-search mechanisms used by registered university graduates were, in order of importance, as follows: advertisements in the press, personal application, response to announcements in *Courrier Cadres* (a bulletin issued by APEC), personal contacts, the national agency for employment (ANPE) and competitive tests. For graduates of non-university institutions, the order is different: personal applications come first, followed by press announcements and the *Courrier Cadres*, as shown in Table 3.

It can be noted that, when ANPE and APEC are excluded, the role of government offices declines, and friends, contacts, and response to advertisements have more importance than the government employment offices. Some authors tend to minimize the importance of ANPE as a method of job search, estimating that on its own it places no more than 10–15 per cent of the job seekers. According to these writers, registration itself does not mean that the job seeker is using this as a method of finding employment.[10] Not all employers take advantage of the different institutional arrangements for placement. Agriculture, energy, transport and the chemical industry, for instance, do not use the agencies. The number of young job seekers using the institutional arrangements for jobs in the steel industry, naval construction and financial institutions is diminishing. The use of these arrangements is moderate in the glass, automobile and textile industries. In food processing, commerce and the capital and consumer goods industries,

Table 3: *Principal job-search mechanisms used by graduates in France*

Method	University graduates (%)[1]	Non-university graduates (%)[2]
Press	89	86
Personal application	85	83
Personal relations	54	35
APEC	77	83
ANPE	41	26
Competitive test	30	6
Interim apprenticeship	16	11
Institution attended or former students' association	–	52
Other	8	6

1   Based on a survey of 1,304 university graduates registered at APEC during the period September 1980 to August 1981. Number of respondents was 1,242. Conducted in 1982.

2   Based on a survey of 1,800 non-university graduates during July 1981 and June 1982. Number of respondents was 812. Conducted in 1983.

Source: APEC document: 'L'insertion professionnelle des jeunes diplomés des écoles supérieures'.

One can observe the importance of the role of the institution in finding employment for non-university graduates. However, the media and personal application remain the principal methods of obtaining work for new university graduates. Since the survey was conducted by APEC among APEC-registered candidates, the role of this institution may have been overemphasized in finding employment for graduates.

however, use of these agencies for recruitment is extensive. In France, apprenticeship training, job orientation programmes for new graduates, and the abolition of social charges in certain cases are some of the measures recently adopted for providing a larger number of graduates with employment.

It can be observed that the problem of unemployment in general and that of graduate unemployment in particular has prompted countries to take measures to make the transition from education to work less difficult under the circumstances of reduced job opportunities. This applies even in the countries enjoying the most favourable higher education and employment situation. In the countries where the situation is only moderately favourable, such measures are not very well organized yet. However, one can note a variety of methods being used by the graduates to find employment. These vary from informal personal contacts to newspaper advertisements and public employment offices. In Egypt, for example, the Ministry of Labour has been used by 34 per cent of the graduates to find their first employment, whereas 26 per cent used newspaper advertisements and 16 per cent used their education institution. Personal contacts, friends and relations played a minor role. According to the employers, it is advertisements which attract both the largest number and the highest quality of graduates at present. However personal contacts are also very important in providing the best personnel, according to the employers. In this country, the students, graduates and employers all think that placement services established at the place of training (department, faculty or university) would be the best method of providing employment for graduates.[11]

A similar situation was observed in Tanzania, where the Government Manpower Allocation Committee found the first employment for 36 per cent of the graduates, and employment bonding provided jobs for another 32 per cent of the graduates surveyed. Institutions of education also played an important role in placing graduates, by providing jobs for 18 per cent of the graduates. The colleges of National Education, Dar es Salaam Technical Colleges and the Fisheries Institute took more initiative in placing their graduates than others. In Tanzania, placement of graduates is a government responsibility, as it is in the centrally planned economies, and the problem of employment has been one of scarcity of graduates rather than a surplus as was common in other countries at the time of the survey. The role of government in finding jobs is much smaller in the Philippines, India, Zambia and Peru. In the Philippines, personal contacts ranked highest as the method of getting a job followed by company personnel offices, government placement offices, and lastly, advertisements. In Peru personal contacts were responsible for the placement of half of the ESEP[12] graduates, whereas advertisements were the means used by 13 per cent of the other graduates. Government employment offices played the least important role (with only 3 per cent of graduates). In India, newspaper advertisements were used by nearly half the graduates to obtain employment, and personal contacts provided jobs for only 9 per cent of the graduates. Government employment offices played a very insignificant role. In Zambia newspaper advertisements and personal contacts were the most important means of recruitment. The government employment exchange office plays a very minor role here also. The parastatal organizations favoured newspaper advertisements in recruiting the best graduates, whereas the private companies preferred personal contact for recruiting the best workers.

Among the least favoured countries, Botswana is exceptional in that employment bonding plays the most important role in the placement of graduates. Of the graduates surveyed 92.5 per cent cited this as the way in which they obtained their first employment. In the Sudan, the government employment office plays the most important role, placing 43.85 per cent of the graduates, whereas personal contacts and the institutions of education are of secondary importance, at 22.5 per cent and 16.6 per cent respectively. In Sri Lanka, the sources are the 'Job Bank' (a government arrangement to find intermediate-level placement for unemployed persons, including graduates), political contacts, the university, and friends and relatives, in that order.[13] Those graduates who obtained work through the 'Job Bank' were the most likely to accept jobs for which higher education was not necessary. In Bangladesh, those who were employed in the public sector mostly obtained their jobs through newspaper advertisements, whereas personal contact was more often the means used by the private sector employers. In all, 53 per cent of the graduates surveyed received their information on potential employment through newspapers; friends and relations were the source for 14 per cent, and the employment exchange office placed none of them.

In the countries where the higher education and employment situation is less favourable, the organization of placement services is mostly informal, particularly in the private sector. Information on employment opportunities passes through friends and relations, and employment takes place through personal contact. In all these countries except Tanzania, Sudan and Egypt, the role of government in helping graduates to make the transition from higher education to work has been minimal.

The recruitment criteria

As far as criteria for recruitment are concerned, there are some interesting differences between industrialized and developing countries and between centrally planned and market economies. In the centrally planned economies (USSR and Poland) academic performance is the most important criterion for recruitment, but membership of the party also plays an indirect role. In the Federal Republic of Germany, according to a survey conducted in 1978/79 in the south-western area, it was observed that grade points in higher education credentials played a smaller role than personal impression, occupational experience gained during education, and foreign language proficiency.[14]

In the developing countries, however, the situation is different. In a survey made in the Philippines, according to the employers work experience and academic record were ranked as the most important, with personal impression playing a very insignificant role. In India, according to the graduates, academic record and performance in aptitude tests or interview are the most important criteria for recruitment. Work experience ranked fifth in a list of seven criteria. In Peru likewise, academic performance is the most important criterion for recruitment among the ESEP graduates. In Zambia, interview results, work experience and academic record rank first, second and third in order of importance, according to the employers, in a list of seven criteria. In Egypt, according to the graduates, the most important criterion in obtaining a job was 'academic record', followed, far behind, by aptitude test and interview performance. The employers, however, indicated that 'aptitude test' was the most important, followed by practical experience and interview performance. By calculating a 'standardized difference' score, the responses for graduates and employers can be arranged as shown in Table 4.

In Tanzania, although the ranking of the different criteria varies between the graduates and the employers, academic record retains its position as the top criterion according to both. The rank of personal impression also remains unchanged for the two groups, as can be observed in Table 5.

The most striking differences are in the importance of past experience and aptitude tests, as perceived by the graduates and employers: graduates attach much less importance to 'past experience' and more to 'aptitude tests' than employers. While there is no convincing explanation for it, it is interesting to note this discrepancy between the criteria that are actually important to the employers, and those thought by the graduates to be important.

In Indonesia as well, academic record, interview performance, aptitude tests and past experience dominated as the criteria for recruitment. The other factors, such as personal impression, did not have much importance.

In the countries of the third group (least favourable relationship between higher education and employment), a similar trend is noted. In the Sudan, for example, 90 per cent of the employers considered academic record as either important or very important. Interview performance was seen as the next most important criterion, followed by past experience and aptitude test results. Personal impression was ranked fifth in a list of six criteria. In Sri Lanka academic performance (defined by course followed and achievement in it) and performance in extracurricular activities ranked highest as criteria for recruitment, followed by past work experience, and knowledge of English. Personal impression ranked seventh in a list of eight criteria. In Botswana 66.7 per cent of the graduates noted academic record as very important for getting a job and 61 per cent of them noted past experience in a similar job as very important. Aptitude test followed these with 58.5 per cent seeing it as very important. Personal impression ranked fourth in a list of eight criteria.

In the case of the developing countries, which include the second and third groups studied in our research, the hypothesis of Kenneth Arrow is that '. . . employers do not have perfect information about potential employees. The best an employer with a job vacancy can do is to recruit an applicant with a high probability of job success . . . possession of a degree is a sign of increased probability of having the attributes necessary for the successful performance of a job.'[15] In view of the importance given to academic record for recruitment in these countries, this is probably correct. However, as we have noted, it loses ground in market economies like the Federal Republic of Germany, where personal impression, rather than

Table 4: Comparison of criteria in obtaining a job and selecting employees in Egypt

Factor	Graduates (G)	Employers (E)	Standardized differences (G–E)
Academic record	2.4	2.2	1.9
Aptitude test	1.7	2.7	− 0.9
Interviews	1.6	2.4	− 0.6
Practical experience	1.4	2.4	− 1.1
Letters of recommendation	1.1	1.1	0.7
Physical appearance	1.5	1.9	0.2
Marital status	1.1	1.4	0.1
Sex	1.3	1.9	0.3
Age	–	1.9	–
Other	1.1	–	–

Notes: 1. Calculated as mean using code 'Unimportant' = 1, 'Important' = 2, 'Very important' = 3.
  2. Figures under the heading 'Standard differences' are differences between mean responses for graduates and mean responses for employers, each set of means standardized so as to have a mean of 0 and standard deviation of 1.
Source: Egypt study, *op. cit.*, p. 161.

Table 5: Ranks of the criteria for graduate employment in Tanzania

Criterion	Graduate rank	Employers' rank
Academic record	1	1
Aptitude test	2	5
Interview	4	3
Past experience	5	2
Letter of recommendation	3	4
Personal impression	6	6
Marital status	7	7

Source: Tanzania study, *op. cit.*, p. 246 and p. 295.

academic record or professional experience, is the most important criterion for recruitment.

Expected sector of employment

In studying the transition from higher education to work, it becomes important to know which sector of employment is preferred by the potential employees, though in the case of centrally planned economies, this question does not arise, as there is no private or parastatal sector. In the market economies, such as the Federal Republic of Germany and France, much flexibility exists in the choice of the sector. In the Federal Republic of Germany, the students' specialization influences their future sector of employment. Less than one third of the graduates are actually employed in the private sector, but the majority of engineering and economic graduates expect to be employed in it. Fifteen per cent of the lawyers and 43 per cent of the medical graduates expect to be self-employed. The majority of the arts-based students expect to be employed in schools as teachers or researchers. Less than 20 per cent of the students in all other fields of studies expect to be employed in the public sector. The corresponding figures for some countries in the other groups of countries are given in Table 6. It is observed that in all these countries students expect a job in the government sector. This is because of the uncertainty of the private sector, leading to less secure jobs, whereas government jobs provide security and prestige.

Broken down by discipline, one might find some differences in the preferences. Medicine, law, commerce and engineering specializations could encourage graduates to seek jobs in the private sector, whereas arts and science-based graduates could seek jobs in the government and in the teaching profession, which in most countries is also a public sector profession.

In the Indian State of West Bengal the question of self-employment was studied. Of the students surveyed 49.1 per cent were willing to be self-employed. The majority of them were currently employed on a part-time basis. Those who were against self-employment cited a variety of reasons, the chief among them being lack of ability to obtain capital. This was followed in order of importance by lack of training and, thirdly, lack of a national policy which favoured self-employment. These responses depended to some extent on the socio-economic background of the respondents. Thus lack of capital, for instance, was cited mainly by those whose parents were in teaching, clerical or agricultural jobs. Respondents with past experience of regular employment cited lack of leadership and insecure future as their main difficulties with self-employment, whereas those currently employed thought that acquiring capital was the main obstacle. This response was particularly frequent among managers and scientists, none of whom thought lack of leadership or of industriousness would present a problem.

The relationship between field of specialization and field of occupation

A manpower planner needs to know how many people have to be trained to provide the skills needed in the economy. Different skills have been

Table 6:   *Expected sector of employment*

Country	Government sector[1] (per cent)	Private sector[2] (per cent)
Bangladesh	86.0	14.0
Botswana	97.5	2.5
Egypt	56.0	34.0
India	75.0	25.0
Sri Lanka	86.0	14.0
Sudan	78.0	17.0
Tanzania	73.2	26.4
Zambia	84.0	16.0

(1)   Including semi-government or parastatal organizations.
(2)   Includes self employment.
Source: IIEP *country studies.*

aggregated according to the occupations to which they lead. Some fields of education lead directly to a small number of specific occupations, but many lead to a large variety. For example, an individual graduate with a specialization in medicine could normally be a health professional, whereas a graduate in an arts-based subject would have a wider choice of occupations. To forecast the output of an education system on the basis of occupational needs, the relationship between field of specialization and the field of occupation within the country concerned should be known. One way to analyse this relationship is to observe the way individuals in each educational category are distributed over the occupational categories and vice versa, in other words to construct an education-occupation matrix.

In the market economies, in a situation of structural unemployment, enterprises are encouraged to look for ways in which a particular occupational requirement could be met by individuals of different education and training background. At a time of accelerating technological development it also becomes important to identify the educational programmes and occupational roles which are more flexible. This also applies to the centrally planned economies where the problem of economic stagnation causes a large number of graduates with one kind of training to be employed in roles needing a different kind of training.

In the Federal Republic of Germany, this phenomenon of substitution in the face of a surplus of graduates, coupled with the determinants of occupational flexibility, has led to the 'flexibility approach' in developing higher education. This approach is based on 'latent substitution', measured by questioning the employers about the extent to which jobs in their area of responsibility could be carried out by persons having a training and educational level different from that of those presently employed. 'Realized substitution' is measured by enquiring into the predecessor's and successor's training. This approach has been applied to several fields of study in the Federal Republic of Germany.

In Egypt an education-occupation matrix was constructed for all education and occupation categories containing at least ten cases. The criterion of ten cases resulted in a matrix containing 18 categories of education and 15 categories of occupation. The uncertainty coefficient was used as a measure of the extent to which the cases falling within a given educational category were evenly distributed over the occupational categories and vice versa. This coefficient is 0 when cases are exactly evenly distributed over all categories and 1 when all cases fall into a single category. The uncertainty coefficients for types of education are given in Table 7 below. It can be seen from this table that the uncertainty coefficient varies greatly from category to category. It is highest for education and medicine — more than 0.80. This means that graduates having studied education and medicine are distributed over a small number of occupational categories. Not surprisingly, the bulk of them are to be found in the professions of education and medicine. Arts, commerce, and economics and political science, however, have relatively low values (under 0.40). Graduates from these fields tend to be distributed across many different occupational categories.

The uncertainty coefficients for the occupational categories are given in Table 8. Again, there is great variation in the categories. Values are highest for certified accountant and lawyer. This means that almost all graduates in these fields have the same educational background. Lowest is the value for teacher — 0.16. Thus teachers come from a wide variety of educational backgrounds, which is in the nature of the teaching profession. It can be seen in Tables 8 and 9 that some types of education offer many choices after graduation, while others offer few. Similarly, some occupations are comparatively open, while others are closed.

In Zambia the graduates were given the following fields of specialization and asked to indicate (a) the field in which they specialized for their highest qualification, and (b) the field which was most relevant to their present job: natural sciences, engineering/technology, social sciences/humanities, health/medicine, business/commerce, agriculture, law, other. Excluding the unknown category, 143 out of 781 Zambian graduates (18 per cent) indicated that the field most relevant to their present job was different from that in which they had obtained their highest qualification. Of the group which had changed their field of specialization, business/commerce was the most important, receiving 7 per cent of those who had made a definite change (mostly from those trained in the humanities and social sciences). Only about 10 per cent of those who indicated that their fields were different were women.

In Tanzania, 75 per cent of the graduates specializing in health were working in the health field at the time of the survey. Among the graduates who held jobs in the health area, 60 per cent had had specialized training in

Table 7: Uncertainty coefficient for types of education distributed over occupations in Egypt

Type of education	Uncertainty coefficient
Arts	0.32
Law	0.45
Commerce	0.34
Economic and political science	0.29
Medicine	0.85
Science	0.42
Pharmacy	0.60
Architecture	0.54
Technology (Matua)	0.61
Agronomy	0.46
Education	0.83
Language	0.47
Fine arts (Cairo)	0.49
Social affairs	0.41
Physical education (men)	0.83
Physical education (women)	0.72
Arts education (not including Cairo)	0.88
Agriculture	0.62
Mean	0.56

Source: Egypt study, *op. cit.*, p. 157.

Table 8: Uncertainty coefficient for occupations distributed over types of education in Egypt

Occupation	Uncertainty coefficient
Architect, engineer	0.40
Medicine	0.80
Mathematician	0.44
Economist	0.76
Certified accountant	0.91
Lawyer	0.94
Teacher	0.16
Writer	0.57
Other arts and sciences	0.26
Legislator	0.61
Director	0.48
Civil administrator	0.31
Bookkeeper	0.89
Telecommunications worker	0.51
Other office	0.27
Mean	0.55

Source: Egypt study, *op. cit.*, p. 158.

health, 20 per cent in social science and 20 per cent in natural science. Thus health as a field of occupation seems to be interdisciplinary in Tanzania. All the graduates with jobs in the field of law had specialized in law, but only 58.3 per cent of the graduates with a law degree held jobs in this field. This shows both the rigidity of the labour market and the flexibility of the higher education system in this field. The same is seen in other professions, such as social science, agriculture and engineering, but in humanities, health, business and commerce, and administration the converse is true.[16]

In the Sudan, all natural scientists had specialized in natural science, but some natural science graduates were working in other fields, showing the rigidity of the labour market for natural scientists. Similar was the case with health, where the education was also rigid, as none of the health graduates worked in other areas. The same was true of engineering. The market for social scientists, teachers, and business administrators was more flexible, as can be seen in Table 9.

The above analysis can be of help to manpower planners in forecasting educational intakes for occupational roles. It can also indicate ways in which training could be changed to make graduates more flexible in regard to employment, and show which subjects should have more students because of their substitution potential.

Problems of employment

In our earlier discussion of the general problem of unemployment among higher education graduates we emphasized only one of its two main aspects, namely the incidence of unemployment, which is the percentage of unemployed people in a given population group. This is the usual 'unemployment rate'. The second aspect of unemployment is duration. It has a calendar time attached to it, and usually takes the form of 'absorption rates × years after graduation' or simply mean years or months spent unemployed by educational level. We have noted before that the incidence of unemployment among university graduates is lower than for those with other levels of education. We have also noted that the rate of growth of unemployment is higher among university graduates than for lower level graduates. The material collected in different countries of our project allows us to draw another conclusion, which is that the incidence of unemployment is not particularly pronounced among general course graduates. Evidence from the countries of the different typologies of our report is as follows.

In the Federal Republic of Germany, Table 10 shows that graduates of law, journalism, library sciences, teacher training, social work, economics and social sciences have lower unemployment rates than those of agriculture, engineering and science graduates.

Table 9: Percentage of graduates in various professions according to their specialization, in the Sudan

Specialization	Natural scientist	Engineer	Social scientist	Liberal profession	Health profession	Teacher	Businessman manager	Agriculturist	Lawyer	Other
Natural science	100.0	2.08	0	0	0	8.16	2.04	6.45	0	0
Engineering	0	93.76	0	0	0	4.08	0	0	0	0
Social sciences	0	2.08	78.31	2.27	0	6.12	6.12	0	0	24.14
Humanities and arts	0	0	15.66	90.91	0	28.57	2.04	0	0	41.38
Health	0	0	0	0	100.0	0	0	0	0	0
Education and teacher training	0	0	1.21	2.27	0	53.07	0	0	0	6.90
Business and commerce	0	0	3.61	0	0	0	87.76	0	0	3.45
Agriculture	0	2.08	0	0	0	0	0	93.55	0	0
Law	0	0	0	0	0	0	0	0	100.0	0
Others	0	0	1.21	4.55	0	0	2.04	0	0	24.14

Source: Sudan study, p. 222.

Table 10: Unemployment of college graduates by field of study in the Federal Republic of Germany (May 1978)

Fields of study	University graduates unemployed			Graduates of short-cycle institutions unemployed		
	Absolute	Percentage of recent graduates	Percentage over 1 year unemployed	Absolute	Percentage of recent graduates	Percentage over 1 year unemployed
Agriculture, forestry	366	34.4	26.0	148	24.3	17.6
Engineering	2,908	29.9	26.7	6,090	30.2	21.5
Science	3,257	27.3	25.5	363	40.2	22.8
Law	1,186	18.5	12.6	–	–	–
Journalism, library science, etc.	568	16.0	14.2	194	20.6	14.9
Music, performing arts, etc.	562	18.3	23.8	1,105	25.6	23.1
Medicine, pharmacy, etc.	1,641	5.5	14.1	–	–	–
Social work	571	50.1	16.3	1,869	21.6	12.4
Teacher training	7,303	27.3	13.9	88	25.0	13.6
Economics and social sciences	4,385	42.2	24.8	998	41.9	15.7
Other humanities	1,067	35.2	30.7	–	–	–
Total	23,768	28.5	21.0	12,408	27.5	19.5

Source: TEICHLER, U., and SANYAL, B.C., op. cit., p. 37.

In the Philippines 100 per cent of the law graduates and 95 per cent of the liberal arts graduates are absorbed five years after graduation. Agriculture graduates, on the other hand, have the lowest absorption rate, with only 64 per cent. The own-field/all-fields distinction in Table 11 is useful in assessing the flexibility of different kinds of graduates to enter jobs for which they have not been specifically trained. Thus business administration graduates are easily absorbed in 'other jobs', whereas civil engineering graduates do not seem to have the same flexibility. The Sudan (Table 12) presents a rather different picture, in that agriculture graduates exhibit a lower unemployment rate than law graduates. However, one cannot generalize from this case because of the small number of observations.

Table 11:   Absorption rates of the University of the Philippines graduates five years after graduation

	Absorption rate	
Field of specialization	All fields	Own field
Agriculture	0.64	0.85
Business administration	0.90	0.60
Chemical engineering	0.72	0.48
Civil engineering	0.75	0.75
Liberal arts	0.95	0.81
Mechanical engineering	0.79	0.67
Physical science	1.00	0.91

Source: PSACHAROPOULOS, G., and SANYAL, B.C., *Higher Education and Employment: The IIEP Experience in Five Less Developed Countries*, Paris, Unesco, IIEP, 1981, p. 40.

Duration of unemployment is shown here to be principally a youth problem. In France this is shown for two points of time as follows:

Table 12:   Number of unemployed graduates as percentage of total number of graduates, Sudan, 1973

	Faculty				
	Agriculture	Arts	Economics	Law	Sciences
Percentage unemployed	7.9	32.7	39.5	54.8	30.9

Source: PSACHAROPOULOS, G., and SANYAL, B.C., *op. cit.*, p. 41.

Table 13:   Unemployment by age (percentages)

Source	1978 ANPE figures Annual rate	Employment survey March 1980 Monthly rate
Total unemployment	12.7	4.3
Unemployment among youth under 25 years of age	42.1	15.2

Source: Agence Nationale pour l'Emploi and Association pour l'Emploi des Cadres, Paris.

Table 14 shows that in the Philippines the majority of graduates wait less than six months.

Similarly, 62.4 per cent of the Egyptian higher education students expected to find a job within a year of graduating. The mean expected time of search in the sample is 1.1 years.

On the basis of this evidence, we may say that what appears to be an unemployment problem among university graduates is in fact largely a job-searching process.

The material collected in the project permits a distinction to be made

Table 14:   Number and percentage distribution of employed graduate respondents by waiting period in the Philippines

	After finishing the course		After actively looking for work	
	Number	Percentage	Number	Percentage
Less than 1 month	6	0.2	4	0.2
1–2 months	1,116	38.0	990	54.4
3–4 months	441	15.0	242	13.3
5–6 months	350	11.9	164	9.0
7–12 months	505	17.2	216	11.9
1–2 years	294	10.0	130	7.1
More than 2 years	224	7.6	74	4.1
Total	2,936	100.0	1,820	100.0
Not applicable (working students)	698		1,802	
No data	1,026		1,033	
Grand total	4,655		4,655	
Weighted average waiting period	5–6 months (3.68)		3–4 months (3.16)	

Source: Philippines study, *op. cit.*, p. 232.

between differential waiting periods and fields of specialization, as in the case of the Sudan. However, the evidence is too mixed for a general conclusion to emerge.

Table 15: Expected delay in finding permanent employment, Egypt

Time	Percentage
Less than one year	62.4
Less than two years	23.2
Less than three years	9.3 Mean time: 1.1 years
More than three years	5.0

Notes: 1. Owing to rounding, figures do not sum to exactly 100 per cent.
2. Mean calculated using code 'Less than one year' = 0.5; 'Less than two years' = 1.5; 'Less than three years' = 2.5; 'More than three years' = 4.

Source: PSACHAROPOULOS, G., and SANYAL, B.C., *op. cit.*, p. 43.

Table 16: Waiting period between graduation and first job by profession, employment sector and degree level, Sudan

	Waiting period		
Characteristic	Under 6 months (%)	6–12 months (%)	Over 12 months (%)
Profession			
Agriculturist	100	0	0
Business manager	80	18	2
Engineer	96	4	0
Lawyer	10	60	30
Liberal professions	52	34	14
Natural scientist	93	7	0
Social scientist	77	14	9
Teacher	86	12	2
Employment sector			
Administration	62	27	11
Agriculture	97	2	2
Education	73	20	7
Industry	85	13	2
Degree			
B.A., B.Sc.	72	24	4
M.A., M.Sc., Ph.D.	73	27	0
Overall	79	16	5

Source: Sudan study, *op. cit.*, p. 219 ff.

The following conclusions can however be drawn with greater certainty:

1 Unemployment concentrates in the first months of entry into the labour force.

2   The duration of job search among university graduates is 'short' in the sense of not substantially affecting a lifetime efficiency measure.

3   What appears to be an 'unemployment problem' among higher education graduates is to a large extent a 'job-searching process'.

So, the effect of the oversupply of college graduates is temporal in nature, although the acuteness of it has been increasing lately. The reactions of the system of higher education to this problem have taken various forms. Views vary about how far-searching the educational reforms are and the extent to which they can be considered to make the transition from higher education to work easier. In any case, it is obvious that the changes in response to the labour market cannot alone make the transition smoother. Some areas of higher education have reacted only marginally to the labour market, and some educational reforms were made to trigger off substantial changes in the employment system, while others rely on corresponding reforms in the labour market or in the organization of work.

Reactions of the higher education system to the problem of improving the transition process

There was a large supply of college graduates in the mid-1970s, accompanied by general uncertainty about economic development. One of the most dramatic effects of this was the rapid spread of a very negative attitude towards higher education expansion and a surprisingly irrational debate on the changing relationship between education and employment. This debate cannot just be dismissed as a short emotional interlude in the process of adjustment to social change, and it certainly revealed some widespread views of the public on education.

Three catch-phrases became very popular: 'inadequate employment' of graduates, 'coupling or de-coupling' of education and the employment system, and 'competition for displacement' on the part of the college-trained manpower and others.[17]

The term 'inadequate employment' has been used frequently to describe the fate of graduates who cannot obtain a job of the kind traditionally held by university graduates. Also often used is the term 'academic proletariat', which in the early 1970s predicted a more sinister fate for these graduates. This expression contradicted arguments and findings according to which the substitution processes in intermediate positions seemed to be more frequent than an extreme discrepancy between the additional jobs for graduates on the one hand and the traditional positions they could expect on the other.

The expression 'inadequate employment' is based first on the assumption that there are clear-cut, permanent elements of appropriateness in the relation between education and employment. Second, it assumes that more or less all graduates in the past held 'adequate' positions. Third, it assumes that the graduates in general want to find a privileged position. Fourth, it takes for granted the traditionally strong impact of education on the jobs held and on the status generally thought to be desirable, although the same persons frequently take an opposite view when using other phrases mentioned above. Fifth, it is based on a model according to which the traditional positions will remain unchanged in the case of a high supply of graduates, so that the 'superfluous' graduates must be placed somewhere else. Sixth, it supposes a co-variation of the different indicators of 'adequate' occupations such as income, security, prestige, power, interesting work, decision-making power in regard to organization of one's own work, other persons and materials, career opportunities, etc. The argument also has been frequently addressed to youth, claiming that they would harm themselves if they enrolled in institutions of higher education.

Obviously these six suppositions are based on an exaggerated contrast between the traditional and the possible new positions of graduates. They do not take into account the dynamics in the development of jobs, and they ignore the fact that there are many jobs now which are quite demanding in terms of reasonable utilization of skills acquired at colleges, although they might not offer the desired status. According to the argument of 'inadequate employment', changes in the assumed clear-cut division between the traditional occupations of graduates and other 'inadequate' positions are neither likely nor desirable.

The phrases 'coupling' and 'de-coupling' became popular during the mid-1970s in the political debates, especially in some developed market economies, on trends and policies regarding the relationship between the education and employment system in general. 'Coupling' refers to a system in which education is geared completely to the qualification requirements of the employment system, and socio-economic status is determined by educational achievement.

The political debate in which these phrases were used was related to academic controversies in the early 1970s on the question of the extent to which development in the employment system leads to corresponding changes in education or leaves room for alternative educational policies. It was also questioned whether requirements for education could be determined by analysing the development of the economy and the occupations.

The phrase 'de-coupling' was used first of all in connection with the aims of learning, usually with negative overtones. Employers' representatives, for example, accused the proponents of educational reform of having 'de-coupled' education from the needs of the economy.

Subsequently, 'de-coupling' was usually referred to as a positive goal, implying that graduates ought not necessarily to expect rewards for their educational accomplishments and employers ought not to rely on education in their recruitment and personnel policy. Many employers and politicians hoped that in this way the problems of the labour market for graduates could be solved, either through easier absorption of graduates or through a decline in aspirations due to the uncertainty of reward. Many educators hoped that this would free education from the pressures of selection and at the same time increase public support for education beyond the occupational requirements.

The debate on 'coupling' and 'de-coupling' showed the difficulties people had in understanding the correlation between education and occupation, turning it into a situation of either utter dependence or complete independence. The demand to 'couple' education and employment in terms of content and to 'de-couple' in terms of status distribution indicates indifference towards the educational policy which favours equal opportunity. Education beyond economic needs was considered desirable, and rewards for educational accomplishments seemed, according to these views, unnecessary. This debate shows how the strong reliance of the public sector on educational credentials is often seen as completely overshadowing the development of higher education and the labour market of graduates.

The phrase 'competition for displacement' gained popularity among very disparate groups, with hardly any outlook in common on matters of education and employment. According to this expression, those graduates not finding an appropriate occupation would finally climb down one step on the ladder of occupations and thus force another person who had been trained for this position to climb down the ladder too. In this way they claimed that persons not having graduated from colleges would be deprived of positions they would have obtained if there had been a balanced labour market for college graduates.

The phrase was used for the first time in the mid-1970s especially in the Federal Republic of Germany, by those who disapproved of the educational reforms of that period. According to this argument the expansion of higher education was not only contrary to the interests of the economy (oversupply) and useless for the increasing number of students (inadequate employment), but also harmful even to the disadvantaged: it robbed them of the opportunities that they would otherwise have had.

'Competition for displacement' is a misleading phrase, in so far as realities are concerned. If the occupation structure and the relationship between the educational level and occupational rank remained constant, a college graduate taking a position normally held by a non-graduate would in all likelihood have obtained more or less the same position had the expansion of education not taken place. The major difference would be evident in a higher educational level, but probably not in fewer job prospects. Thus, displacement as a consequence of educational expansion would only take place within one generation if the weight of credentials grew in general. This could not be attributed to the rationale of the employment system but would be forced by the growing supply of graduates. A 'displacement' process could be assumed between the generations, for the younger generation would have a better chance to enroll at institutions of higher education. It can be noticed, however, that the higher the education level, the more established career patterns dominate, protecting the older working population from being replaced by younger people. Other criteria for occupational success, such as physical strength in the case of manual labour, are much more liable to cause problems for the older generation.

It might be justified in concluding that the popularity of the phrase, in view of its doubtful basis, reveals a strong element of underlying sentiments. Promotion of equal opportunities through education might have been accepted in a period of growth which fostered hopes of upward mobility among many people, but when these conditions were lacking, the legitimacy of social advancement through educational success seemed to be questioned. In addition, there seems to be widespread disapproval of a general upgrading, i.e., a rise in the level of competences considered typically to be a prerequisite for performing certain job tasks. This is also implied by the other catch-phrases. 'Inadequate employment', 'coupling or de-coupling' and 'competition for displacement' are all phrases which tended to take for granted certain ideas about a desirable relationship between higher education and employment instead of provoking a debate on what principles are desirable in this relationship. Thus they contributed to the difficulties that the politicians and representatives of the employment and higher education systems faced in reconsidering the relationship between higher education and employment.

Adaptation processes on the labour market for highly qualified manpower depended partly on the change of attitudes among graduates. The private employers in the Federal Republic of Germany, for example, considered a higher intake of graduates likely, provided the graduates developed more moderate expectations.

There are three widespread and perhaps complementary views on the attitudes of the majority of students towards the labour market. According to the first, most students harbour traditional concepts of appropriate occupations. The diminishing interest of students, in some countries, in pursuing higher education may support this view. The second view is that the students adapt their expectations to the changing market conditions. Among other things, a large number of graduates who are not unemployed but do not find appropriate positions reinforces this view. The third view is that students wish primarily to have interesting and intellectually challenging jobs (see the following chapter), but accept also a certain loss of income and status. It has not been possible to prove that any one of these views is more plausible than the others.

Reactions of the employment system to the problem of improving the transition process

Modifications in the relationship between higher education and employment in response to the large supply of graduates also have to be sought in the employment system. Three major types of change could be expected, if we exclude for the moment changes in the organization of work and the tasks involved:

1 A reduced weight of credentials in determining the general career;
2 Processes of vertical substitution, whereby the additional graduates take over positions previously held by non-graduates;
3 A reduction in the advantages of college-trained manpower in terms of income (without any change in the relation of educational attainment and positions).

In the debates on the processes of adjustment to the rising supply of graduates in the labour market, a clear-cut distinction between the types of adjustment process can seldom be found. There seems to be, however, a widespread belief that vertical substitution might be the most prevalent pattern.

Substitution processes are much more frequent than experts who warned about the danger of an academic proletariat tended to believe. Most experts seem to agree today, however, that the prevailing trends of the labour market for graduates will not be sufficient to absorb the growing number of graduates without serious friction. The private employers might turn towards a more flexible practice of recruiting graduates, but there are doubts as to whether this will lead to a rapid increase of job openings for graduates, because there are counterbalancing forces such as the interests of persons in intermediate ranks and especially because, as some observers predict, methods of rationalization to save labour costs reduce intermediate positions more than others.

In the 1970s the public employers did not give sufficient attention to restructuring the training and career system so that educational level would have less influence on the career and people with a higher level of education could easily substitute for those with a lower level.

There have been some measures to ease horizontal and vertical substitution to a certain extent, but in general there was still a fairly close relation between subject of training and occupational field. It was also true for the level of education and access to positions.

Therefore, it seems reasonable to ask if the expansion of the number of graduates will be accompanied by a corresponding increase of flexibility in the employment system. There have been increasing signs of counteracting measures; thus, many experts consider special measures to be necessary if friction is to be avoided, either through measures to increase flexibility or through special programmes for the employment of graduates.

Finally, the income advantages of college graduates have been somewhat reduced by special wage increases for persons in lower ranks and due to substitution effects. However, there have not been any substantial changes in the pay-scale in general. Action has been taken, however, in some of the countries of our survey, to reduce the wages of highly qualified persons indirectly, by providing positions on a part-time basis.

Summarizing the observations of this section, we might conclude that there are adjustment processes in the labour market towards the new pattern of supply, but this still does not lead to a sense of perfect 'match'.

The role of organization of work in improving the transition process

As the high supply of graduates has not been neutralized by changes in enrolment, structure of education, curriculum, or adjustment processes in the labour market, we may assume that the supply creates a pressure for change in job roles and even in the organization of work.

Several research projects raised the question of how much changes in supply affect the work both of graduates and non-graduates. A few surveys concluded that graduates were not only absorbed into positions previously held by non-graduates but in many cases also took over tasks that did require their level of training. The results of other research projects showed that the personnel policy of enterprises is to a very large extent responsive to the availability of manpower. Furthermore, many surveys showed large margins of potential for substitution, both horizontally and vertically. The pattern of co-operation within enterprises has sometimes changed considerably as a consequence of an increased percentage of qualified manpower. Such findings might support the view that the increased number of graduates affects the work itself, but there is very little information available which might help us measure the extent to which such impulses from higher education shape the roles of college-trained manpower and the organization of work in general.

Five different kinds of such changes at the workplace in response to the larger supply may be mentioned:

1   The extension of the number of existing job-roles for highly qualified manpower: the most obvious example of this was the increase of positions for schoolteachers in some countries, like France and the Federal Republic of Germany. The large supply of

graduates, their demand to be employed and the problems in the schools under the existing pupil-teacher ratios obviously have led the governments to employ more teachers than otherwise would have been expected. In this way, some improvement was made possible in schools, and certain deliberations about cutting back the number of teachers came to a halt for the time being.

2 Many proposals have been made to utilize the additional supply of graduates for new tasks which have been generally considered to be important, but were neglected previously. A long list of possible programmes such as innovation through research, increase in the quality of social work, health, the press, preparation of political decision-making, counselling services, military, police, city planning, security of the workplace, etc., has been prepared in some countries. It was generally accepted that there were 'requirements' which had not been transformed into a 'demand' on the labour market. To encourage caution about such ideas, the phrase has sometimes been employed: 'Demand is what we can pay for.' In recent years, arguments comparing the costs of establishing new positions to those of keeping people unemployed have changed attitudes to some extent, supporting the idea that new positions for highly qualified manpower in science and technology ought to be paid predominantly by public funds over a limited time span. This would promote technological innovation and establish new positions for graduates.

Special programmes for creating new positions for college graduates met many criticisms, too. For example, some trade union representatives argued that these measures, if they were not incorporated into general programmes for full employment, would only serve to reduce some minor problems of the privileged few. Trade unions also argued that many special programmes offering lower remuneration and job security would lead to a cut-back of both income and the rights of employees in general. There is also criticism on the costs involved in carrying out the programmes, and their utility. Many graduates who obtain jobs within the framework of special programmes are quite unhappy about the special status and the tasks involved.

3 Jobs previously considered to be suitable for non-graduates might change their characteristics after being taken over by university graduates. Obvious examples include the upgrading of training (in social work or pre-school education, but also in occupational fields less structured by credentials, such as the press or the support staff of politicians). It is generally assumed that certain occupational roles previously assigned to persons with intermediate education

are liable to undergo substantial changes with the advent of new personnel, because many of these roles are only partially structured by regulations, routine organization and continuous controls. There are some worries among employers that the employment of college graduates can often result in less efficiency rather than useful innovation. Lack of data does not permit us to estimate the extent to which the take-over of positions by graduates proves innovative, but known cases might justify the view that there are ample opportunities of this kind.

4 The large supply of college-trained labour might change the division of labour in the long run. When graduates actively shape their work roles, which were previously considered not to require a college education, such changes will often influence other roles too, either in new tasks partly taken over by others, or new divisions of job tasks. Also it is known that employers' programmes to rationalize work take into account, to some extent, the availability or scarcity of skills, as well as the motivation of the work force. Therefore, some long-term effects can be expected. Again, lack of information prevents us from giving an account of the range of such changes.

It is also difficult to establish whether these changes will have the overall effect of supporting the vertical or horizontal division of labour more strongly. One research group points out that changes can be expected in both directions. On the one hand, a non-graduate might be deprived of the more interesting parts of his or her work if an additional college graduate is employed; but on the other hand, the employment of more qualified persons in administration might have the effect of distributing responsibilities more widely.

5 Finally, the large supply of college-trained labour might have an effect on interchange within the employment system, i.e., the system of organized gainful work and other spheres of socially relevant work. The increasing number of college-trained persons has an effect on the patterns of unremunerated activities, for example the extension of political and cultural activities, new types of counselling services, voluntary social work, experiments in alternative living modes and new leisure activities. These changes in activities obviously have very divergent feedback effects on the employment system, such as increased interest in part-time work, reduction of paid jobs because of the transfer of tasks from paid to voluntary work, reduced motivation for self-realization in the work role, newly remunerated jobs in the service sector and the establishment of positions in the public administration. There is a growing awareness of changes of this kind, but it is difficult to

predict the impact that these developments could have on the employment of higher education graduates.

In summary, one has to note that the effects of the large supply of highly qualified manpower on work are clearly visible in the case of actions taken by public employers to increase the number of positions for graduates and the special programmes to induce unemployed college-trained labour to utilize their skills. Information is lacking on the gradual changes in job roles, utilization of the abilities of additional graduates employed in the private sector and the interchange between work in the employment system and unpaid work. The lack of information is certainly detrimental for a labour policy which must take into account not only the visible demand and supply of the labour market, but also the potential utility of 'mismatches'.

Notes

1 NUMBER, C., and KRINGS, I., *Abiturienten ohne Studium*, Frankfurt, Athenaeum, 1973, p. 301.
2 'Rahmenvereinbarung über die Zusammenarbeit von Schule und Berufsberatung: Beschluss der Kultusministerkonferenz vom 5. February 1971', *Amtliche Nachrichten der Bundesanstalt für Arbeit*, Vol. 19, No. 3, 1971, pp. 132–3; cf. also Käte Mahrt, 'Zusammenarbeit von Schule und Berufsberatung', in AURIN, K., GAUDE, P., and ZIMMERMANN, K. (eds.), *Bildungsberatung*, Frankfurt, Diesterweg, 1973, pp. 87–95.
3 See BISPING, P. 'Zur Bedeutung Berufs und studienkundicher Vortragsreihen der Berufsberatung,' in LANGE, E., and BUSCHGES, G. (eds.), *Aspekte der Berufswahl in der modernen Gesellschaft*, Frankfurt, Aspekte, 1975, pp. 305–354, esp. 305–312.
4 Bundesanstalt für Arbeit, *Daten Fakten 78*, Nürnberg, 1978, pp. 16–17.
5 GRIESBACH, H., HINSENKAMP, J., and REISSERT, R., 'Einstellungen von Studenten höherer Semester zu Beruf und Arbeitsmarkt', *HIS Kurzinformationen*, No. 5, August 1978, pp. 5–7. However, 38 per cent of the students believed that the unemployment quota of university-trained manpower was above the average of that for the total labour force.
6 See FAULSTICH-WIELAND, H., KÖHLER, G., and MÜHLER-KOHLENBERG, L. 'Beratung im Bildungswesen: Aufklärung oder Anpassung?' In Gewerkschaft, Erziehung und Wissenschaft (ed.), *Hinter den Barrikaden: Zur Verteidigung der Bildungsreform*, Frankfurt, Aspekte, 1976, pp. 195–210, esp. 204–5.
7 See for example, GEORG VON LANDSBERG, 'Unter Wert beschäftigt?' *UNI*, Vol. 3, No. 1, 1979, p. 32.
8 *Dziennik Ustaw*, No. 8/1964, Item 48.
9 See USSR study, *op. cit.*, pp. 137–152, for the details of this process.
10 ROSE, J., *Contribution à l'analyse de formes sociales d'accès aux emplois: l'organisation de la transition professionnelle*, doctoral thesis, University of Paris-X, Nanterre, 1982, p. 163.
11 See Egypt study, *op. cit.*, Tables 85 and 87.
12 Higher professional schools.
13 See Sri Lanka study, *op. cit.*, Table 8.4.
14 See Federal Republic of Germany study, *op. cit.*, Table 34.

15 Quoted from WILLIAMS, G., *Credentialism and the Labour Market*, 3rd International Conference on Higher Education, University of Lancaster, September 1975.
16 See Tanzania study, *op. cit.*, p. 259 and Table 71.
17 See Federal Republic of Germany study, *op. cit.*, page 135.

8   The World of Work

In the previous chapter we discussed the transition of school leavers from higher education to work. Education continues to play a role while the graduates are in the world of work. This is the subject of analysis of this chapter. We shall deal with the issues of the characteristics which are conducive to job satisfaction among graduates, the extent to which training is utilized on the job, occupational mobility, and the salary structure, with special emphasis on the role credentials play in the incentive system.

The characteristics which make a job satisfactory

In the case of market economies, such as the Federal Republic of Germany, the percentage of students supporting egalitarian views on society, especially in the labour market, is much higher than that of the general public. Economic incentive comes as the second most highly valued characteristic of the job, as is shown in the following table.

Table 1:   Attitudes towards selected characteristics of jobs, opinion polls 1977–78 (percentages), Federal Republic of Germany

Question	University students 1978	Adults 1977	Youth 16–19 years old 1977
Which of the following phrases do you prefer?			
'Achievement ought to be rewarded'	37	58	46
'More equality of income'	47	31	43
Others, no answer	16	11	11
Total	100	100	100

Source: Noelle-Neumann, E., 'Wie demokratisch sind unsere Studenten?' *Frankfurter Allgemeine*, 2 October 1978.

In another survey of values placed on jobs, graduates considered that for themselves good co-operation with colleagues, independent organization of one's own work, changes to develop and apply one's own ideas and interesting and varied work were the most important factors. A comfortable life outside one's working life was also considered important by some. It is noted that economic incentive is not the most important characteristic of satisfactory employment in the Federal Republic of Germany.[1]

In Poland some more detailed data are available, although they relate to a survey carried out some time ago.

In a study carried out in 1970 among 1965 and 1966 graduates, job preference was dealt with in a semi-open question: 'What guided your choice of your first job after graduation?' Respondents were presented with a choice of eight suggested answers and could add further criteria. The suggested answers can be classifiied as follows:

1　Related to professional qualifications
　　(i)　　　Interesting work;
　　(ii)　　Work relevant to qualifications;
　　(iii)　　Prospects of rapid promotion.
2　Related to material rewards
　　(iv)　　Good prospects of obtaining housing;
　　(v)　　Good income.
3　Related to geographical location of job
　　(vi)　　Job in the place of permanent residence;
　　(vii)　　Job away from the place of residence;
　　(viii)　Attractive locality (with additional question: 'In what way?').

Irrespective of how these responses were interpreted (whether counting all the factors indicated, or only the 'essential' ones) correlation of the answers to this question with other characteristics of the respondents showed that two factors played the principal, and almost equally important, role:

　(i)　work relevant to qualifications (22.3 per cent);
　(ii)　work at the place of residence (24.8 per cent).

Other factors in order of importance were:

　(i)　interesting work (14.5 per cent); and
　(ii)　good prospects of obtaining housing (9.1 per cent).

The above four factors accounted for 71 per cent of the responses. What is interesting to note is the apparent lack of importance of 'economic incentives' as a satisfying characteristic of the job. Accommodation an important factor, as is indicated in two items: work in the place of residence and provision of housing. Work relevant to qualifications scores higher in Poland than in the Federal Republic of Germany, perhaps because in Poland the gap between the qualification of the graduate and the skill needed on the job is higher than in the Federal Republic of Germany.

In the second group of countries the situation is different. In India the students indicated several factors as either very important or important for job satisfaction, and hardly any preference for a particular factor was evident. Despite the career and employment motivation for higher education among the students surveyed, 'good income' is just as important as other factors such as 'possibility of higher studies'.

In Indonesia the employers' opinions on factors considered to be very important in making jobs satisfactory and meeting career objectives place more emphasis on work and mental capability. This probably reflects the employers' own interests and concerns. They would normally like to see their industries growing, developing and producing the best possible results — qualitatively, quantitatively and commercially. The graduates' opinions, on the other hand, place more emphasis on other things related to work, and their primary concerns and interests are to ger maximum satisfaction from their jobs. The students' views are different again: apart from giving weight to work, they also place more emphasis on the benefits produced by their jobs, not only for themselves but also for others and for society in general. It is obvious that the students' views on these factors, compared with those of the other two groups, are more idealistic and contain other values worth defending (see Table 2).

A similar analysis was carried out in Egypt for the different factors of job satisfaction, and the mean ratings of the factors were calculated for students, graduates and employers. They are given in Table 3. It can be observed that for students, use of special talents on the job was the most important single factor, with self-fulfilment following closely behind. Good income received a moderate rating. Career-related factors were also important, while matters such as time for family and opportunities for travel were of less importance. For graduates, good income received a moderate rating in comparison to the other factors. Career-related factors were important, while time for family was of low importance. Working conditions were important, but supervision of others or absence of supervision by others was of little importance. Employers believed that good income was the most important factor for employee morale, and that considerations about the future were also important.

A direct comparison between students', graduates', and employers' responses has been made in Table 4. The most interesting comparisons are probably between graduates and students, on the one hand, and graduates and employers, on the other. From Table 4 it can be seen that both students and employers rate use of special talents higher than graduates do. Likewise with opportunity for further study. Employers rate good income much higher than either students or graduates. They also rate creative work as more important than either students or graduates do.

Table 2: Indonesia: Distribution of job characteristics satisfying students

Factor	(1)	(2)	(3)	(4)	(5)
(a) Interesting work	133	84	5	572	2.6
(b) Use of special talent	67	136	16	489	2.14
(c) Creative work	77	130	13	504	2.21
(d) No supervision	11	96	103	328	1.44
(e) Further studies	48	142	26	454	1.99
(f) Improve competence	43	158	14	459	2.01
(g) Helpful to others and to society	32	156	26	434	1.9
(h) Work with people	33	120	62	401	1.76
(i) Good income	119	98	4	557	2.44
(j) Travel	11	75	131	314	1.38
(k) Supervise others	19	103	92	355	1.55
(l) Better prospects	103	116	3	544	2.38
(m) Secure future	110	101	7	539	2.36
(n) Time for family and hobbies	43	146	28	449	1.97
(o) Use of skill learned in formal schooling	73	128	19	494	2.16
(p) Good working conditions	132	83	6	568	2.49
(q) Good supervisor	63	144	11	488	2.14
(r) Good mental capability	104	113	3	541	2.37
(s) Proper attitude towards work	56	157	6	488	2.14
(t) Opportunity to be productive in work	85	129	4	517	2.26

(1) very important ($=3$); (2) important ($=2$); (3) unimportant ($=1$); (4) total score; (5) average score. Columns (1) to (3) give number of cases.

Source: NOTODIHARDJO, H., and SANYAL, B.C., *Higher Education and the Labour Market in the Java Region, Indonesia*, Paris, IIEP, p. 89.

In the Philippines, the graduates ranked the satisfying characteristics of the job in the following order of preference: ability to utilize talents, good employee relations, good prospects for career advancement, future security, self-fulfilment, good income, time for family and hobbies and opportunity to travel.[2] It can be noted that 'income' is of low importance in the Philippines, as well.

The analysis was carried out in some depth in the case of Zambian graduates. Table 5 gives the weight of each characteristic of the job and its rank. Highest weights and ranks represent those held to be most important and the lowest represent those held to be least important. Several points of interest emerge from this analysis. Generally speaking, supervision of others and freedom from supervision by others are ranked low. Availability of further studies is generally ranked high, at least by the majority of the graduate population who can still look forward to further education. Some of the other factors have a high degree of variability: prospects for advancement, income, and working with people, for instance, depend upon the particular group under consideration. The differences by sex are not

Table 3:   Egypt: Comparison of importance of factors in job satisfaction, job choice and employee morale

Factor	Students	Graduates	Employers
Use of special talents	2.4	1.8	2.2
Creative work	2.0	1.6	2.5
Opportunity for further study	2.2	2.0	2.2
Opportunity to improve competence	2.2	1.9	2.5
Being helpful to others	2.2	2.1	2.4
Good income	2.1	1.7	2.8
Opportunities for travel	1.8	1.5	2.0
Secure future	2.2	1.8	2.7
Time for family	1.9	1.4	2.2
Working conditions	2.1	1.9	2.7
Self-fulfilment	2.3	2.0	2.6
No supervision from others	–	1.2	–
Work with people	–	1.8	–
Supervision of others	–	1.4	–
Prospects for advancement	–	1.7	–
Better future	–	–	2.7

Note: Calculated as mean using code 'Unimportant' = 1; 'Important' = 2; 'Very Important' = 3.
Source: Egypt study, *op. cit.*, p. 174.

Table 4:   Egypt: Factors influencing job satisfaction: differences among students, graduates, and employers

Factor	Students graduates	Students employers	Graduates employers
Use of special talents	1.5	2.5	1.0
Creative work	0.1	– 1.0	– 1.1
Opportunity for further study	– 0.5	1.3	1.9
Opportunity to improve competence	– 0.1	0.1	0.2
Being helpful to others	– 1.0	0.5	1.5
Good income	0.2	– 1.7	– 1.9
Opportunities for travel	– 0.6	– 0.2	– 0.4
Secure future	0.4	– 0.7	– 0.1
Time for family	0.4	– 0.4	– 0.8
Working conditions	– 0.7	– 0.9	– 0.2
Self-fulfilment	0.5	0.3	0.3

Note: Scores for the eleven common items in the previous table were standardized so that the mean responses for students, graduates and employers had a mean of 0 and standard deviation of 1. Figures in the present table are calculated as differences between means for students and graduates, students and employers, and graduates and employers.
Source: Egypt study, *op. cit.*, p. 175.

great, although women rank 'working with people' and 'time for family and hobbies' somewhat higher than men do, whilst men rank creative work higher than women do.

There are some interesting differences between institutions. Graduates of the University of Zambia tend to follow the same patterns as the total population, with the exception that they give less importance to opportunities for further study and more importance to prospects of advancement. As might be expected this is because there are few opportunities currently available through employers for post-graduate studies. Graduates of Nkrumah Teachers College show a similar pattern to teachers in general. Northern Technical College graduates place far less emphasis on being helpful to others and society and much more emphasis on creative work, security, and good prospects for advancement.

In Tanzania the degree of importance was assigned by a graduate on a three-point scale, namely 'very important', 'important' and 'not important', with a score of 1, 0.50 and 0 respectively for the different characteristics. The percentage of respondents considering a factor with the different degrees of importance was computed. The product of this percentage and the score would convert the total score of each factor into a 0–100 point scale. The scores for each factor are given in Table 6.

Table 5: Importance of selected factors in job satisfaction by sex, in Zambia

	Over total population		Sex			
			Males		Females	
Factor	Weight	Rank	Weight	Rank	Weight	Rank
Interesting work	11.1	14	10.9	14	11.1	14
Helpful to others and society	9.7	13	9.4	13	10.3	13
Further studies available	9.6	12	9.1	12	9.2	12
Improves competence	9.2	11	8.8	9.5	9.1	10.5
Use special talents	9.1	9.5	8.8	9.5	8.7	9
Creative work	9.1	9.5	8.9	11	8.2	7
Secure future	8.8	8	8.5	8	8.3	8
Good prospect for advancement	8.7	6.5	8.4	7	8.1	6
Work with people	8.5	6.5	8.0	6	9.1	10.5
Good income	7.2	5	7.0	5	5.5	4.5
No supervision from others	5.6	4	5.1	4	4.5	3
Supervise others	4.9	3	4.5	3	3.6	1
Time for family and hobbies	4.7	2	4.0	2	5.5	4.5
Opportunity to travel	4.5	1	3.9	1	4.0	2
	N = 1,005		N = 820		N = 133	

Source: Zambia study, *op. cit.*, p. 197.

It can be noted that 'secure future' is the most important factor in making a job satisfactory, with a score of 92.84 on a 0–100 point scale. This is very closely followed by the factor 'interesting work', which has a score of 90.30. Scope for further studies, improving competence, creative work, and use of skill learned in formal schooling — all of which are related to human cognitive skill development — follow the above two very closely. It was very interesting to note the low score that 'good income' receives as a factor to make a job satisfactory (score: 63.21, rank 11). Supervision of others has the lowest rank, with a score of only 17.56. Table 7 tests the same 15 factors with the characteristics for which a difference changes the degree of importance.

The characteristics listed are age, sex, home district, highest qualification of the graduate (duration of studies, institution attended, university faculty of a graduate, specialization, field of specialization relevant for the present job), sector of employment, present monthly salary, and starting monthly salary. Among those for which the responses to the 15 factors were analysed, only home district and starting salary of the graduate caused a variation in responses for the 'interesting work' factor. Present salary has a significant degree of association with the 'creative work' factor. The higher the present salary, the more important studies become as characteristics which cause the influence of the 'further studies' factor to vary. The lower the age, the higher is the proportion of graduates giving this factor the highest degree of importance; this is because they still aspire to rising higher in their careers. On average, the shorter the duration of studies of the graduate, the higher is the degree of importance attached to this factor — except in the case of a post-graduate diploma or certificate where the graduates show that they have a lower income than others with the same duration of studies. They think that perhaps an additional degree or course of studies would give them a better career and make their jobs more satisfactory. The institution attended by the graduate has a significant degree of association with the degree of importance of the factor 'scope for improving competence' in a job. The score varies from 50 in the case of Olmotonyi Institute of Forestry graduates to 100 in the case of the Fisheries Institute of Dar es Salaam graduates. The graduates of the University of Dar es Salaam gave this factor a score of 76.8. The higher the age of the graduates, the higher is the score given to the factor 'helpful to others and society' to make a job satisfactory. It is interesting to note that although it is graduates of lower age who normally have a more altruistic spirit, it is the contrary in the case of Tanzania.

Although very few graduates attach any importance at all to the factor 'supervision of others' to make a job satisfactory, there is some significant association between the degree of importance and characteristics such as age, specialization and faculty, in the case of a university graduate. The higher the age of the graduate, the lower is the degree of importance given to this factor. The temptation of power may have diminished with

Table 6:   Average scores of the factors which make a job satisfactory in Tanzania

Factor	Average score (%)	Rank
Interesting work	90.30	2
Use of special talent	71.00	10
Creative work	73.09	6
No supervision	33.55	14
Further studies	77.19	3
Scope for improving competence	75.65	4
Helpful to others and society	71.40	8
Work with people	73.95	5
Good income	63.21	11
Travel	36.28	13
Supervise others	17.65	15
Better prospects	71.02	9
Secure future	92.84	1
Time for family and hobbies	54.37	12
Use of skill learned in formal schooling	71.98	7

Source: Tanzania study, *op. cit.*, p. 281.

Table 7:   Characteristics significantly influencing factors which make a job satisfactory in Tanzania

Factor	Characteristics
Interesting work	Home district,[1] starting salary[1]
Use of special talent	–
Creative work	Present salary[2]
No supervision	–
Further studies	Age,[1] highest qualification[2]
Scope for improving competence	Institution attended[2]
Helpful to others and society	Age[1]
Work with people	–
Good income	–
Travel	–
Supervise others	Age,[2] faculty,[2] specialization[1]
Better prospects	Specialization[1]
Secure future	Specialization[1]
Time for family and hobbies	Sex,[1] institution attended,[1] specialization relevant to job[1]
Use of skill learned in formal schooling	–

1   Significant at 5 per cent level.
2   Significant at 1 per cent level.
Source: Tanzania study, *op. cit.*, p. 282.

149

experience! The medical graduates give it a higher degree of importance than others. The nature of the job of medical graduates in Tanzania at present keeps them very busy with the details of work which could be delegated to subordinates.

The graduate's specialization also has an influence on the degree of importance attached to the factor 'better prospects' in making a job satisfactory. The scores vary from 63.9 in the case of humanities graduates to 90.35 in the case of business and commerce graduates. The doctors and engineers also give a very high score to better prospects. The same characteristic also has a significant degree of association with the degree of importance attached to the factor 'secure future'. The agricultural graduates give this factor the lowest score, at 56.30, and the business and commerce graduates give it the highest, at 88.45.

The only factor for which the sex of a graduate has any significant degree of association with the degree of importance is that of 'time for family and hobbies', where the female graduates give it a higher score than the male graduates. Institution attended and specialization relevant to present job also have a significant degree of association with the degree of importance attached to 'time for family and hobbies'. The score varies from 16.65 in the case of law graduates to 70.0 for medical graduates. The humanities graduates also give it a higher score, of 65.70. The explanation may be different for the different graduates. The medical graduates do not usually have much time and the humanities graduates enjoy the time they do have for family and hobbies.

In the third group of countries, however, the situation was different in Bangladesh, where earnings received the highest average score among a survey of 510 employees who had higher than secondary education. Prestige of the work received the second highest score and security came third. Among the graduates (first-degree holders), prestige and security alternated, but among the post-graduates 'prestige' was the most preferred characteristic of a job, followed by earnings. In Sri Lanka as well, income becomes an important characteristic to make a job attractive.[3] Security and career prospects are other important characteristics. For Botswana, Table 8 gives some idea of the characteristics of job satisfaction.

An examination of the table shows that a good income, good prospects for advancement, secure future and interesting work are thought to be very important. The likelihood of improvement of competence and the possibility of further studies are also an important consideration. Helpfulness to society is of some importance, since almost 50 per cent thought that this was a very important factor.

It can be noted that the importance of characteristics which make a job satisfactory differs from country to country. In almost all the countries of the first two groups, good income was not an important factor whereas in all the three countries of the third group 'income' was an important factor for job satisfaction.

Table 8:   Order of degree of importance of significant factors leading to job satisfaction in Botswana

Factor	Percentage
Good income	68.1
Good prospects for advancement	65.9
Secure future	64.1
Interesting work	63.4
Improves your competence	60.7
Further studies available	59.4
Helpful to others in society	49.4

Source: SETIDISHO, N.O.H., and SANYAL, B.C., *Education for Social Harmony — A Study of Education and Employment in Botswana*, IIEP, 1984, p. 292 (mimeo.).

Mobility in work

Mobility during the period of education and mobility in the transition between education and work has been discussed in the earlier chapters.

The objective of this section is to find out the extent to which geographical and occupational mobility can help to improve the absorptive capacity of the labour market in the face of structural unemployment problems or to supply emerging needs for manpower when there are shortages in certain regions of the country. Another objective in analysing mobility in the world of work is to identify the reasons for such a phenomenon and use them to make adjustments in the process of insertion of graduates in the labour market, by either promoting or reducing their influence through policy measures. The extent of mobility in the world of work is reflected in the degree of uncertainty of manpower forecasts which ignore this phenomenon in relating education with employment. As with the other issues, this has been the subject of research in the three different types of countries.

First group of countries

In the Federal Republic of Germany a high level of substitution of both a latent and realized type[4] between the specialization of graduates and their occupation was observed. Sixty per cent of the jobs which were considered to require graduates with a degree in mathematics could be done by people with degrees in other subjects or by people with no college degree. A detailed breakdown of this flexibility in the requirements of jobs and the specialization of graduates is given in Table 9.

This evidence suggests that there is a large amount of flexibility in the career position of graduates in higher education in the Federal Republic of

Table 9: Latent substitution and realized substitution[1] of highly qualified manpower in the Federal Republic of Germany, 1970 (percentage)

University and college degree in	Latent substitution				Realised substitution			
	Passive: could be substituted by persons with:		Active: could substitute for persons with:		Passive: has been substituted by persons with:		Active: has substituted for persons with:	
	Other subjects	No college degree	Other subjects	No college degree	Other subjects	No college degree	Other subjects	No college degree
Economics and social sciences	12	41	60	30	–	–	–	–
Law	42	19	53	–	40	30	17	33
Mathematics	58	23	65	13	29	20	58	4
Physics	58	19	67	12	44	7	33	15
Chemistry	43	10	34	16	6	2	5	2
Biology	38	–	45	6	61	–	46	–
Architecture	15	36	11	42	7	17	9	22
Applied engineering, mining and metallurgy	38	22	50	23	12	8	24	11
Mechanical engineering	46	31	33	41	16	21	17	20
Electrical engineering	47	32	33	40	25	21	28	17

1. See page 124 for explanation.
Source: Institut für Arbeitsmarkt- und Berufsforschung der Bundesanstalt für Arbeit, Berufliche Flexibilität und Arbeitsmarkt, Nürnberg, 1977, pp. 14 and 20 (Quintessenzen aus der Arbeitsmarkt- und Berufsforschung, No. 7).

Germany. In fact, this type of mobility provided a sense of optimism in the potential absorptive capacity of the labour market in the face of the structural unemployment problem.

In the USSR, a large amount of manpower has moved from other regions to the region of Siberia and the far east of the country, to exploit the natural resource potential of that region. The population increased by 32.7 per cent in the Tyumen region (western Siberia) and by 14.3 per cent in Khabarovsk (far eastern region) during the period 1971 to 1979.[5] The proportion of high-level graduates to the work force moving to these regions would be at least as high as elsewhere. The reason for this mobility is the need for the economic development of the region.

In another survey of teachers, the reasons for changing jobs were noted to be as follows: family reasons, 41.7 per cent; job unsatisfactory, 22.6 per cent; housing difficulties, 18.3 per cent; others, 5.8 per cent.

In the USSR, such mobility among the high-level manpower, particularly among the teachers, apparently, has affected the quality of instruction in the institutions of higher education.[6]

In Poland, surveys of graduates indicated that between 50 and 60 per cent of graduates changed their job after three years of work, the period prescribed by the planned employment system. The first year of 'free choice', i.e. the fourth year of work, saw more changes than the subsequent ones. The mobility was not significantly different for different academic institutions or for different forms of planned employment.

In addition to the environment they find at their place of work, the young graduates' permanence in the job is determined by the closeness of their links with the locality. In our research we categorized the graduates' geographical transfers under three headings:

- place of residence before taking up higher studies (a);
- place of study (b);
- place of work (c).

These give five possible combinations: complete identity of the three locations, complete disparity between the three, and three cases in which two of the three are the same. (The territorial unit taken for this purpose was the province, of which there are now 49 since the 1975 administrative reform.)

Their order on the stabilization index after three years of work was as follows:

1. Studied and worked in a different place from where they had originally lived (58.2);
2. Did not change residence to study or to work (57.6);
3. Changed residence in order to study but not in order to work (55.7);
4. Changed residence in order to study and again to work (53.5);
5. Studied without changing residence but moved to take up their job (43.4).

Relating this spatial mobility to the method of job placement, it was found that sponsored grant recruitment resulted in the most movement and directed placement in the least.

Much clearer differences in the permanence index are found in a breakdown by economic sectors. With an average index of permanence after three years of 55 per cent for eight economic sectors, its maximum value is found to be 81 per cent and its lowest, 44 per cent. Top permanence indices are recorded for graduates directed to jobs in higher educational establishments and institutions of the Polish Academy of Sciences (PAN), the lowest for those directed to agriculture and the food processing industry. According to the data obtained in 1975, as compared with 1969 results, the permanence of young graduate workers in commerce and construction had increased, whereas it had fallen in education and agriculture.

The results of these studies on permanence in the first job need to be supplemented with whatever information is available on those graduates who have changed their jobs. Such information, as supplied by the employing institutions and enterprises, is often incomplete. In the 1975 study, as in the 1969 survey, the real reasons why graduates left their jobs were frequently obscure, either because no definite reply was given (in approximately 22 per cent of the cases) of because it was masked in the statement that the contract of employment was rescinded at the request of the employee or by mutual consent (about 35 per cent). Between them, these two types of response account for about 57 per cent of the graduates who left their jobs before the expiry of the obligatory three-year period of service.

Termination of employment contracts in conflict situations, i.e. through failure of the employer to fulfil his obligations, or through disciplinary dismissal of the employee, jointly account for 8 per cent of cases (with only 0.8 per cent for disciplinary dismissals).

Among all the instances of job transfer, job changes for important economic or social reasons amounted to 25 per cent. These cases are a result either of administrative transfer or of release from the contract approved by the Department of Employment, by the Delegate for Graduate Employment Affairs, or by a higher agency. An earlier survey of graduates, made in 1970, showed economic considerations (such as poor chances of obtaining accommodation, or low pay) were responsible for 47 per cent of those changes, and non-utilization of qualifications was responsible for 33 per cent. Nevertheless, it seems clear that job changes motivated by 'nature of work not relevant to training specialization' and 'poor housing conditions' could largely be prevented, if some of the malfunctioning in the process of job placement were eliminated and if employer organizations could be made to fulfil their obligations to the graduates they recruit.

There was a strikingly large percentage of answers indicating conflicts at work, and particularly unsatisfactory relations with superiors, as the reason for changing jobs. This might be indicative of shortcomings not only in the process of work but also in the training of the graduates.

Second group of countries

In India better service conditions and facilities motivated most (43 per cent) of the responding graduate employees to change their jobs. They also referred to other motivating factors, but these were mentioned in far fewer responses. Factors like 'scope for further studies', 'secure future' and 'scope to improve competence' were each cited in about 13 per cent of the responses. About 11 per cent of the respondents also referred to the better use of training as a factor motivating job changes.

In relation to the age of the respondent, one finds (in conformity with expectations) that a larger number of younger graduates are still interested in using their training and in the pursuit of higher studies. While 10 per cent each of the employees in the 50–59 age group refer to 'better use of training' and 'scope for further studies' as factors which motivate changes in jobs, 18 per cent of employees in the 20–24 age bracket mention these motives.

Concern for better service conditions and facilities seems to grow generally with age and possibly with work experience. This is borne out by the fact that while only 24.4 per cent of the responses of the youngest age group correspond to this factor, the percentage of such responses in each of the higher age groups is greater than 40, and 48 in the oldest age group (50–59 years). The proportion of responses mentioning 'scope for further studies' as a factor of occupational mobility is found to decline gradually with age. Considerations of secure future and of scope to improve occupational competence are more frequent among the middle-aged people of 40–49 years.

'Scope for further studies' is mentioned by a much larger percentage of females than males as a factor motivating change in job, although in both groups 'better service conditions and facilities' is the most frequently cited response, 43 per cent of males and 39 per cent of females mentioning this factor as a motive for change. Males are slightly more concerned about better use of training and scope to improve competence.

Except among technology graduates, the highest percentage of responses in all the subjects of graduation referred to better service conditions and facilities as a factor motivating change in occupational profile. Among technology graduates, 29.7 per cent referred to scope for further studies, as against 27.0 per cent who mentioned better service conditions and facilities. Twenty-four per cent of the graduates in biology and 18.1 per cent of the general science graduates also referred to the scope for further studies. The concern for scope to improve professional competence seems to be more common among engineering and language graduates. All three medical graduates in our sample refer only to better service conditions and facilities as the motivating factor. Of the four graduates in law, two referred to better use of training, one referred to secure future, and one gave a reason not listed in the questionnaire. It thus transpires that the possibility of better utilizing knowledge and training already acquired, and of pursuing further studies, is a motive for changing jobs for about 20 per cent of those who graduated in engineering, social sciences, arts, language and commerce. The corresponding figure is over 30 per cent for graduates of biological and general sciences and agriculture. This motive was given by 48.6 per cent of the technology graduates and 26.9 per cent of the physical science graduates.

Among some employees with post-graduate degrees in management, scope to improve professional competence was the factor most often cited. Among all the other post-graduates, the most important motivating factor seems to be 'better service conditions and facilities'. Except in the cases of technology, language and some branches of science, the percentage of responses referring to pursuit of higher studies and better utilization of acquired knowledge and training is lower among post-graduates than among graduates. All four respondents with postgraduate qualifications in medicine referred to service conditions and facilities as factors motivating job changes.

In Egypt, 13 per cent of the graduates sampled lived in different communities from the ones in which they worked. Sixty per cent of the respondents indicated that the region in which they worked was different from the region in which they originally lived. This regional mobility seems to be of sufficient magnitude to represent a kind of internal brain-drain problem. It should be seen in the light of the dominance in our sample of employees of the government and parts of the public sector. Reasons for not working in the region of origin are shown in Tables 10 and 11. The most important reason was that the family moved. Other important factors concern availability of appropriate work in the region of origin. Least important was unwillingness to work in one's own region. Eighty-three per cent of the respondents indicated that this reason was unimportant.

Twenty-eight per cent of the graduates indicated that they had changed jobs. The main reasons for these changes are shown in Table 11. Most important was 'better working conditions', which more than half of those who had changed jobs regarded as 'very important'. The other important reasons were related to career development: 'better utilization of training', 'better promotion prospects', 'more suited to personal talents'.

In summary, regional mobility was very high in the graduate sample. The most important reasons are personal, but labour market factors are also important. Job mobility was moderate. The most important reasons concerned working conditions, but labour market factors were also important.

In the Philippines, the length of stay in the first job was in all instances

Table 10:   Reasons for migration in Egypt

Reason	Degree of importance	N
Could not get a job in your own region	1.7	566
Could get job, but not relevant to your training	1.7	560
Transferred by your employer	1.5	560
Did not want to work in your own region	1.3	560
Better career prospects outside your region	1.7	560
You knew the region and wanted to work there	1.6	560
Your family moved	1.8	560
Other	1.1	552

Notes: 1   Calculated as mean using code 'Unimportant' = 1; 'Important' = 2; 'Very Important' = 3.
       2   Calculated over only those who changed jobs.
Source: Egypt study, *op. cit.*, p. 186.

Table 11:   Reasons for job change in Egypt

Reason	Degree of importance
Better working conditions	2.2
Better promotion prospects	2.0
Better utilization of training	1.9
Difficulties with colleagues	1.3
More suited to personal talents	1.9
Lost previous job	1.1
Other	1.1

Notes: 1   Calculated as mean using code 'Unimportant' = 1; 'Important' = 2; 'Very Important' = 3.
       2   Calculated over only those indicating that they have changed jobs.
Source: Egypt study, *op. cit.*, p. 186.

shorter or equal to the length of stay in the second and current job. The majority of the changes in jobs took place within major occupational groupings. For example, there had been greater mobility within the professional and technical group than from clerical and related workers to professional and technical groups. Professionals with the highest income (judges and lawyers) were least mobile in respect of their jobs. However, teachers were also less mobile, even though they had low pay. In general, those who had lower pay on their first job moved more often than others.

For Tanzania, job mobility can be summarized as follows:

1   Approximately one out of seven graduates in Tanzania changes jobs at some time in his or her working life.

2   The most frequent reason for change is better use of skills — both training and personal talents. Better conditions of service comes next in order.

3 Better use of training is more frequently cited as the reason for change among the graduates over 30 years of age, and better conditions of service and better use of personal talents are cited more frequently by the graduates in the 25–30 age group.
4 The higher the age of graduates, the higher is the probability that they have changed jobs.
5 Neither change nor the reasons for change are a function of sex.
6 Those who specialize in social science and those who work for the parastatal sector have a higher probability of changing their jobs for one reason or another.

In Zambia, of the total respondents some 58 per cent of the graduates state that they had changed their occupation.

The percentage claiming to have changed occupation varies between the different current occupational categories. The administrative, clerical and sales employees stand out as containing lower proportions of people who changed their occupation, while the agriculture/forestry and professional/technical categories contain a higher proportion.

The field of specialization for highest qualification also appears to have a strong effect on changes in occupation. Forty-five per cent of graduates who specialize in business and commerce and 30 per cent of those who specialize in law stated that they had changed their occupation. Those are below the average. An above-average proportion of changes was stated by graduates of natural sciences (68 per cent), engineering/technology (70 per cent), and health/medicine (65 per cent). This may reflect the more occupation-specific nature of business, commerce and law training, and the more favourable working conditions for graduates of these fields.

The propensity to change occupation does not appear to vary greatly between graduates with different types of qualification. The only variation is a slightly higher proportion of changes among two-year diploma holders and a somewhat lower proportion for one-year diploma holders. The one-year courses do tend to be more definitely occupation-oriented. The most frequently cited reasons for changing were those concerned with better use of personal talents and training. Conditions of service and promotion prospects came second, while dissatisfaction with and loss of previous employment were rarely given as a reason for change. The choice of reasons for change in occupation differed slightly between male and female respondents, with the females laying greater emphasis on jobs suited to their particular talents, but less emphasis on promotion prospects than the males.

Reasons for change also varied according to the current occupation of the respondents. Those who had changed to professional or technical occupations tended to place greater emphasis on the use of their talents and less on promotion prospects, whilst those in administrative posts stressed promotion prospects more strongly.

The industry in which the respondents were employed also appeared to affect reasons for change of occupation. The graduates in the mining and transport and communications industries placed less stress on the use of special talents but more on the better use of their training. Those in government administration and community and business services indicated just the opposite, in addition to regarding promotion prospects as generally less important. Graduates in trade and industry gave conditions of service and promotion prospects as their major reasons for change, with better use of their talents and training as correspondingly less important.

In Peru, 23 per cent of the ESEP graduates who had changed their job had done so to obtain better working conditions, 14 per cent had been promoted and 39 per cent had changed for a better salary. These changes were observed in 1981 among those who graduated in 1977, 1978 and 1979.[7]

Third group of countries

Bangladesh had a significant proportion of its educated employees change their jobs.

Of the 515 employees who responded to the question on the number of jobs they had had, 73 per cent indicated more than one job. Table 12 gives the structure of changes of jobs by academic qualification of the employees.

Twenty-eight per cent of the employees were working on their second

Table 12: Distribution of employees according to number of jobs they have held and levels of education in Bangladesh

Level of education	Number of jobs held					
	1	2	3	4	5 and more	Total (% to total)
S.S.C. Pass	55	35	21	14	10	135
	(41)	(26)	(16)	(10)	(7)	(26)
H.S.C. Pass	34	27	23	7	12	103
	(33)	(26)	(22)	(7)	(12)	(20)
Polytechnic graduates	6	11	3	4	4	28
	(22)	(39)	(11)	(14)	(14)	(5)
Bachelor's degree holder	25	51	34	25	26	161
(graduates)	(16)	(32)	(21)	(16)	(16)	(31)
Master's degree and above	18	19	17	12	22	88
(post-graduate and above)	(20)	(22)	(19)	(14)	(25)	(17)
Total	138	143	98	62	74	515
	(27)	(28)	(19)	(12)	(14)	(100)

(Figures within parentheses indicate per cent to row total.)
Source: Bangladesh study, *op. cit.*, p. 209.

job, 19 per cent on their third, 12 per cent on their fourth and 14 per cent had experience of at least five jobs in their employment career. The table also reveals that there is an association between levels of education and the mobility of the employees on the job market. Although 27 per cent of all 515 employees were found to retain their first job, the percentage is highest in the case of S.S.C. pass employees (41 per cent) and lowest in the case of bachelor degree graduates (16 per cent) followed by those having the academic qualifications of master's degree and above (20 per cent). On the other hand, the proportion of employees who had had four or more jobs is lowest in the case of S.S.C. pass employees (only 7 per cent) and highest in the case of post-graduate employees (25 per cent). The position of graduate employees in this case is second. Using data of Table 12 above we estimated the average number of jobs held by an employee of each educational category. The estimated averages are given below.

				Level of education		
	All	*S.S.C.*	*H.S.C.*	*Polytechnic graduates*	*Bachelor's (graduates)*	*Master's (post-graduate)*
Average number of jobs held by an employee	2.59	2.18	2.38	2.61	2.85	3.01

Source: Bangladesh study, p. 210.

The average number of jobs of each level of education is lowest for S.S.C. pass employees and highest for post-graduate employees. Employees with higher educational qualifications appear to be more dynamic than employees with lower educational qualifications.

In Sri Lanka 35.1 per cent of graduate employees changed their jobs after graduation (males 45.3 per cent; females 18.2 per cent).[8]

Satisfaction with the job was most frequently cited by the professional graduates (law, business, engineering, etc.) and special science graduates whereas insecurity of employment was more frequently cited by the general arts and science graduates, and earnings are cited most frequently by the special arts graduates as reasons for changing their jobs. According to types of jobs held by graduates, it is observed that better salary is the most frequent reason for change to jobs presently held by senior and junior executives and university academic staff, clerks and technicians. Job satisfaction is the most frequently cited reason for jobs presently held by directors and heads of departments, and security of employment is the reason most frequently cited by those presently employed as teachers (see Tables 13 and 14).

In the Sudan, the maximum number of graduates who changed their jobs did so for better future prospects. The factor of next highest

Table 13: Percentage distribution of frequency of responses given by employed graduates regarding the reasons for moving into the present job by course followed, in Sri Lanka

| | Course followed | | | | | |
| | Arts | | | Science | | |
Reason for moving into the present job	Professional	General	Special	General	Special	Total
1. Better salary	13.3	13.8	16.2	12.9	9.4	14.0
2. Better promotion prospects	12.2	11.4	12.1	11.8	12.8	12.0
3. Security of employment	13.7	15.6	13.3	16.8	12.8	14.1
4. Job satisfaction	15.2	12.5	13.7	14.6	15.4	14.4
5. Greater scope to use knowledge/skills acquired through university education in job situation	10.7	9.6	10.2	8.4	11.1	10.1
6. Scope for use of acquired additional qualifications	12.6	13.1	12.5	14.6	15.4	13.1
7. Job more in keeping with graduate status	8.5	10.2	10.2	10.7	10.3	9.7
8. Better work environment	12.0	10.2	9.6	7.8	9.4	10.2
9. Others	1.8	3.6	2.2	2.4	3.4	2.4
Total	100.0	100.0	100.0	100.0	100.0	100.0
	(460)	(167)	(481)	(178)	(117)	(1,403)

Notes: 1. Frequencies of responses given in parentheses.
       2. The question being one with provision for multiple responses, the total number of responses exceeds the total sample responding.
Source: Sri Lanka study, op. cit., p. 268.

Table 14: Percentage distribution of frequency of responses given by employed graduates regarding the reasons for moving into the present job by present employment, in Sri Lanka

| Reasons | Frequency of responses | Present employment | | | | | | | |
		Directors/ Heads of departments/ Professionals	Senior executive	Academic staff	Junior executive	Clerical, technical and allied	Teachers	Others	Total
1. Better salary	191	12.7	15.6	14.5	15.5	17.7	10.8	14.3	13.9
2. Better promotion prospects	166	11.2	12.2	13.8	13.9	15.2	7.0	14.3	12.1
3. Security of employment	193	12.9	14.3	12.5	14.6	10.1	18.9	14.3	14.0
4. Job satisfaction	197	16.2	13.6	11.8	13.0	12.6	15.2	14.3	14.3
5. Greater scope to use knowledge/skills acquired through university education in job situation	140	10.9	10.2	11.8	9.8	10.1	7.6	14.3	10.2
6. Scope for use of acquired additional qualification	180	13.6	12.9	11.8	12.7	8.9	15.7	14.3	13.1
7. Job more in keeping with graduate status	135	9.7	11.6	10.5	10.1	7.6	9.2	–	9.8
8. Better work environment	139	10.5	8.2	11.2	8.6	11.4	11.9	14.3	10.1
9. Others	34	2.3	1.4	2.1	1.8	6.4	3.7	–	2.5
Total	1,375	100.0 (489)	100.0 (147)	100.0 (152)	100.0 (316)	100.0 (79)	100.0 (185)	100.0 (7)	100.0 (1,375)

Notes: 1. Frequencies of responses given in parentheses.
2. The question being one with provision for multiple responses, the total number of responses exceeds the total sample responding.
Source: Sri Lanka study, op. cit., p. 269.

importance is the better service conditions. The other important factors that encouraged graduates to change their jobs are the opportunity for better use of training and the suitability of the present job to their personal aptitudes.

The change of jobs seems to be rare in the cases of graduates with post-graduate diplomas, M.A., M.Sc. M.Com. or Ph.D. degrees, or professional degrees such as B.Ed., B.L., B.Sc. (agriculture) and B.Vet.Sc. It is the graduates with a B.A., B.Sc. or B.Com. who change jobs the most; 41.94 per cent changed their jobs because the new job offered a better future; 24.19 per cent changed to obtain better service conditions; 17.74 per cent did so to make better use of their training; and only 8 per cent changed to suit their personal aptitudes.

The relative importance of the factors causing the change of jobs is different for graduates who had a job whilst studying and those who did not. The former placed better match with personal aptitudes, while the latter gave better use of training as the third most important motive for changing. Both types of graduates ranked better future prospects and better work conditions first and second, however.

In Botswana, 13.8 per cent of the graduates had changed their occupational career. Better conditions of service, government transfer on promotion, better promotion prospects, and better use of training are the most important motives for change (see Table 15).

Table 15:   Reasons for changes of occupation in Botswana

Reasons	Percentage
Better conditions of service	43.8
Better prospects for promotion	28.4
Government transfer on promotion	32.3
Better use of training	23.8
More suited to personal talents	3.7
Lost previous job	0.2
Did not get along with work colleagues	0.1

Source: Botswana study, *op. cit.*, p. 300.

One can observe from this analysis that changes of job are common to all types of country studied in our survey, including the centrally planned economies. Flexibility of needs in jobs was found to be an important feature of a market economy like that of the Federal Republic of Germany, thus mitigating the rigid quantitative relationship between education and employment and indicating the potential adjustment of the labour market in the face of oversupply of graduates in some fields or shortages in others. Geographical mobility of graduates can ensure the supply of manpower in areas where they are needed, as in the USSR. Poor housing conditions and mismatch between training acquired and the needs of the job are the most important reasons for change of job in centrally planned economies like the USSR and Poland.

In the second group of countries, better service conditions and better use of skills have been the most frequently cited reasons for job mobility. However, most of these changes have occurred within the major occupational groupings and not from a lower level occupation to a higher one. Better working conditions and better career prospects have been important reasons for change of job in the third group of countries. In one of them, namely Bangladesh, the higher the education of a graduate the higher the mobility, which also indicates the lower probability of mobility from a lower level of occupation to a higher one, since in most cases such mobility occurs with better service conditions.

This, then, is the situation of mobility in work and the apparent reasons for it. In some ways, mobility in work creates problems in relating educational output to the needs for skills in the economy. However, such occupational mobility is often necessary if graduates are to keep their productivity increasing and if a country is to have a balanced economic development (as is the purpose of centrally planned economies). Such changes in jobs are often vertical in the same occupation, as has been noted above. One moves higher up the ladder while keeping the same specialization. When such changes are horizontal, from one type of job to another, changing the field of specialization, the problem of relating education to employment in quantitative terms becomes more complex. Identification of the extent of such changes in jobs may help in reducing this complexity. Knowledge of the reasons for the mobility may also help the planner to adjust supply of education to demand for employment.

Utilization of training on the job

In the analysis of the characteristics which make a job satisfactory to the graduates, we have learnt that use of skills on the job is a recurring feature. From the human capital point of view as well, training given to the students should be utilized to make it cost effective. In reality, it is very rarely that the qualifications achieved by the graduates can be matched with the jobs, however efficient the system is. Often, many of one's qualifications remain unutilized on the job. We were interested in identifying the extent of such under-utilization in the different countries of our study.

First group of countries

In the Federal Republic of Germany a survey of graduates of commerce was conducted, in which 60 per cent of the respondents considered a graduate in the field of economics to be required for this position. Sixteen per cent considered that the jog could be performed by a graduate of another field, and 22 per cent thought that the job could be performed by persons not holding a college degree at all, which implies that they did not think their training in commerce was being utilized.

It has also been observed that in terms of under-utilization of training, the graduates of mechanical engineering suffered most in the 1970s, because of the enormous increase in the supply of mechanical engineers due to economic stagnation.

In the USSR a survey of engineers on the job in the enterprises demonstrates a high degree of discontent, mainly because of the under-utilization of training. Such dissatisfaction is observed to be highest among the civil and mechanical engineers and textile engineers, and lowest among the research institutes, as shown in the following table.

Table 16: Degree of satisfaction of engineers with their job in the USSR (%)

Degree of satisfaction	Overall (all industries)	Construction manufacturing	Chemical industries	Textile and others	Research institutes
Very satisfied	21.2	18.7	18.8	19.2	23.0
Satisfied	41.6	39.0	40.0	43.6	42.8
Indifferent and no opinion	9.9	9.7	9.2	9.6	10.2
Dissatisfied	27.3	32.6	32.0	27.6	24.0
Total	100.0	100.0	100.0	100.0	100.0

Source: USSR study, *op. cit.*, Table 31, page 112.

Polish studies have shown a substantial divergence between the opinions of graduates and those of their employers concerning the adequacy and the relevance of the former's training. In 1975, 60 per cent of the employers expressed the view that their employees with post-secondary degrees had been fully trained for their jobs, whereas a 1970 survey of gradates revealed that only 23 per cent believed that the knowledge they had acquired was adequate. Moreover, while 81 per cent of the employers believed that graduates' qualifications were being fully utilized, almost half (47 per cent) of the graduates expressed the view that their knowledge was insufficiently used in their jobs.

In processing the 1970 survey data, relationships between the graduates' own assessment of the extent to which their qualifications were being utilized and several other assessments were examined (see Tables 17, 18, 19). The strongest relation proves to be between the utilization of general professional training and the consistency of employment with the course of education completed. The extent to which qualifications were being utilized correlated more weakly with the type of employing organization, the greatest utilization being recorded for higher education institutions and

Table 17: Assessment of extent to which training is utilized related to consistency of work content with study content in Poland

Consistency of work with study course and specialization	Knowledge acquired (%)		
	Adequate to job performed	Insufficiently used	Required supplementing
Consistent with specialist studies	33.3	38.0	29.7
On the whole consistent with specialist studies	20.2	54.0	27.3
On the whole not consistent with specialist studies	16.4	57.9	27.6
Not consistent with specialist studies but consistent or consistent on the whole with study course	15.4	56.2	29.6
Not consistent with either	7.5	59.5	29.8

Source: Poland study, *op. cit.,* p. 237.

Table 18: Assessment of training related to type of employing organization in Poland

Type of organization	Knowledge acquired (%)		
	Adequate to job performed	Insufficiently used	Required supplementing
Production	18.2	59.7	23.6
Applied research	24.0	38.0	38.0
Higher education and science	30.4	15.5	53.7
Education	37.4	38.3	24.7
Provincial and central administration	26.1	47.6	28.7
Others	23.1	44.0	30.5

Note: Difference from 100 per cent — question not answered.
Source: Poland study, *op. cit.,* p. 238.

research centres, and the smallest for production enterprises. The weakest correlation found was between the extent to which knowledge was being utilized and hierarchical position in the organization. The survey was concerned with the allocation of working time. Graduates were asked what proportion of their time was occupied with tasks not requiring a higher education. On the basis of responses from 86 per cent of the population surveyed, it was found that tasks not requiring higher education took up approximately 40 per cent of working time. The correlation of this assessment with other factors is very similar to that of the utilization of qualifications. Table 20 shows data on the interdependence of the job being performed with the specialization of the individual graduate.

Table 19:   Assessment of training related to position held in Poland

	Knowledge acquired (%)		
Position	Adequate to job performed	Insufficiently used	Required supplementing
Non-executive	24.3	49.2	27.5
Middle management	18.5	58.7	24.2
Senior management	24.5	53.9	23.4
Scientific worker	32.8	15.4	51.8

Note: Difference from 100 per cent — question not answered.
Source: Poland study, *op. cit.*, p. 238.

Table 20:   Time spent on tasks not requiring higher education related to degree of consistency of training with job content in Poland

	Tasks not requiring higher education occupy:		
Consistency of work with study course and specialization	Up to 20% of time	From 21% to 50% of time	Over 50% of time
Consistent with specialist studies	15.4	38.7	28.0
On the whole consistent with specialist studies	11.3	37.5	41.5
On the whole not consistent with specialist studies	8.1	33.4	47.6
No consistent with specialist studies but consistent or consistent on the whole with study course	10.0	34.9	45.9
Not consistent with either	5.9	26.1	59.0

Note: Difference from 100 per cent — question not answered.
Source: Poland study, *op. cit.*, p. 240.

Perhaps surprisingly, it is not easy to interpret the figures for time spent on tasks not requiring higher education. This is because specialists, even under an optimal system for time use, are bound to perform certain tasks which do not require high qualifications but are directly related to their activities within their employer's organizational and social structure. It follows that only by deducting some 15, 20 or 25 per cent of inevitably, and therefore 'justifiably', wasted time, can we begin to assess how much time graduates could save in jobs which correspond to their training and specialization, and try to identify any additional waste resulting from the lack of such correspondence.

In the 1970 study the only further information on the training acquired in higher education was confined to a question on any fundamental gaps in this education with respect to a few specified subject groups. Replies to this question can be summed for the entire population surveyed. Over 40 per cent of the graduates pointed to gaps in practical or specialized knowledge, and knowledge of foreign languages and management and organization methods. Only about 5 per cent of the respondents indicated additional gaps in basic theoretical knowledge and in the fundamentals of their professions. These answers, too, were highly correlated with the nature of the job. It is not possible to deal broadly with the other questions in the same survey, concerning subjects which had proved to be the most and the least useful in the job, or suggestions for changes in the content and methods of training, as these are too specifically linked to particular fields of study.

An attempt to analyse more fully the usefulness of knowledge acquired in higher studies, using a multi-grade scale of assessment, was made in a survey carried out in 1973 among graduates of technical colleges. This showed that some of the respondents — approximately one third — considered their training in basic theoretical subjects (e.g. mathematics, physics, etc.) to have been 'too extensive'. About a quarter of the respondents had the same opinion of general economic subjects. Subjects in which training was described as insufficient or inapplicable were, principally, foreign languages, sociology and psychology, management and organization methods, and certain specialized technologies. About a quarter of the respondents mentioned specialized technologies.

Second group of countries

In India, analysis of the relationship between formal academic qualifications and their present job requirements revealed that 58.6 per cent of the graduates found their academic qualifications to be both useful and adequate. Another 27.7 per cent felt they were useful but not adequate and hence should be supplemented by other forms of training and education. According to 12.2 per cent of the employed graduates, their educational qualifications were simply irrelevant to the needs of their present jobs, while 19 (1.5 per cent) respondents characterized these qualifications as even detrimental to the needs of their current jobs.

The experiences of male and female graduate employees did not differ much, except that slightly more males (86 per cent) found their educational qualifications to be adequate and/or useful for meeting their present job requirements. Fifteen per cent of the females (as against 13 per cent of the males) considered that such qualifications were neither useful nor adequate (see Table 21).

None of the graduates in medicine, technology, law and unlisted subjects found their educational background to be useless or inadequate for meeting their current job requirements. Besides this, no graduates in engineering, languages and science considered their academic qualifications to be detrimental. All the medicine graduates, 83 per cent of the technology graduates and 71 per cent of the science graduates had the

Table 21: Distribution of employed graduates according to the perceived relevance/adequacy of their education in West Bengal, India

Opinion	Sex		Total
	Male	*Female*	*Total*
Useful and adequate	703 (58.7)	40 (56.3)	743 (58.6)
Useful but not adequate	332 (27.7)	20 (28.2)	352 (27.7)
Irrelevant	145 (12.1)	10 (14.1)	155 (12.2)
Detrimental	18 (1.5)	1 (1.4)	19 (1.5)
Total	1,198	71	1,269

Source: West Bengal study, *op. cit.*, p. 208.

impression that their academic attainments were not only useful but adequate for their jobs. The figure is over 60 per cent in biological sciences, engineering and agriculture as well. However only a third of the graduates in languages and other unclassified subjects had this impression. Law and language graduates point more to the inadequacy of their formal education, which is pointed out by sizeable segments of the respondents in other subjects as well (see Table 22).

A cross-classification of respondents according to the extent to which their educational qualifications were necessary for obtaining their current jobs and the extent to which these were found useful, adequate or relevant brings out some important points. Among graduates to whom these qualifications were 'very necessary' for obtaining their current jobs, the qualifications were found to be 'useful and adequate' for meeting their job requirements by 72.6 per cent of the respondents. The corresponding figure is 55.6 per cent for those who looked upon their qualifications as just 'necessary' for securing jobs and is only 35.2 per cent for those who regarded these as 'not necessary' for this purpose. Conversely, little more than 30 per cent of the graduates in the latter two categories saw their education as 'useful but not adequate' to meet job needs. The percentage of respondents who found their formal education to be 'irrelevant' to their current job requirements increases from among those who felt their degrees to be 'very necessary' to those who felt them to be just 'necessary' and is much larger (27.0 per cent) among those to whom the degrees were unnecessary. Similarly, 5.6 per cent of the respondents who regarded their degrees as unnecessary for securing their current jobs characterized their educational qualifications as 'detrimental' in meeting the needs of their jobs. Very few (not more than 1 per cent) of the respondents in the two other groups had such a negative assessment of their academic qualifications in relation to jobs. Out of the 756 employed graduates who found their qualifications 'not necessary' or just 'necessary' for securing their current jobs, 144 (19 per cent) reported their qualifications to be irrelevant or even detrimental to their job needs. This indicates a possible mismatch between

Table 22: *Distribution of employed graduates according to the perceived relevance/adequacy of education and graduate level course in West Bengal, India*

Graduate level course	Need for education				
	Useful and adequate	Useful but not adequate	Irrelevant	Detrimental	Total
Natural science	98 (52.1)	62 (33.0)	25 (13.3)	3 (1.6)	188 (15.9)
Bioscience	35 (63.6)	11 (20.0)	9 (16.4)	0	55 (4.7)
Social science	185 (58.7)	86 (27.3)	38 (12.1)	6 (1.9)	315 (26.7)
Engineering	86 (64.2)	33 (24.6)	14 (10.4)	1 (7.5)	134 (11.3)
Technology	15 (83.3)	3 (16.7)	0	0	18 (1.5)
Agriculture	5 (62.5)	2 (25.0)	1 (12.5)	0	8 (6.8)
Commerce	167 (56.4)	82 (27.7)	41 (13.9)	6 (2.0)	296 (25.1)
Language	5 (33.3)	6 (40.0)	4 (26.7)	0	15 (1.3)
Arts	59 (59.0)	29 (29.0)	11 (11.0)	1 (1.0)	100 (8.5)
Science	37 (71.2)	12 (23.1)	3 (5.8)	0	52 (4.4)
Total	692 (58.6)	326 (27.6)	146 (12.4)	17 (1.4)	1,181

Source: West Bengal study, *op. cit.*, p. 209.

Table 23: *Distribution of employed graduates according to the perceived relevance/adequacy of education and credentials in recruitment in West Bengal, India*

Credential in recruitment	Relevance/adequacy of education				
	Useful and adequate	Useful but not adequate	Irrelevant	Detrimental	Total
Very necessary	349 (72.6)	105 (21.8)	26 (5.4)	1 (0.2)	481 (27.8)
Necessary	291 (55.6)	164 (31.4)	63 (12.0)	5 (1.0)	523 (41.1)
Not necessary	82 (35.2)	75 (32.2)	63 (27.0)	13 (5.6)	233 (18.3)
Total	722 (58.4)	344 (27.8)	152 (12.3)	19 (1.5)	1,237

Source: West Bengal study, *op. cit.*, p. 211.

job requirements and prescribed qualification requirements for various jobs (see Table 23).

In Egypt, the graduates generally indicated that the education they had received was 'necessary' and 'useful' in their work. Nevertheless, some 15 per cent indicated that their education was 'not necessary' and 'not useful' in their work. Perception of the degree of necessity and the degree of usefulness can be seen to vary according to the field of education, as shown in Tables 24 and 25.

The highest degree of necessity and usefulness of educational qualifications is expressed by graduates having arts education: 83 per cent indicated that their education was 'very necessary' and over 90 per cent indicated that it was 'very useful'. Next came graduates from the field of

Table 24: Necessity and utility of education in the job in Egypt

	Necessity (%)	Utility (%)
Not necessary/useful	15.7	14.3
Necessary/useful	16.2	21.9
Very necessary/useful	68.0	63.8
Total	100.0	100.0

Note: Owing to rounding off, totals may not sum to exactly 100 per cent.
Source: Egypt study, *op. cit.*, p. 164.

Table 25: Degree of necessity of educational qualifications for job by faculty graduated from in Egypt

Faculty	Not necessary	Necessary	Very necessary	Degree of necessity
Social science and humanities	15.7	20.3	63.9	2.5
Science and medicine	10.3	7.1	82.6	2.7
Engineering	13.2	10.1	76.7	2.6
Arts education	5.7	11.3	83.0	2.8
Technology	30.8	9.2	60.0	2.3
Agriculture	19.4	15.8	64.8	2.5
Other	18.2	15.2	66.7	2.5
All	15.5	16.4	68.1	2.5

Note: Degree of necessity calculated as mean using code 'Not necessary' = 1; 'Necessary' = 2; 'Very necessary' = 3.
Source: Egypt study, *op. cit.*, p. 165.

Table 26: Degree of usefulness of education in the job by faculty graduated from in Egypt

Faculty	Not useful	Useful	Very useful	Degree of usefulness
Social science and humanities	13.8	25.7	60.5	2.5
Science and medicine	9.5	14.4	76.1	2.7
Engineering	16.3	13.2	70.5	2.5
Arts education	1.9	7.5	90.6	2.9
Technology	26.2	26.2	47.7	2.2
Agriculture	18.6	21.7	59.6	2.4
Other	24.2	15.2	60.6	2.4
All	14.2	22.0	63.8	2.5

Note: Degree of usefulness calculated as mean using code 'Not useful' = 1; 'Useful' = 2; 'Very useful' = 3.
Source: Egypt study, *op. cit.*, p. 165.

science and medicine: 83 per cent indicated their education was 'very necessary', and 76 per cent indicated it was 'very useful'. Lowest were graduates of technology: 31 per cent indicated their education was 'not necessary', and 26 per cent indicated it was 'not useful' (see Table 26).

In Zambia, graduates were asked to rate the education they had received in relation to their current jobs, and to state whether their educational qualification was necessary for obtaining their current jobs. The responses are tabulated in Table 27. Approximately 2 per cent of the respondents said either that the education they had received in relation to their current job was not useful or that their educational qualification was not necessary for obtaining their current job. On the other hand, slightly more than 75 per cent of the respondents stated either that their education was very useful or that their educational qualification was very necessary.

Slightly more women than men thought that the education they had received was 'very necessary' to their current job. This of course may be due to the somewhat larger proportion of women in jobs for which the training is task-oriented, e.g. secretarial work. On the other hand, both men and women agreed, with almost equal frequency, that their educational qualifications were necessary for obtaining their current job. The responses are tabulated in Table 28.

Table 27:   Education received in relation to needs to present job in Zambia

	Very necessary	Necessary	Not necessary	Total
Very useful	582	91	6	679
Useful	93	107	7	207
Not useful	5	7	6	18
Total	680	205	19	904

Source: Zambia study, op. cit., p. 188.

Table 28:   Educational qualification necessary for obtaining present job in Zambia

Sex	Educational qualification necessary for getting present job			Education received in relation to needs of present job		
	Very necessary	Necessary	Not necessary	Very useful	Useful	Not useful
Male	623	189	22	574	193	16
Female	103	31	1	111	19	2
Total	726	220	23	685	212	18

Source: Zambia study, op. cit., p. 189.

It is interesting to note that graduates in health/medicine, agriculture, law, and, to a lesser extent, engineering/technology, rated their education as useful more frequently. This difference is probably accounted for by a combination of job-oriented training and professionalism developed during their training. Natural science graduates tend to rate their training less highly.

When the responses are analysed by institution, graduates of the University of Zambia and the Evelyn Hone College tend to give a lower rating to the importance of their qualification. Again, this may be due to a somewhat broader education received by a large proportion of the graduates of these two institutions.

A matrix of occupation versus education received in relation to present job confirms that those persons who either have undergone training in professional areas or are in highly task-oriented jobs tend to rate their training more highly.

In the Philippines, the rationalization of training was analysed on the basis of the graduate survey considering two variables: (1) formal training and (2) supplementary out of school training. Many of the respondents (36.2 per cent) had had supplementary training. On the content and method of instruction in their formal training, 49.2 per cent of the employed graduates felt that the content was adequate, and 48.9 per cent felt the method was adequate. Those who rated content and method of instruction as 'very adequate' account for 36.75 per cent and 35.18 per cent respectively, and 'excellent' content and method of instruction, 9.26 per cent and 9.62 per cent respectively. A negligible number expressed dissatisfaction with their college training.

As stated earlier, the demand for education is stimulated by employment prospects. This section of our study assesses whether education judged as highly satisfactory is indeed necessary in securing a job. A majority (56.94 per cent) considered their educational qualification to be 'very necessary'; 24.15 per cent considered it 'extraordinarily necessary'; and 24.66 per cent 'necessary'. A small percentage asserted that educational qualifications were 'barely necessary' (2.79 per cent) and 'not necessary' (1.09 per cent). Those who placed greater emphasis on educational qualifications and formal training included professional and technical workers, clerical and related workers, production and transport workers. In terms of industrial classification, graduates employed in community, social and personal service, manufacturing and mining and quarrying attached greater significance to educational qualifications and formal training.

Furthermore, the graduates of proprietary institutions, Catholic schools, the UP system and the other state colleges and universities attached more importance to educational qualifications and formal training. In none of the above cases was non-formal training ranked first or second.

Regarding non-formal training, respondents are distributed according to their perceptions as follows: 'very necessary', 52.2 per cent; 'necessary', 19.5 per cent and 'extraordinarily necessary', 16.6 per cent. Of the total 1,704 respondents, only 2.3 per cent judged it 'unnecessary' and 5.2 per cent 'barely necessary'. The evaluation of non-formal education differs from that of formal education in two ways. First, there were more (in the sub-sample of 1,704) who felt that non-formal training was 'not necessary' or 'barely necessary' than who rated formal training in this way. Second, while there were 34.9 per cent who judged formal training to be more useful than non-formal training, only 13.8 per cent considered non-formal education to be more useful than formal.

In Tanzania the assessment of the usefulness of the education to meet the needs of the job is revealed in the following table.

Table 29: Tanzania: Degree of usefulness of the education to meet the needs of the job

Degree of usefulness	Frequency	Percentage
Very useful	248	59.3
Useful	153	36.6
Useless	17	4.1
Total	418	100.0

Source: Tanzania study, *op. cit.*, p. 254.

In Tanzania we tried to identify the degree to which the education graduates had was needed for their jobs, in order to (i) diagnose the performance of the education system in meeting the needs of the job, and (ii) assess the specialization needed for different kinds of jobs. The above table gives the results.

It is noted that only in 4 per cent of the cases was the education received not useful for the job, which means that there is a high degree of relevance in the education received by the graduates for their working life. The responses were analysed for the different background characteristics of the graduates. It was observed that the nature of responses varied between male and female graduates; all the female graduates thought that their education was useful for the needs of the job, whereas 5.3 per cent of the male graduates thought that it was useless. It was interesting to note that the specialization of the graduates did not have any association with their reactions as regards the general usefulness of the course. Also of interest was that all the graduates who specialized in humanities, health and agriculture found that their educational qualifications met the needs of the job. However, 15 per cent of the law graduates and 10 per cent of the engineering graduates thought that their courses (which are more pro-fessional than the others) did not meet the needs of the job. It is in these two areas that attention should be given to relating education more closely to work needs. Similar conclusions were reached when we analysed the responses according to the field of specialization most relevant to the graduates' current jobs. In this case, the nature of responses varied significantly with specialization. Those who thought academic record was very important for getting their jobs also thought that the education received was very useful for the needs of the jobs. The dependence of the choice of career on success in studies was also found to be associated with the degree of usefulness of the education with the needs of the job.

In Peru the majority (57 per cent) of the ESEP graduates surveyed indicated that there was a good relationship between their specialization and the needs of the job. However, a significant proportion (35 per cent) suffered from under-utilization of their training.

Third group of countries

In Bangladesh 59.09 per cent of the employed graduates thought their training to be 'very useful' while only 9.66 per cent of them thought it to be of no use in performing their current job. While all the medical graduates considered their training to be very useful none of the management graduates did. Similarly, 71.88 and 72.58 per cent of the engineering and agriculture graduates respectively considered their training to be very useful in performing their current job. On the other hand, a significantly small proportion of the arts, commerce and social science graduates had a similar response, as can be seen in Table 30.

From this, it is clear that training in some specializations (e.g., medicine, agriculture and engineering) is quite relevant for the needs of the labour market while that in others (e.g., arts, commerce, social sciences) is not. This is to be expected, in view of the fact that in the latter cases training is of a general nature, not oriented towards the needs of any particular job, while in the former, the training is much more specific and meant for particular jobs only. We have also seen earlier that the degree of correspondence between specialization and actual occupation is quite high in the case of medical and engineering graduates.

In Botswana 64.6 per cent of the graduates indicated that their qualifications were very necessary for the job; 10.5 per cent felt that even though their qualifications were not very necessary, the acquisition of their qualification had helped them to get the job and to cope with its demands; and 24.9 per cent regarded their qualifications as having been necessary.

Of the graduates who felt that their qualifications were very necessary for the job 89.1 per cent had entered a specific professional field of study (such as lawyers, doctors, engineers, nurses, teachers and agricultural workers). Of those who responded 'necessary' 93.4 per cent had jobs in the general administration of their sector of employment and they had not been specifically trained for what they were doing, as was noted in the case of Bangladesh.

One can again observe a kind of complacency in the less favoured countries with respect to the utilization of training on the job as measured by its importance in performing the task. In the countries which enjoy a

Table 30: *Distribution of employed graduates by specialization and their opinion about the usefulness of the training received in performing the job in Bangladesh*

Specialization	Very useful	Moderately useful	Not at all useful	Uncertain	Total
Science	14	10	5	1	30
	(46.67)	(33.33)	(16.67)	(3.33)	(100)
Engineering	23	8	1	0	32
	(71.88)	(25.00)	(3.12)		(100)
Agriculture	45	12	4	1	62
	(72.58)	(19.35)	(6.45)	(1.61)	(100)
Medical	8	0	0	0	8
	(100.00)				(100)
Management	0	1	0	0	1
		(100.00)			(100)
Commerce	1	2	1	0	4
	(25.00)	(50.00)	(25.00)		(100)
Arts	3	9	2	1	15
	(20.00)	(60.00)	(13.33)	(6.67)	(100)
Law	3	1	2	0	6
	(50.00)	(16.67)	(33.33)		(100)
Economics	4	2	0	0	6
	(66.67)	(33.33)			(100)
Social science	3	6	2	1	12
	(25.00)	(50.00)	(16.67)	(8.33)	(100)
Total	104	51	17	4	176
	(59.09)	(28.98)	(9.66)	(2.27)	(100)

Note: Figures within parentheses represent percentages of row totals.
Source: Bangladesh study, *op. cit.*, p. 202.

favourable relationship between education and employment (the industrialized countries) the graduates' dissatisfaction with the utilization of training was noted to be higher. The most striking fact was the under-utilization of training in the centrally planned economies. Among the factors which make an assessment difficult is the specificity of skills needed by the employing organization for any job and the diversity of knowledge sought to be given in any graduate level course. Of course, the problem is much less serious — though not altogether absent — in the professional field and in technical subjects, and it is in these fields that one can assess the degree of utilization with slightly more accuracy. In several cases we have found that the graduates gave a clear indication of the utilization of their training in these fields. Even in the less favoured countries graduates have indicated under-utilization of their training on the job.

The salary structure

Traditionally, the benefits of education have been measured approximately by the salaries of employees with different qualifications. Such a method is not without its problems but it is sufficient for our purposes here to mention that this approximation procedure has not been invalidated by the empirical evidence.

What we know already on the relative salary structure is that more-educated persons earn more than less-educated persons world-wide, and almost without exception. In developing countries the earning advantage of university graduates is 2.7 times that of secondary school graduates and 6.4 times that of the primary school graduates.[9] This structure is confirmed by the IIEP studies. For example, in Zambia there exists a net salary hierarchy even within the post-secondary level (see Table 31).

In the Sudan, there is a strong degree of association between the duration of studies and the starting salary.[10] The same result has also been obtained in the Philippines, Sri Lanka, Bangladesh, India and the People's Democratic Republic of Yemen.[11]

This shows that even in a period of rapid university expansion, higher education graduates have an earnings advantage.

Table 31: Monthly salary by educational qualification, Zambia, 1974

Educational qualification	Monthly salary (in kwachas)	Educational qualification	Monthly salary (in kwachas)
Diploma[1]	238	M.A., M.Sc.	343
B.A., B.Sc.	327	Ph.D	393

1 Weighted average one- to three-year diploma courses.
Source: Derived from Zambia study, *op. cit.*, p. 354, Table 4.18.

For example, in the Philippines, the advantage of university graduates over secondary-school graduates is 1.4 times.[12]

This can be interpreted in several ways. It may mean that there is a high degree of substitution between university and other kinds of graduates for the earnings structure to remain stable while the relative skill-mix changes. It could also mean that the demand for university graduates keeps pace with the expanding supply in such a way as to produce a 'reduced-form' solution with constant differentials.

The consideration of salaries by the level and kind of education brings out a number of interesting points. For example, a distinction between graduates of different university faculties shows that general or non-technical graduates do as well as and sometimes better, in terms of labour market earnings, than vocational or technical course graduates. This might be surprising to those who think it is technical or vocational education that mainly commands a premium in the labour market. But whether one looks at it from the point of view of the course completed (e.g. Tables 32 and 33) or the occupation of the graduate (Tables 34 and 35), non-technical skills are rewarded as much as vocational skills in most cases. Differences exist, however, between selected fields, as in the case of engineering and medicine on the one hand and arts on the other.

Table 32:   Specialization and salary in Tanzania

Specialization	Gross monthly starting salary (in shillings)		Gross monthly salary at time of survey (in shillings) (1976)	
	Average	*S.D.*[1]	*Average*	*S.D.*[1]
Natural scientist	1,067.231	456.196	1,450.583	709.262
Engineer	1,371.895	365.681	1,941.905	516.299
Social scientist	1,113.803	357.003	1,653.627	602.429
Humanistic professional	942.438	425.659	1,407.848	377.879
Health professional	1,623.286	420.323	2,119.000	736.001
Business and managerial	1,103.964	336.060	1,702.889	644.405
Agriculturist	1,245.857	418.424	1,709.000	733.228
Lawyer	1,227.857	68.550	1,813.714	582.881
Others	1,179.600	154.802	1,662.727	502.940

[1]   Standard deviation.
Source: Tanzania study, *op. cit.*, pp. 265 and 266.

Table 33:   Annual earnings by field of study in Egypt

Field of study	Annual earnings in Egyptian pounds
Agronomy	663
Arts	540
Engineering	622
Science and medicine	683
Social sciences and humanities	587
Technology	583

Source: Egypt study, *op. cit.*, p. 177.

Table 33 reveals that no dramatic discrepancies exist between the mean salaries of graduates of different higher-education fields in Egypt. Science and medicine are at the top of the earning scale and arts and technology at the bottom.

Table 34:   Monthly salary by occupation, Philippines, 1977

Occupation	Monthly salary (in pesos)
Applied scientists	943
Medical scientists	615
Physical and natural scientists	657
Accountants	925
Judges	1,087

Source: Psacharopoulos, G., and Sanyal, B., *op. cit.*, p. 28.

Table 35:   Monthly salary by occupation, Zambia, 1974

Occupation	Monthly salary (in kwachas)
Administrative	400
Agriculture	211
Clerical	201
Production and transport	215
Professional and technical	255
Sales	318
Service	156

Source: PSACHAROPOULOS, G., and SANYAL, B., *op. cit.*, p. 29.

This indication is strengthened when one considers the differential growth of earnings by subject (Table 36). The fact that the earnings of arts and law graduates grow more than for other fields is indicative that employers must be deriving some benefit from them after they have been under observation for some time.

Table 36:   Mid-career to starting-salary ratios by subject, Tanzania, 1974

Subject	Growth ratio
Agriculture	1.40
Arts	1.49
Engineering	1.36
Law	1.50
Medicine	1.29
Science	1.42

Source: PSACHAROPOULOS, G., and SANYAL, B., *op. cit.*, p. 29.

Age is the wage leader. All other factors remaining the same, the more aged graduates are the higher is their salary. For all the countries surveyed in our series, this is true. This, of course, is due to the strong association between age and experience and the salary scales are mechanistically related to seniority on the job. In the Philippines the graduates holding administrative positions earned most, whereas age was the second most important variable in explaining salary differentials. In the Sudan it ranked first in explaining salary differentials, in other countries it was a significant explanatory variable, although its rank in order of importance varied.

It might be said that the earnings of graduates grow because of the substantial role of the public sector in the market for them. We have dealt above with the role of the public sector in the employment of graduates. In all the developing countries (of the second and third group of our typology), and of course in all the centrally planned economies of the first group, most of the graduates are employed in the public sector. However, when a distinction is made between private and public employment, a clear division emerges. In the market-dominated economies, the private sector pays more. For example in Zambia, mean earnings by sector are as follows: public sector, 241 kwachas; private sector, 262 kwachas. In Sri Lanka, the sector of employment is the second most important variable in explaining salary differences, and this is due to the higher salary paid in the private sector. In India, as well, the private sector pays more. In the planned economies, however, the situation is different. There the private sector pays less, as can be seen in Tanzania, where at the time of our survey the situation was as follows:

Table 37: Monthly salary (in shillings) by sector of work in Tanzania

Sector working	Gross monthly starting salary	Standard deviation	Monthly salary at time of survey	Standard deviation
Government	1,121.440	401.960	1,567.173	613.951
Parastatal	1,148.015	442.869	1,816.536	731.783
Private	912.500	292.083	1,165.917	431.627

Source: Tanzania study, *op. cit.*, p. 269.

Another interesting result in the analysis of the salary structure is the gender gap in salaries. For planned economies like Poland, an analysis of earnings of technicians by sex and period of work experience gives the following result:

Table 38: Earning of technicians by sex and period of work experience in Poland

Sex	Period of work experience			
	2 years	2.1–4 years	4.1–6 years	6 years +
Women	78.3	78.7	81.7	85.1
Men	94.5	99.3	109.7	138.4

(Figures are percentages of average wages)
Source: KLUCZYNSKY, J., and SANYAL, B.C. (Eds.), *Education and Work in Poland*, Warsaw, PWN, and Paris, Unesco, 1985.

In Tanzania the mean salary at the time of the survey was 337 shillings higher for men than women and in Zambia 60 kwachas more for men than women. As in the case of age, gender has also been a very common significant variable in explaining earnings differentials. One can therefore conclude that despite policy statements on eliminating the gender gap in the labour market, it is still discriminatory.

It was also noted that earnings differentials are not significant in most of our studies for differences in region of home, parental occupation and parental income. However, in some cases (Sri Lanka and Philippines, for example) the institution attended by the graduate has an influence on the salary structure of a graduate.

We may sum up our section on salary structure by stressing that although more highly educated people are better paid throughout the world, a more professionally specialized education does not necessarily yield a higher salary in the long run. The most significant source of salary differences among those with a third-level education is age. Other major differences stem from the gender gap, still very pronounced in many countries, and the fact that in all except the centrally planned economies the private sector pays more than the public sector.

Notes

1   Federal Republic of Germany study, *op. cit.*, p. 138.
2   Philippines study, *op. cit.*, p. 219.
3   See Sri Lanka study, *op. cit.*, pp. 271–273.
4   See page 124 for explanation.
5   See USSR study, *op. cit.*, p. 86.
6   *Ibid.*, p. 111.
7   See Peru study, *op. cit.*, Table 40, page 111.
8   This figure includes all categories of employed graduates, such as casual, temporary etc.
9   See Psacharopoulos, G., *Returns to Education: An International Comparison*, Elsevier, 1973, p. 132.
10 Sanyal, B.C., and Versluis, J., *Higher Education, Human Capital and Labour Market Segmentation in the Sudan*, IIEP/ILO Working paper, 1976, pp. 15–16.
11 See the IIEP case studies on these countries.
12 Psacharopoulos, G., *op. cit.*, p. 132.

9 Conclusions: Implications for Higher Education Planners

In the foregoing chapters we have analysed the following four aspects of the relationship between higher education and employment for a selected set of countries around the world: the determinants of demand for higher education, the delivery system and response to the demand, the transition from higher education to work, and the world of work itself as perceived or experienced by three groups of people — students, graduates and employers. The findings of these analyses provide us with some hints for planning higher education, which will be discussed for each aspect of the relationship mentioned above.

Implications of the analysis of the determinants of demand

Our analysis shows that the phenomenon of 'mismatch' between the development of higher education and the employability of graduates exists in varying degrees in both the centrally planned economies and the market economies. The centrally planned economies, with manpower forecasts as a technique for planning education, are facing problems of employment revealed through under-utilization of qualifications and 'misemployment' of graduates. The market economies, on the other hand, have overexpanded their higher education system because of increased social demand and lack of concern for the employability of graduates. It has been observed that, in spite of extreme care taken in making manpower forecasts in the centrally planned economies, estimates are not always accurate. The first problem is the forecast of manpower needs. The defects of the method of estimation have been described as follows:[1]

- The inability of the method to take into account changing technology, which makes the estimates of future demand unreliable by changing the inputs of the modern sector of the economy, changing productivity, substituting some kinds of manpower for others or increasing capital.

- The development plans for countries, where they exist, are not implemented within the time period specified. The gaps are often very wide, owing to unexpected shortages of professional, technical and skilled manpower; unexpected delay in obtaining the financial resources; or unforeseen circumstances such as weather failure, political crises, etc.
- The composite nature of the economic sectors and sub-sectors as components of the development plan creates difficulty in the accurate estimation of manpower demand for each component of the sub-sector.
- The rural-urban imbalance, which overcrowds the cities with qualified manpower of some types and causes the rural areas to be neglected, creating unemployment in the cities and scarcity of the same type of people in the villages, is ignored in the above-mentioned method.
- The identification of the right kind of education for any type of job is difficult for the employer, so that the estimates do not satisfy the needs of the employers, even if they are consulted. Although performance on the job may not be related to the academic performance, the employers use the academic performance as the tool for recruitment, since no other criterion is available.
- The occupational mobility of qualified manpower is difficult to assess and has not been given due recognition in the techniques. The relationship between training and subsequent occupational career depends not only on the type and content of training and job description, but also on the attitude of graduates towards conditions of work which, in turn, depends upon their social and economic background. In many countries, there are high levels of substitutability between types of training and the relationship between educational experience and career patterns undergoes particularly rapid changes. Very little is known about the exact dimension of this relationship.
- The changing participation rates of output from the education sector among different social groups also create problems. These participation rates vary from one training situation to another and also depend on the attitudes of the graduates towards the education system and the labour market. Again, very little is known about this phenomenon.
- During the time period between the manpower forecasts and the output of the forecast number of graduates, the economic situation may change the demand significantly.

The above defects of manpower forecasting limit the applicability of purely quantitative techniques. Gross calculations about the scale and scope of investment programmes can be used as a rough guide for the levels of future demand for certain broad categories of manpower. As such, it can be one useful — if limited — tool in manpower planning to match the higher education system. But there is no justification for using an investment programme as the sole basis for calculating in detail the future requirements for different types of skills. The major alternative approach for estimating the future requirements involves asking the employers about the estimates of future requirements for various numbers and types of professional, technical and skilled workers with a broad or narrow coverage by mailed questionnaire or by interview. However, this method also has its defects: employers respond in terms of their own judgement about the future trend of business in general and their business in particular, and the longer the time period, the less valid their forecasts will be. So, except in the very short run, such an approach cannot help in formulating the strategy for development of higher education.

The second problem is the identification of the role of the rural sectors, which consist mainly of the subsistence agricultural sector and the commercial sector — the former playing a larger role in most of the developing countries in a very special and complex way, to be analysed and included in socio-economic planning for development. The traditional customs and beliefs, attitudes and value systems, which cannot be measured precisely, are the main planning difficulty in this area.

The third problem is the difficulty in reconciling the needs of a job with individual interests and attitudes towards work. Theory has lagged behind in analysing this relationship. Educational psychologists have ignored considerations of working life when specifying educational objectives and developing evaluation criteria. The industrial psychologists have not gone far either in identifying the cognitive, affective and psycho-motor skills needed for different kinds of jobs. Very rarely have the interests and attitudes of workers been analysed to reconcile them with the needs of the job. A labour market unit aiming to make its human resources effective should have a tool for harnessing the talent and knowledge of its most versatile resource, which is the worker. The increasing need for 'knowledge workers' rather than 'manual workers' in the labour market aggravates the problem.

The fourth problem is the new concept of development. So far, contribution to the gross national product has been the sole criterion for measuring the performance of an economic sector. Questions are being raised now about the validity of such a measurement, especially as it relates to the well-being and happiness of human beings. Better distribution of economic benefits throughout the population, eradication of poverty, improvement of health care systems, opportunities to participate meaningfully in civic and community affairs and extended life expectancy are considerations which make the task of the operation of the labour market more complicated.

The above problems make manpower forecasting as a basis for educational planning extremely difficult. The broader goals of education which generate the social demand for higher education are, by definition, not employment oriented. Whatever the context in which an educational planner works, the rising expectations of citizens cannot be ignored, nor can the social goals of democratization, or the cultural appetite of the people for education. One may therefore come to the following conclusion:

Planning for higher education should be based on a combination of manpower and social demand approaches. For the guidance needed as to the direction that the development of education in general, and higher education in particular, should take in quantitative terms to cater for the future needs for skills, the manpower approach is helpful if unemployment and underemployment are to be controlled. At the same time, to meet rising expectations and to achieve democratization in the society, social demand for education has to be looked at. The disciplines to be used in applying one or the other approach must be chosen to suit the different objectives.

This is reinforced with the advance of technology around the world, especially in the industrialized countries. The size of employment, as it has been traditionally defined, may not increase to the extent that the economicaly active population in the world will increase.[2] In the developing countries, however, there is still some scope for increasing employment by enlarging the modern sector of the economy. Higher education will have a role in increasing economic activities by relating itself to economic and social development. Even then, the size of employment may not cover the entire economically active population who seek an identity in the society through employment. To achieve full employment in any country, it will be necessary to redefine employment as any useful social role that an individual plays in the society for its preservation and development, and governments will have to formulate policies to recognize these roles economically and socially, thus strengthening the part played by social demand in educational planning.

Hints for planning higher education also emerge from the individual determinants (micro-characteristics) of demand for higher education (see Chapter 3, pp. 33–9). Results of our surveys show that professional career motives are the most important in creating individual demand for higher education. Bursary incentives play an insignificant role in creating demand for specific types of higher education. This last finding, which has direct policy implications in meeting manpower demand for specific skills, has to be qualified. Without bursaries the overall demand for higher education would be reduced. On the other hand, if bursaries are introduced to attract students to specific disciplines with less upward career prospects, the result may not be satisfactory.

The analysis of the individual demand for higher education leads us to another important consideration. Study for its own sake comes next in importance after career reasons as a determinant for such demand, with variations according to the sex of the student; females give this a higher score than males in some countries. This again reinforces the socio-cultural role played by education. In the choice of disciplines, also, factors such as student's sex, economic and occupational status of parents, and region of home, play important roles. Medicine and teaching are more popular with girls, boys being more interested in engineering and agriculture. In most developing countries, arts-based disciplines are more popular with girls and science-based disciplines are more popular with boys. This also has implications for the planning of higher education and leads us to the next hint for planners.

Socio-economic status of students influences choice of discipline in higher education. Urban, male and higher income group students demand career oriented higher education more than rural, female and lower income group students.

This leads to a further consideration: achievement of a better match between supply and demand calls for the inclusion of the individual socio-economic characteristics of students in the context of the country concerned in the analysis of the relationship between higher education and employment.

Implications of the analysis of the delivery system

To respond to the demand, each country has developed its delivery system for higher education. However, the developing countries have in most cases followed the system of the industrialized countries. The access policy, organizational structure and method of operation in the developing countries have been largely influenced by the existing structure and methods of the industrialized countries. Although, on the one hand, this has allowed for some sort of equivalence of credentials among different countries, on the other it has to some extent ignored the special context of the countries and, in some cases (especially the decolonized ones), caused conflict with national objectives.

One example is the role of the medium of instruction in perpetuating the hierarchy inherited from the colonial rulers, which had often barred lower social groups from admission to higher education. Experiential background had also played a role in perpetuating the social hierarchy in some countries through the instrument of discriminatory access policies. However, in recent years, changes have been introduced in access policy in many countries so as to achieve the social objective of democratization and the economic objective of supplying manpower.

Our analysis of the countries indicates the following:

Centrally planned economies have emphasized the manpower approach for the development of higher education and have adopted access policies principally to meet the manpower objectives, whereas the market economies have adopted access policies oriented towards meeting the individual demand for higher education. Most of the developing countries (except countries like Tanzania) have taken the latter approach.

Another feature of the access policy is related to the process of democratization where socio-economic background is increasingly playing a role in the admission policy through the 'quota system' or assignment of 'preferential points' to traditionally deprived sections of the society. However, academic performance still plays a dominant role in admission to higher education, and this fact leads us to the following consideration:

The access policy to the systems of higher education is used as a screening device to regulate both academic quality and social mobility.

Given the problem of employment of higher education graduates, access policy should differ according to discipline. Professionally oriented disciplines should place more emphasis on manpower needs, while the liberal disciplines should place more emphasis on meeting the individual demand for higher education.

Again, a feature of the access policy to higher education is the increasing recognition of work experience as an admission requirement. Experience in the developed and developing countries shows some of the benefits of this recognition, and we may conclude that work experience in a related field should have some weight in the admission policy to higher education.

Regarding the structure of the higher education system, one may note the diversity that is developing in the delivery of higher education. Traditional university-type education is being supplemented by short-cycle programmes in higher education. All over the world, a large number of non-university institutions are being set up which do not offer degrees but diplomas at a lower level. This tendency is more evident in industrialized and oil-exporting countries, though the reasons for it are different.

In the industrialized economies, at present, demand for higher education goes beyond the desire for higher income; it is increasingly sought for cultural reasons such as prestige, or a role to play in society. In predominantly Islamic countries, higher education had traditionally been an outlet for cultural aspirations, but the oil boom in some of these countries has made it necessary to have more and more qualified persons to provide the skills for developing these natural resources. One way to achieve this quickly is to provide short-cycle programmes, as in Africa, where a country like Mali does not have any university, although expansion is taking place in the non-university institutions.

Changes in the higher education system are also taking place in the offering of more science- and technology-based programmes. In the 1960s and early 1970s, countries like Benin, Mali and Tanzania had hardly any students in the science- and technology-based disciplines, whereas in the later 1970s, enrolment in these disciplines was increasing rapidly. For example, Tanzania had increased its share of science-based enrolment from 56 per cent in 1977 to almost 73 per cent in 1979. In the Sudan, the proportion of science-based students is nearly 30 per cent — the same as in India. The tendency for diversification towards economic development-oriented fields has been continuing in spite of the scarcity of resources needed to develop these fields. In the Eastern European countries, the proportion of engineering enrolment is in general much higher than in other country groups.

Another development is the increasing number of post-graduate programmes being offered in the developing countries around the world. In addition to the development of higher education in the traditional format mentioned above, many countries are attempting to restructure their systems of higher education.

In some countries, the education system is being adapted to make it more relevant to changing social needs, in others, 'shadow education systems' are developing in the world of work. In Europe, including the USSR, the most common form is 'recurrent education', usually undertaken in alternation with work after leaving school. West Germany, Sweden and the United Kingdom in the Western world have developed these programmes to suit the changing needs of the employment market. The increasing need for workers to participate in management, the growing tendency of companies to meet their employment needs by upgrading the work force within the company rather than depending on the external labour market, and the specific types of skills needed by different industries, have been the motivating factors for the organization of adult education in the Federal Republic of Germany; as a result, about 40 per cent of all the firms with 50 employees or more were already making provision for such education in 1974. Training could take place, depending on the purpose, either 'on the job' in the firm, or 'off the job' with paid educational leave. Because of the high level of unemployment in Sweden, the development of recurrent education among youth has been encouraged. An additional stimulus has been the experiments in 'industrial democracy' for increasing workers' participation in decision-making on the conditions of work. A joint project between the University of Lund, in Sweden, and a regional trades union has formalized an education-employment linkage whereby course content and teaching are adapted to trade union needs and the union supports research relevant to its interests.

In the United Kingdom, recurrent education has developed against a background of skill obsolescence, lagging productivity, high unemployment among youth, shifts in occupational distribution and changing labour/management relations. The Employment and Training Act of 1973 has given rise to courses making education more responsive to the world of work. In the mid-1970s, about two-thirds of the total labour force were covered by the Industrial Training Boards, which were responsible for this training. In addition to the ITBs, there was also the programme of Training Within Industries (TWI), offering short courses under the direct responsibility of the government. Medium and long-term 'off the job' recurrent education was provided under the Training Opportunities Scheme (TOPS). These programmes proved so popular that between 1973 and 1976, the number of courses nearly doubled. Flexible hours, compressed work courses and part-time employment enable the workers to undertake such training more easily.

In the United States, the total budget for training and development in business and industry now runs to about $80 to $100 billion per year. American Telephone and Telegraph alone spends approximately US$1.3 billion per year on training. There are nearly 700,000 full and part-time educators in business and industry.[3] The type and scope of the training today varies from industry to industry, but the core of the programmes consists of active student involvement through simulation exercises and end-of-course critical evaluation, individually-oriented course content, duration and instructional method, the increased use of programmed materials, advanced instructional technologies and the appreciation of the student's sensibilities, behaviour and attitudes. The Fund for the Improvement of Post-Secondary Education, a federal government fund, has been established to relate education to work with the objective of providing more avenues for routeing out-of-school adults back into education and through education to work, providing new openings for youth who are typically in school and need to get into contact with work, and providing guidance on problems of substance and outcome. The Fund works in co-operation with voluntary agencies, educational associations and institutions for higher education.

In Eastern European and many developing countries, there are similar programmes for the training of the work force. In some of them, investment in such training will exceed investment in formal education.

The above review demonstrates that education today has ceased to be the monopoly of a formal education system. Nevertheless, attempts to relate education to work are also going on in the formal education system. Reference has already been made to universities recognizing work experience for admission, partly as a substitute for formal education. We also saw that as early as 1974, Tanzania had adopted work experience as an entry requirement to universities, and the Faculty of Agriculture at the University of Dar es Salaam is a training-cum-production centre. Academic programmes are interwoven with field-work experience, not only in professional subjects but in liberal arts courses as well. Examples of integrating continuing education and work in various ways are also in abundance in many other developing countries.

Many new models for structuring higher education as a response to societal changes are being developed. One model involves setting up a cell, centre or institute in relation to a particular problem faced by a country. A second model has been developed around problem-centred interdisciplinary schools. A third model involves setting up universities for national development, each of which is a prototype based on several university-area divisions which in turn are broken down into a number of problem-oriented departments.[4] For universities to be concerned with national development is certainly a step in the right direction.

Discussions on new structures of higher education would be incomplete without mentioning two innovations that are being tried out in the United Kingdom and in the United States: the 'Open University' and 'Co-operative Education', respectively.

The Open University was established in 1969 with the primary objective of giving to those who would not otherwise have access to it the opportunity to pursue higher education. Provision was made for 'open entry' admission of mature students (21 years and upwards) as part-time, non-residential students who would work at home in their spare time. The instruction can lead to a degree (BA Ordinary or Masters), but non-degree programmes are also available. 'Foundation courses' must be taken by most students, but those who have the basic qualifications needed for a particular programme are exempt. Instruction takes different forms. A variety of correspondence units and television and radio broadcasts provide students with information and guidance in a standard package. The packages are prepared by a course team composed of regional and central academic staff, the BBC, and educational technologists. In addition to working at home, students can attend, on a voluntary basis, 'study centres' located throughout the country, usually in other educational institutions. These centres are the focal points for the undergraduate students' meetings with their tutors or counsellors, who play the role of general educational adviser at the local level throughout the student's educational course. Assignments by correspondence, corrected by tutors, are the major means of improving upon the student's work. Computer-marked assignments complement these. Degrees are awarded to students who have achieved a given number of credits in the programme. In addition to continuous assessment through assignments, every course has a final examination for the degree. Since the Open University was established, such distance learning systems are spreading to many countries in the developing world, centred around the correspondence courses already in existence. This illustrates an important factor to be taken into account in education planning:

New structures are providing many individuals with a chance to upgrade their social roles as well as to pursue higher education for its own sake.

The American programme, 'Co-operative Education', is an academic strategy that integrates on-campus classroom study with off-campus work experience. Although the term is more common in the United States, such programmes are prevalent in many other countries. Students in co-operative education alternate between periods of study in the colleges and universities, and periods of employment in business, government and non-profit-making organizations. Employment areas are directly related to academic areas. Depending on the situation, such work experience is given due academic credit and may be remunerated (as in the USA and the United Kingdom) or voluntary (Federal Republic of Germany). The main characteristic of these programmes is that they are organized from within the education system in an attempt to develop a closer relationship between the education system and the world of work.

These various structures demonstrate that efforts are being made to relate higher education more closely to the world of work. Experiences with alternative structures of higher education could indicate new directions which would increase its relevance.

As these trends develop, the task of educational planners becomes more complicated. Before the planning process starts, the diversification of the delivery systems of education needs to be studied carefully and understood. The functional differentiation between various educational programmes — i.e. their complementarity, supplementarity and conflict — must be identified before one can plan for the development of one or the other educational programme.

While attempting to develop educational programmes for scientific and technological development, one has to look, on the one hand, into the methods of adjustment by the training system to needs determined by technical changes imported from other countries and, on the other, into the need to adapt this imported technological know-how and develop local technology.

In responding to the demand for education in quantitative terms, planners also have to keep in mind the following:

In the developing countries, it will be particularly difficult to control adequate growth in higher education, because the lower levels of education are expanding and thus creating disproportionately high expectations.

There is an additional point the planners must take into consideration:

In spite of the difficulties in the production sectors of the economy, the allocation of resources to education in general, and higher education in particular, has not been drastically reduced so far. The poorer countries are still struggling to develop their systems of higher education to achieve democratization, relate them to the economic need for skills and increase enrolment in science and technology in order to decrease economic dependence on the industrialized countries.

It has been observed from our studies that non-government and private sources play an increasingly significant part in financing higher education. This, combined with the observation that career motives play an important role in generating demand for higher education, leads us to the following suggestion:

A positively discriminatory fee-paying system in higher education, in which fees would be payable according to the student's financial capacity, might redress financial inequity in developing countries.

The analysis of the operation of the education system as perceived by the students, graduates and employers reveals that professional career guidance in all types of countries leaves much to be desired. It has also been noted that student mobility within the education system is significant in most of the countries studied. It is one of the areas which has been least studied in the analysis of the relationship between education and employment, and brings us to a further consideration:

If sufficient information on the potential mobility of students between fields is available, it is possible for the planner to take account of such mobility in order to adjust intakes to different specializations.

Regarding the arrangement of instruction to make it more responsive to the needs of the world of work, there is a clear indication for educational planners which is as follows:

The incorporation of work experience in formal training programmes is the arrangement preferred by students, graduates and employers. It is also observed that out-of-school training cannot replace formal training, but can supplement it.

Planning higher education for a smoother transition of graduates to the world of work

The dominant cause of graduate unemployment is, of course, the stagnation in economic growth. Compared to the period 1960–1970 the average annual growth rate of gross domestic product decreased during the period 1970–1982, from 5.1 to 2.8 per cent in the industrial market economies and from 6 to 5.4 per cent in the middle-income countries. Except for China and India among the low-income countries, the growth rate decreased from 4.3 per cent during the period 1960–1970 to 3.4 per cent during that of 1970–1982.[5] Slower economic growth in the face of faster growth in the supply of graduates from the institutions of higher education around the world is at the heart of the problem. But the growth model adopted by different countries favouring more capital investment than labour investment is also a major cause of the unemployment problem.

In market economies, if salaries were fixed on the basis of demand and supply of graduates, the larger output of graduates would have reduced the salary structure for graduates, thus reducing the demand for higher education. However, as we have seen, in developing countries all graduates so far have ended up with some kind of employment after waiting for a certain time, and a university graduate has a higher probability of employment than a non-graduate. Since most of the graduates in developing countries are employed by the public sector, and since the public sector salary structure cannot be adjusted quickly to follow the law of demand and supply, a longer waiting period does not reduce the private rate of return on higher education in the long run.[6] So the demand for higher education continues.

The situation in Europe is slightly different, where one reason cited for unemployment is the high and rising wage cost. This is revealed in the steadily increasing capital/labour ratios. As real wages have risen relative to the value of output, this has had an adverse effect on profits and the decline in profitability has led in turn to stagnation in investment and job creation. However, views differ on this process. Some researchers, for instance, are of the opinion that 'substitution of capital for labour takes place because of factor prices and that given a certain technology, labour and capital are largely complementary, especially in large-scale industries with a high technology content. As a consequence, unemployment is more likely to be caused by deficiencies in the process of capital accumulation — i.e., lagging investments'.[7]

Another reason for rising graduate unemployment is the increased labour force participation rate among graduates. This is true mainly for women. In developing countries, until recently, the participation rate of female graduates in the labour force had remained remarkably low because of attitudes, traditions and social customs. The participation rate of women, many of whom are graduates, is also increasing at a high rate in the industrialized countries. The effect of the overall labour force participation rate on graduate unemployment may decrease in the near future because of falling birth rates. However, this decrease is likely to be offset by increased participation of female graduates in the labour force.

Lack of interaction between employers and institutions of higher education is another problem cited by a large proportion of graduates in some developing countries. Also, lack of proper information about where the jobs are available and how to obtain them is cited as a reason for graduate unemployment. At a more aggregate level, lack of information on manpower needs for developmental efforts is a more or less universal phenomenon. In spite of defects in the accuracy of manpower forecasts, it is believed that these forecasts can indicate some broad direction as to the development that higher education should take. Educated unemployment is also due to a mismatch between aspirations and opportunities. The examination results which provide terminal qualifications do not have any correspondence with the needs of the world of work. Nevertheless, these terminal qualifications raise the job aspirations of those who have them, though they do not help in obtaining productive employment.

Finally, there is often a preference among employers for non-graduates rather than graduates, and this is another cause of graduate unemployment. If the job conditions allow, employers prefer to employ people with a lower academic qualification and train them on the job.

Identification of the causes of graduate unemployment helps us to formulate some suggestions as to the means of reducing the problem. These have to be different in the developing countries from those used in the industrialized countries, because of the differences in the nature of the employment market and in the level of educational development. The employment market of the developing countries is not yet saturated, because the modern sector still has considerable scope for expansion. With a proper choice of technology, growth in the modern sector might greatly contribute to the creation of employment for graduates. Adjustments in the salary structure of the graduates, relating it to demand-supply consider-ations, could also help. There is much scope for improvement in the recruitment pattern of employers, as well as of career information, professional guidance and placement services. The admission patterns to different disciplines can be related to the needs for professional skills in the economy, at least in broad terms. New structures of higher education combining education with work experience in different forms may be developed to relate the world of higher education to the world of employment. Attempts may be made to involve the institutions of employ-ment with the institutions of higher education in formulating policies.

The choice of technology in development policy should take into account the employment possibilities. The cost of labour in the developing countries is still low and it would be unwise to follow the Western model of capital intensive economies, where the cost of labour is high and capital had been made artificially cheap through a variety of devices such as low interest rates, amortization procedures, public subsidies for investment in depressed regions, subsidizing loans to modernizing sectors, etc., without a rigorous analysis of the employment situation. With the development of the industrial sector and the service sector, employment opportunities in developing countries can be increased to a great extent. Attempts to reorganize the curricula of the higher education system, oriented towards the development needs of the economy in respect of cognitive skills and such affective skills as would encourage self-employment of the graduates, will also contribute to reducing the problem of graduate unemployment. The higher education system has a role to play in these attempts.

In the centrally planned economies, the organizational forms of enterprises, the manner in which work is organized, the system of wages, and the recruitment practices have to be reformed on the basis of sociological analysis of the behavioural patterns of those concerned. The schooling system has to adjust to such needs as well. The issue of 'work ethic' is also important for a socialist citizen who is guaranteed an employment situation.

The industrialized countries, particularly those of the West, will have to return to 'true' prices for both capital and labour to achieve a balance among the production factors that would be more favourable to labour. The present approach of 'cheap' capital and 'costly' labour will require some modification.

The service sector of many of the industrialized countries has reached a saturation point beyond which further increase in employment growth is difficult to achieve. It has to be understood also that today a substantial part of the service sector in the industrialized countries is directly related to the productive industrial sector. Technological advancement has led fewer and fewer people to produce, but more people are needed to invent, design, distribute and sell. In this sense, the service sector still has possibilities to create employment. In addition, there has been some thinking about the generation of a non-commercial service sector which would concentrate on the services and needs unfulfilled by the existing public and private sectors.[8] Decentralized operations and initiatives, low investment costs per job, labour-intensive projects, labour costs partially compensated by a reduction in public outlays for social security benefits, and users of services charged for the costs of the services rendered, are some suggestions for organizing this new sector, which has been termed the 'quaternary sector'.

The movement towards a new 'dualism' in the economies of the industrialized countries, characterized by increased labour productivity in the 'open' internationally competitive sector comprising industry and closely related services, together with the creation of employment in those parts of the industrial and service sectors which are sheltered from international competition, has been suggested in some countries as another measure for creation of graduate employment. Such measures as reduction in labour costs by means of temporary exemption from social security contributions by the employer for newly hired workers (in France), employment premiums in the form of a flat subsidy paid to the firms to avoid lay-off, and 'employment tax credit' offered to the employers have all shown some signs of increasing employment opportunities in industrialized countries. Suggestions have also been put forward to reorganize job content and work organization so as to improve work performance and increase employment opportunities in the long run. Decentralization of decision-making and a more even distribution of conceptual tasks have been suggested as ways to fit the needs and capacities of the increasingly sophisticated and highly trained labour force in the industrialized countries. It is believed that these measures would encourage 'entrepreneurship' and self-employment, which may have to play an enhanced role in future job creation.

An employment policy oriented towards the eradication of discriminatory procedures, the creation of stable jobs in large quantities and the systematic provision of mobility channels between the various segments of the employment market in order to reduce the segmentation of the labour market would allow for an easier adjustment between the output of the education system and high-level manpower needs. Reduction of working time combined with an adjustment in wages is also suggested as a measure to reduce graduate unemployment. According to one study in the Federal Republic of Germany, reduction of working time created employment for 824,000 persons in 1979 and registered unemployment was reduced by 549,000. An increase in part-time work could directly reduce unemployment, which implies that there would be benefits to be gained from splitting full-time work into part-time jobs.

The above suggestions mostly relate to adjustments in economic policy and the labour market itself. The education system also has a role to play in the reduction of graduate unemployment. A number of possibilities are suggested by the findings we have discussed in the previous chapters, particularly the following.

College and university officials could (1) exercise greater direct data management so as to avoid decisions which add to imbalances between supply and demand in labour markets, (2) respond to indicators of imbalance where appropriate, (3) work in co-operation with secondary schools to delineate functions, reduce overlap and assure programme continuity, (4) seek to assure as much learning value as possible from college work-study assignments, field experiences and internships, and (5) indicate to students, especially those firmly committed to the liberal arts or teaching, how to combine subject matter interests with the development of marketable skills. Development of non-traditional alternatives to the acquisition of credentials in the trades and professions, implying closer links between institutions of higher education on the one hand and business and industry on the other, is also worth exploring. In this respect, work-education programmes with clearly defined objectives should involve carefully selected motivated students and link experiential learning to work in classrooms and laboratories.

Another suggestion is that employers, employee organizations and educators should work together in ways that are mutually beneficial to the learners. The employers should provide part-time student job opportunities and faculty staff development programmes, and they should articulate clearly the qualities they seek in the graduates. Educators should see that the learners acquire and practise skills of value in employment. Special emphasis should be given to the establishment of educational information centres, the strengthening of guidance and counselling, and the development of occupational information systems for states and regions.

From the experience obtained through the present research, one can observe the complexity of the relationship between higher education and employment. To reduce the 'mismatch' between them one cannot stop at simple formulation of policy measures. The countries concerned have to pass legislation to adopt such measures formally, and then their implementation has to be followed up through a built-in monitoring system.

The foregoing suggestions only hint at general directions and have to be adapted to the specific context of each country.

Notes

1   For a discussion of the methodology, see: JOLLY, A.R., and COLCLOUGH, C., 'African manpower plans: an evaluation', *International Labour Review*, Vol. 106, Nos. 2–3; and, for a fuller discussion of the defects, see BASHIR, A., and BLAUG, M. (eds.), *The Practice of Manpower Forecasting: A Collection of Case Studies*, Amsterdam, Elsevier, 1973.

2   According to one estimate (see RUMBERGER, R., 'The job market for college graduates, 1960–90', *Journal of Higher Education*, 1983) robots could replace up to 3 million operative jobs in the next twenty years and could eliminate 8 million operative positions of today by 2024 in the USA. Technologies such as computer-aided design, for example, may eliminate the occupation of draughtsman.

3   DUNN, S.L., 'The changing university: survival in the information society', in: *The Futurist*, August 1983. Also see: *International Herald Tribune*, 4 February 1985.

4   ADISESHIAH, M., in *Higher Education and the New International Order*, by SANYAL, B.C., Franks Printers UK and Paris, Unesco, 1982.

5   WORLD BANK, *World Development Report 1984*, Washington DC.

6   BLAUG, M., *Education and the Employment Problem in Developing Countries*, Geneva, International Labour Organization, 1973.

7   JALLADE, J.P. (ed.), *Employment and Unemployment in Europe*, Staffordshire, Trentham Books, 1981.

8   DELORS, J., *Comment Créer des Emplois*, Paris, Centre de Recherches Travail et Société, 1978.

Appendices

APPENDIX I

Statistical profile of countries involved in the research

Group	Country	Area (thousands of km²)	Population (millions)	Annual population growth (%)	Life expectancy	GNP per capita 1982 in US$	Annual growth of GNP 1962–82 (%)	Share of GDP[1] in Agriculture	Industry	Share of labour force[2] in Agriculture	Industry
I	France	547	54.9	0.5	75	11,680	3.7	4	34	8	39
	FRG	249	61.3	0.1	73	12,460	3.1	2	46	4	46
	Poland[3]	313	37	0.9	73	3,710	–	–	–	31.6	39
	USSR[3]	22,402	273.4	0.9	73	2,605	–	–	–	14	45
II	Egypt	1,001	47.0	2.5	57	690	3.6	20	34	50	30
	India	3,288	726.0	2.3	55	260	1.3	33	26	71	13
	Indonesia	1,920	160.3	2.3	53	580	4.2	26	39	58	12
	Malaysia	330	14.7	2.5	67	1,860	4.3	23	30	50	16
	Pakistan	804	91.0	3.0	50	380	2.8	31	25	57	20
	Philippines	300	53.6	2.7	64	820	2.8	22	36	46	17
	Tanzania	945	20.0	3.4	52	280	1.9	52	15	83	6
	Yemen PDR	290	2.1	2.2	46	470	6.4	12	27	45	15
	Zambia	753	6.4	3.1	51	640	–0.1	14	36	67	11
III	Bangladesh	144	97.5	2.6	48	140	20.3	47	14	74	11
	Benin	113	3.7	2.7	48	310	0.6	44	13	46	16
	Botswana	582	0.96	3.5	60	1,010	6.8	19	35	78	8
	Mali	1,204	7.1	2.7	45	180	1.6	43	10	73	12
	Nepal	141	16.0	2.6	46	170	–0.1	–	–	93	2
	Sri Lanka	66	16.0	1.7	69	320	2.6	27	27	54	14
	Sudan	2,506	21.0	3.2	47	440	0.4	36	14	78	10

Notes: 1. Data relate to 1982.
2. Data relate to 1980.
3. Different accounting system renders economic data uncomparable.
   For comparability 1982 has been shown as target year for all cases except for the labour force.

Some characteristics of the three types of country participating in the research

It may be observed that the countries of the first category, which enjoy a relatively favourable higher education and employment situation, have been going through a difficult period economically. Although their per capita income is high, the growth rate has slowed down. Their traditional natural resources are exploited to a large extent but they are also exploring new resources. Their population growth rate is less than 1 per cent per year, but labour force participation rate is high. The agricultural sector has a very low share in the gross domestic product, employing a small portion of the available labour force (except in Poland where in 1980 31 per cent of the labour force was engaged in agriculture in comparison with 14 per cent in the USSR). The majority of the people in these countries live in urban areas and life expectancy is greater than seventy years. To face international competition these countries have been introducing high technology and automation in the production process of the economy, thereby reshaping not only the occupational structure but also the value systems of these countries. The emphasis on the industrial sector in the past in the centrally planned economies is now being extended to the agricultural sector. There is also a tendency towards opening up the economy to private initiatives in the centrally planned economies, whereas the market economies are reducing their openness by introducing price and wage control mechanisms.

The countries of the second group have a lower life expectancy, the highest being 67 years for Malaysia, and a larger share of agriculture in the gross domestic product, which employs an even larger proportion of the labour force. Natural resources are exploited to a lesser extent than in the first group. However in recent years they have started to change the old international division of labour, based on export of primary commodities to the industrialized countries and import of manufactured goods from them, to a new international division of labour based on the export of popular consumer goods manufactured by abundant and cheap manpower in these countries and import of more sophisticated but less essential goods manufactured with highly advanced technology in the countries of the first type. Some of these countries have enjoyed a higher growth rate in GNP per capita than those of the first group. Their population growth rate is more than 2 per cent per year, and for Pakistan and Zambia it is 3 per cent of more. The majority of the people live in rural areas. Labour force participation rate is lower than the first group of countries.

The countries of the third group are in the worst situation. Their per capita income is lowest, and in most cases is growing at the lowest rate. These countries are still dependent on external resources. They are exporters of primary commodities with little or no import substitution industry. Their population growth rate is high, most of them living in rural areas with a minimum of basic facilities. Agriculture is the most important component of the gross domestic product, employing the largest share of the labour force although exploiting a very small share of the land for agricultural purposes. Exploration of natural resources has occurred only to a limited extent and exploitation is rare. With a low participation rate in the labour force, the people face severe unemployment and underemployment problems.

APPENDIX II

Tables of variables

Table 1: List of variables and types of information and statistics collected

Variables	Required information statistics	Sources
1. SOCIO-ECONOMIC FRAMEWORK OF THE COUNTRY		
(i) Economic potential of different regions	(1) Estimates of reserves of natural resources.	(1) Geological surveys, agricultural surveys, economic surveys: government and non-government agencies.
	(2) Physical characteristics of the regions	(2) Geographical surveys: government and non-government agencies.
	(3) History of the economic and social development of the country.	(3) Historical studies in the country: government and non-government agencies and individual authors.
(ii) Economic sectors, their growth and degree of balance with the resource potential, bottlenecks for development. The role of the rural sector in national development.	(1) The economic structure of the modern sector: the industrial origin of gross domestic product, level of saving, wage employment, the role of the subsistence sector, income *per capita*.	(1) Economic surveys, reports from national government agencies, international agencies and private agencies, and national economic and social development plans.
	(2) Their relevance with the natural resource potential: degree of exploitation of the natural resources and in-country processing: implications for types of skills needed.	(2) Same as above and manpower reports if available, and other studies on relating skills with techniques needed for exploitation and development of natural resources including agricultural resources.

(iii) Population characteristics by regions, social groups and sex.

(1) Regional distribution of population by social groups, sex and age.
(2) Growth of population: implications for educational policy.
(3) Allocation of capital expenditure per head, by region.
(4) Formal employment as percentage to total population
(5) Attitudes and value systems of the people of different regions.

(1) Census, sample surveys.
(2) Same as above, and studies relating education with population.
(3) Economic surveys and government reports, estimates of public expenditure of the government.
(4) Census, sample surveys.
(5) Historical and social studies on the country, government and non-government.

(iv) Characteristics of the labour force: employment situation.

(1) Labour force in the formal sector by sex, region, occupation level and income — participation rates by sex and age.
(2) Same information by different industries of the moder sector.
(3) Estimates of labour force in the informal sector and their earnings.
(4) Estimates of productivity by sector.
(5) Unemployment in the formal and informal sector.
(6) Shortage of national skills in the modern sector.
(7) Role of expatriates in the national development.

(1) Economic report, census, sample surveys: government and non-government.
(2) Same as in (1).
(3) Census, sample surveys of the rural sector — if any.
(4) Economic survey, census of manufacturing industries conducted by central statistics agency or by any other agency.
(5) Employment exchange offices, sample surveys of employed graduates or waiting period of the graduates for getting a job, census figures, manpower surveys from Ministry offices, central statistical office or any other source.
(6) Same as above and also a survey of the employers.
(7) Census, statistics on localization programmes of different agencies.

Table 1: List of variables and types of information and statistics collected (continued)

Variables	Required information statistics	Sources
(v) Types of skill needed for the development of the economy.	(1) Stock of qualified manpower by nationality, educational level, occupation and sector serving.	(1) Manpower report, census statistics, survey of employers.
	(2) National policy guidelines in respect of localization, economic growth and other attitudinal changes (national service scheme, etc.) of the people and social aspects of the country.	(2) Party document, if any, national plans.
	(3) Alternative estimates of needs for highly qualified manpower by educational level, occupation and sector to be served.	(3) Manpower reports, survey of employers with alternative assumptions based on the economic uncertainty in the future.
2. EDUCATIONAL SYSTEM		
(i) Past development of education in general and higher education in particular, its rationale and inconsistencies if any in the pattern of development as related to the socio-economic framework of the country.	(1) Statistics on enrolments by types and level of education — for the past and present — with special reference to higher education.	(1)–(5) Ministry of Education statistics, individual educational institutions, educational research units.
	(2) Enrolment by sex and region.	
	(3) Growth of enrolment particularly for higher level of education.	
	(4) Growth of physical facilities and other facilities, namely teachers, budget, etc.	
	(5) Estimates of flow rates by grade, sex and level of education.	

(ii) Existing organizational structure; its problems, if any, in respect of meeting the objectives.

(1) The facilities for education available at present in the formal system particularly for the higher level of education.

(2) Linkage between the higher education system and the second-level education system.

(3) Role of private and public sector agencies in the control of education in general and higher education in particular, in respect of budgeting, financing, curriculum development, etc.

(1)–(3) Same as above.

(iii) Quantitative development of higher education as related to the socio-economic framework of the country and the national policy guidelines.

(1) Stock of enrolment by type of higher education, by institution, sex and region of home.

(2) The existing admission policy for different types of higher education.

(3) Stock of graduates by specialization, institution, and sex.

(4) Past trend of growth in enrolment and necessary facilities.

(5) Cost per student by type of higher education.

(6) The capacity of the institution to expand or control.

(7) Number of students abroad for training by type and duration of training.

(8) Alternative estimates of graduates to meet the needs of the economy at least quantitatively.

(1)–(7) Same as above.

(8) National policy guidelines, estimates of manpower needs, information on the institutions' capacity to expand and/or control estimated internal efficiency of the higher education system.

Table 1: List of variables and types of information and statistics collected (continued)

Variables	Required information statistics	Sources
	3. ATTITUDES AND EXPECTATIONS OF STUDENTS IN RESPECT OF HIGHER EDUCATION[1]	
(i) Students' socio-economic background.	Sex, age, marital status, nationality, region of home, guardian's occupation, industry and income.	Student survey, see for example: Questions Nos. 5 to 11 and 31 to 34 for the case of Tanzanian students.
(ii) Educational status.	Secondary school attended, type of certificate, year of graduation, desired education career, year of study, reasons for undertaking higher education, reasons for change in the field of study — if any, sources of finance, adequacy of the secondary education, choice of present faculty, degree of satisfaction with present educational career.	Questions Nos. 1 to 4, 12, 15 to 23, 26, 27 and 37 for the case of Tanzanian students.
(iii) Expectations about higher education and employment.	Present employment, if any; estimated earnings if not in educational institution at present, reasons for continuing in the field of study if intending to be employed in a field other than the present field of study, dependence of the choice of career on success in present studies, expected employment sector, conditions for accepting a job in rural areas, importance of factors in the choice of an employment, expected annual earnings at different levels of working life.	Questions Nos. 24, 25, 28 to 30 and 39 to 44 for the case of Tanzanian students.

1 All sources for item 3 are student survey.

(iv) Role of career guidance in higher education.	Sources of information, their adequacy.	Questions Nos. 13, 14, 35 and 38.
(v) Role of employment guidance.	Desirability of the involvement of educational institutions in providing such guidance, their operational mechanism, means of getting better knowledge about jobs.	Questions Nos. 35 to 38.

4. ATTITUDES AND EXPECTATIONS OF GRADUATES[1]

(i) Socio-economic background.	Age, sex, marital status, region of home, present home, education and industry of father.	Questions Nos. 1 to 7 and 30.
(ii) Educational background and expectations about the education system.	Reasons for pursuing higher education, reasons for change in field of study, if any; sources of finance for higher education, diplomas obtained, specialization and present occupation, degree of relevance of educational background with the job.	Questions Nos. 8, 9, 11, 12, 14 to 16, 21, 24 and 31.
(iii) Employment status.	Methods of obtaining first employment, waiting period to get first employment, nature of present employment, changes in jobs, if any, reasons for change, importance of different factors to make a job satisfactory, income in first employment and present income.	Questions Nos. 10, 13, 17 to 20, 22, 23, 25 to 29.

5. ATTITUDES AND EXPECTATIONS OF EMPLOYERS[2]

(i) Background.	Date of establishment, type of control, size, the industry group.	Questions Nos. 2 to 7.

1 All sources for item 4 are graduate survey.

Table 1: List of variables and types of information and statistics collected. (continued)

Variables	Required information statistics	Sources
(ii) Employment characteristics.	Methods of recruitment, criteria for selection, desirability of and difficulties in having job description mechanism. Number of graduates employed by nationality, professional level, forecast of needs of graduates in the near future.	Questions Nos. 7 to 10, 18 to 20.
(iii) Relation between the higher education sector and the labour market.	Degree of correlation between academic performance and job performance, organizational mechanism of in-service training — if any, provision for accepting students on 'sandwich' courses, methods of co-operation with the higher education institutes in the formulation and implementation of their programmes.	Questions Nos. 11 to 17.

2 All sources for item 5 are employers survey.

Table 2: Summary list of common variable groups

	Variable number		
Variable group	*Student*	*Graduate*	*Employer*
Personal characteristics	1	1	–
Community characteristics	2	2	–
Childhood home characteristics	3	3	–
Early occupational and educational desires and expectations	6	4	–
Adult home characteristics	7	5	–
(Current) Educational characteristics (manpower requirements)	10	6	2
Preferred ways of obtaining career information	13	10	–
Attitudes toward work in rural areas	14	11	–
Opinions about work	15	12	8
(Expected/current) Occupational career	16	8	(1)

Table 3: Summary list of conceptual groups of student variables

Group number	*Variable group*
1	Personal characteristics
2	Community characteristics
3	Childhood home characteristics
4	Secondary school characteristics
5	Early career information
6	Occupation desired at end of secondary schooling
7	Adult home characteristics
8	Educational career decision
9	Current employment context
10	Current educational context
11	Institution seeks cooperation in careers information
12	Attitudes and opinions about current education
13	Opinion about careers information
14	Attitudes toward work in rural areas
15	Opinions about work
16	Current occupational expectations

Table 4: Summary list of conceptual groups of graduate variables

Group number	Variable group
1	Personal characteristics
2	Community characteristics
3	Childhood home characteristics
4	Early occupational and educational expectations
5	Adult home characteristics
6	Educational characteristics
7	Early occupational career
8	Current occupational career
9	Opinions about education
10	Opinions about career information
11	Attitudes toward work in rural areas
12	Opinions about work
13	Will co-operate with institution of post-secondary education

Table 5: Summary list of conceptual groups of employer variables

Group number	Variable group
1	Organizational characteristics
2	Manpower characteristics
3	Recruitment practices
4	Correspondence between academic and vocational performance
5	In-service training
6	Opinions toward institutions of higher education
7	Provision of work opportunities within organization
8	Opinions about employee needs

Table 6: Quasi-causal conceptual ordering of student variables.[1]

1 *Personal characteristics*
1.1 Age (5)
1.2 Sex (6)

2 *Community characteristics*
2.1 Tanzanian citizen (11)
2.2 Home district (10a)
2.3 Place of residence rural/urban (10b)

3 *Childhood home characteristics*
3.1 Guardian (31)
3.2 Educational level of mother (33.1)
3.3 Educational level of father (33.2)
3.4 Guardian's occupation (32)
3.5 Guardian's income (34)

4 *Secondary school characteristics*
4.1 Attended secondary school in Tanzania (1)

1. Figures in parentheses are the question numbers of the student questionnaire (Appendix III).

Table 6:   Quasi-causal conceptual ordering of student variables (continued)

4.2   Name of last secondary school attended (2)
4.3   Completed Form VI (3)
4.4   Last year in secondary school (4)

5   *Early career information*
5.1   Received career information before applying for higher education (13a)
5.2   Source of career information (13b)
5.3   Degree of satisfaction with career information (14)

6   *Occupation desired at end of secondary schooling (12)*

7   *Adult home characteristics*
7.1   Marital status (7)
7.2   Have been divorced (8)
7.3   Number of children (9)

8   *Educational career decision*
8.1   Reasons for entering post-secondary study (19)
8.2   Present course was first choice (20)
8.3   Have changed course since entering (22)
8.4   Reason for changing course (22)
8.5   If more career information had been available, would have been willing to change course (37)
8.6   Anticipated earnings immediately after secondary schooling (30)

9   *Current employment context*
9.1   Current employment status (24)
9.2   Current earnings (25)

10   *Current educational context*
10.1   Current course of degree (15)
10.2   Number of years in present course (16)
10.3   Institution currently attended (17)
10.4   If university, faculty attended (18)
10.5   Major sources of financing for present studies (26)
10.6   Boarding student (27)

11   *Institution seeks co-operation in career information (36)*

12   *Attitudes and opinions about current education*
12.1   Like present course (21)
12.2   Secondary school course adequate preparation for present course (23)
12.3   If not expecting employment in major field of study, reason for remaining in present course (29)

13   *Opinions about career information*
13.1   Institution should take interest in employment possibilities of graduates (35)
13.2   Preferred ways of obtaining career information (38)

14   *Attitudes toward work in rural areas*
14.1   Aspects which might induce you to work in rural areas (41)
14.1.1   Importance of financial incentives
14.1.2   Importance of promotion aspects
14.1.3   Importance of greater responsibility
14.1.4   Importance of opportunity for freer life
14.1.5   Importance of other reasons

Table 6:   Quasi-causal conceptual ordering of student variables (continued)

14.2   Aspects discouraging you from work in rural areas (42)
14.2.1   Importance of lack of water, electricity, etc.
14.2.2   Importance of communication and transportation difficulties
14.2.3   Importance of being separated from friends and relatives
14.2.4   Importance of dullness and slowness of rural life
14.2.5   Importance of lack of scope for improving competence
14.2.6   Importance of delays in promotion
14.2.7   Importance of other reasons

15   *Opinions about work*
15.1   Factors in obtaining job satisfaction (44.1)
15.1.01   Importance of interesting work
15.1.02   Importance of using special talent
15.1.03   Importance of creative work
15.1.04   Importance of no supervision
15.1.05   Importance of further studies
15.1.06   Importance of improving competence
15.1.07   Importance of being helpful to others and society
15.1.08   Importance of work with people
15.1.09   Importance of a good income
15.1.10   Importance of travel
15.1.11   Importance of supervising others
15.1.12   Importance of better prospects
15.1.13   Importance of a secure future
15.1.14   Importance of time for family and hobbies
15.1.15   Importance of using skills learned in formal schooling
15.2   Factors in meeting career objectives (44.2)
15.2.01   Importance of interesting work
15.2.02   Importance of using special talent
15.2.03   Importance of creative work
15.2.04   Importance of no supervision
15.2.05   Importance of further studies
15.2.06   Importance of improving competence
15.2.07   Importance of being helpful to others and society
15.2.08   Importance of work with people
15.2.09   Importance of a good income
15.2.10   Importance of travel
15.2.11   Importance of supervising others
15.2.12   Importance of better prospects
15.2.13   Importance of a secure future
15.2.14   Importance of time for family and hobbies
15.2.15   Importance of using skills learned in formal schooling

16   *Current occupational expectations*
16.1   Intend to seek employment in major field of study (28)
16.2   Sector of expected permanent employment (40)
16.3   Extent to which career will depend on success in present studies (39)
16.4   Expected earnings (43)
16.4.1   At start of career
16.4.2   After five years
16.4.3   After ten years
16.4.4   Near retirement

Table 7: Quasi-causal conceptual ordering of graduate variables.[1]

1   *Personal characteristics*
1.1   Age (2)
1.2   Sex (3)

2   *Community characteristics*
2.1   Tanzanian citizen (1)
2.2   Region (4)
2.2.1   Now living (4.1)
2.2.2   Home district (4.2)

3   *Childhood home characteristics*
3.1   Educational level of mother (7.1)
3.2   Educational level of father (7.2)
3.3   Guardian's occupation (30a)
3.4   Guardian's income (30b)

4   *Early occupational and educational expectations*
4.1   Occupation desired at end of secondary school (9a)
4.2   Reason for undertaking post-secondary education (9b)

5   *Adult home characteristics*
5.1   Marital status (5)
5.2   Educational level of husband or wife (6)

6   *Educational characteristics*
6.01   Highest academic qualification (8a)
6.02   Institution from which highest qualification was received (8b1)
6.03   Other institutions attended (8b2)
6.04   If university graduate, faculty attended (8c)
6.05   Year admitted to graduating institution (8d)
6.06   Year received highest qualification (8e)
6.07   Changed field of study during higher education (12)
6.08   Reason for changed study during higher education (12)
6.09   Field of specialization for highest qualification (16.1)
6.10   Field of specialization most relevant to current job (16.2)
6.11   Educational institution had employment office (20.2)
6.12   Source of financing for first post-secondary education (21)
6.13   Trained to be teacher (11)

7   *Early occupational career*
7.1   Waiting period before receiving first employment (13.1)
7.2   How first employment obtained (13.2)
7.3   Salary in first permanent employment (29)
7.4   Changed jobs (18)
7.5   Reason for changing job (19a)

8   *Current occupational career*
8.1   Sector of employment (19b)
8.2   Teacher (10)
8.3   Hours working per week (22)
8.4   Salary in present work (28)

9   *Opinions about education*
9.1   Utility of education received for present job (14)
9.2   Necessity of educational qualifications for getting present job (15)

---

1.   Figures in parentheses are the question numbers of the graduate questionnaire (Appendix III).

Table 7:   Quasi-causal conceptual ordering of graduate variables (continued)

10   *Opinions about career information*
10.1   Preferred way of receiving career information (23)
10.1.1   Rank of job experience during studies
10.1.2   Rank of information from prospective employers
10.1.3   Rank of career publications
10.1.4   Rank of discussions with workers
10.2   Employment office at educational institution would have been useful (20.2)

11   *Attitudes toward work in rural areas*
11.1   Aspects which might induce you to work in rural areas (26)
11.1.1   Importance of financial incentives
11.1.2   Importance of promotion aspects
11.1.3   Importance of greater responsibility
11.1.4   Importance of opportunity for freer life
11.1.5   Importance of low cost of living
11.1.6   Importance of other reasons
11.2   Aspects discouraging you from work in rural areas (27)
11.2.1   Importance of lack of water, electricity, etc.
11.2.2   Importance of communication and transportation difficulties
11.2.3   Importance of being separated from friends and relatives
11.2.4   Importance of dullness and slowness of rural life
11.2.5   Importance of lack of scope for improving competence
11.2.6   Importance of delays in promotion
11.2.7   Importance of other reasons

12   *Opinions about work*
12.1   Factors in obtaining present work (17)
12.1.1   Importance of academic record for getting present job
12.1.2   Importance of aptitude test
12.1.3   Importance of interview
12.1.4   Importance of past experience
12.1.5   Importance of letters of recommendation
12.1.6   Importance of physical appearance
12.1.7   Importance of marital status
12.1.8   Importance of other factors
12.2   Extent to which choice of career depends on success in studies (24)
12.3   Factors in obtaining job satisfaction (25.1)
12.3.01   Importance of interesting work
12.3.02   Importance of using special talent
12.3.03   Importance of creative work
12.3.04   Importance of no supervision
12.3.05   Importance of further studies
12.3.06   Importance of improving competence
12.3.07   Importance of being helpful to others and society
12.3.08   Importance of work with people
12.3.09   Importance of a good income
12.3.10   Importance of travel
12.3.11   Importance of supervising others
12.3.12   Importance of better prospects
12.3.13   Importance of a secure future
12.3.14   Importance of time for family and hobbies
12.3.15   Importance of using skill learned in formal schooling

Table 7: Quasi-causal conceptual ordering of graduate variables (continued)

12.4   Factors in meeting career objectives (25.2)
12.4.01   Importance of interesting work
12.4.02   Importance of using special talents
12.4.03   Importance of creative work
12.4.04   Importance of no supervision
12.4.05   Importance of further studies
12.4.06   Importance of improving competence
12.4.07   Importance of being helpful to others and society
12.4.08   Importance of work with people
12.4.09   Importance of a good income
12.4.10   Importance of travel
12.4.11   Importance of supervising others
12.4.12   Importance of better prospects
12.4.13   Importance of a secure future
12.4.14   Importance of time for family and hobbies
12.4.15   Importance of using skills learned in formal schooling

13   *Will co-operate with institution of post-secondary education* (31)
13.1   As member of advisory group
13.2   Filling in questionnaires
13.3   Attending meetings

Table 8: Quasi-causal conceptual ordering of employer variables[1]

1   *Organizational characteristics*
1.1   Date of establishment (2)
1.2   Sector (3)
1.3   Industrial classification (4)

2   *Manpower characteristics*
2.1   Number of employees (5)
2.1.1   Full time
2.1.2   Part time
2.2   Occupational distribution of employees (7)
2.2.1   Total number of employees
2.2.1.1   Professional, technical and related
2.2.1.2   Administrative and managerial
2.2.1.3   Clerical
2.2.1.4   Sales
2.2.1.5   Services
2.2.1.6   Agriculture, forestry, fishing
2.2.1.7   Production, transportation
2.2.2   Tanzanian employees
2.2.2.1   Professional, technical, and related
2.2.2.2   Administrative and managerial
2.2.2.3   Clerical
2.2.2.4   Sales
2.2.2.5   Services
2.2.2.6   Agriculture, forestry, fishing
2.2.2.7   Production, transportation
2.2.3   Vacancies

1. Figures in parentheses are the question numbers of the employer questionnaire (Appendix III).

Table 8:   Quasi-causal conceptual ordering of employer variables (continued)

2.2.3.1   Professional, technical and related
2.2.3.2   Administrative and managerial
2.2.3.3   Clerical
2.2.3.4   Sales
2.2.3.5   Services
2.2.3.6   Agriculture, forestry, fishing
2.2.3.7   Production, transportation
2.3   Number of employees with education beyond form VI
2.4   Manpower requirements (fields of specialization) (19)
2.4.1   Actual requirements (1968)
2.4.1.01   Natural sciences
2.4.1.02   Engineering
2.4.1.03   Social sciences
2.4.1.04   Technology
2.4.1.05   Humanities
2.4.1.06   Health
2.4.1.07   Business and commerce
2.4.1.08   Agriculture
2.4.1.09   Law
2.4.1.10   Administration
2.4.1.11   Others
2.4.2   Actual requirements (1973)
2.4.2.01   Natural sciences
2.4.2.02   Engineering
2.4.2.03   Social sciences
2.4.2.04   Technology
2.4.2.05   Humanities
2.4.2.06   Health
2.4.2.07   Business and commerce
2.4.2.08   Agriculture
2.4.2.09   Law
2.4.2.10   Administration
2.4.2.11   Others
2.4.3   Anticipated requirements (1977)
2.4.3.01   Natural sciences
2.4.3.02   Engineering
2.4.3.03   Social sciences
2.4.3.04   Technology
2.4.3.05   Humanities
2.4.3.06   Health
2.4.3.07   Business and commerce
2.4.3.08   Agriculture
2.4.3.09   Law
2.4.3.10   Administration
2.4.3.11   Others
2.4.4   Anticipated requirements (1981)
2.4.4.01   Natural sciences
2.4.4.02   Engineering
2.4.4.03   Social sciences
2.4.4.04   Technology
2.4.4.05   Humanities

Table 8: Quasi-causal conceptual ordering of employer variables (continued)

2.4.4.06   Health
2.4.4.07   Business and commerce
2.4.4.08   Agriculture
2.4.4.09   Law
2.4.4.10   Administration
2.4.4.11   Others

3   *Recruitment practices*
3.1   Methods of recruiting largest number of employees (8.1)
3.2   Method of recruiting best employees (8.2)
3.3   Criteria for selecting educated applicants (9)
3.3.1   Importance of academic record
3.3.2   Importance of aptitude tests
3.3.3   Importance of interview
3.3.4   Importance of past experience
3.3.5   Importance of letters of recommendation
3.3.6   Importance of physical appearance
3.3.7   Importance of marital status
3.3.8   Importance of other aspects
3.4   Problems in describing a job for recruiting purposes (10)
3.5   Starting salary of persons with formal education (18)

4   Correspondence between academic and vocational performance (11)

5   *In-service training*
5.1   In-service training facilities (12)
5.2   Type of in-service training facilities (13)
5.3   Staff sent abroad for in-service training (14)
5.4   If no in-service facilities, would like to introduce (15)

6   *Opinion about institutions of higher education*
6.1   Institutions of higher education should become more concerned about your needs (16)
6.1.1   Formulation of curricula
6.1.2   Methods of instruction
6.1.3   Developing new training programmes
6.1.4   Research projects
6.2   Institutions of higher education should have sandwich courses (17.1)

7   *Provision of work opportunities within organization*
7.1   Interested in providing vacation employment to post secondary students (17.2)
7.2   Organization has projects which could be done by students during their training (17.3)

8   *Opinions about employee needs*
8.1   For job satisfaction (20.1)
8.1.01   Importance of interesting work
8.1.02   Importance of using special talent
8.1.03   Importance of creative work
8.1.04   Importance of no supervision
8.1.05   Importance of further studies
8.1.06   Importance of improving competence
8.1.07   Importance of being helpful to others and society
8.1.08   Importance of work with people

Table 8: Quasi-causal conceptual ordering of employer variables (continued)

8.1.09	Importance of a good income
8.1.10	Importance of travel
8.1.11	Importance of supervising others
8.1.12	Importance of better prospects
8.1.13	Importance of a secure future
8.1.14	Importance of time for family and hobbies
8.1.15	Importance of using skills learned in formal schooling
8.2	For meeting career objectives (20.2)
8.2.01	Importance of interesting work
8.2.02	Importance of using special talent
8.2.03	Importance of creative work
8.2.04	Importance of no supervision
8.2.05	Importance of further studies
8.2.06	Importance of improving competence
8.2.07	Importance of being helpful to others and society
8.2.08	Importance of work with people
8.2.09	Importance of a good income
8.2.10	Importance of travel
8.2.11	Importance of supervising others
8.2.12	Importance of better prospects
8.2.13	Importance of a secure future
8.2.14	Importance of time for family and hobbies
8.2.15	Importance of using skills learned in formal schooling

The Questionnaires

I. STUDENT QUESTIONNAIRE
To be completed by students of
post-secondary institutions in
Tanzania

This survey is being carried out
by the
International Institute for
Educational Planning (Unesco),
Paris
in conjunction with the
Ministry of National Education,
Dar es Salaam, Tanzania

All answers are confidential

1. Did you attend secondary school in Tanzania?   Yes ☐   No ☐
2. Name of the last secondary school attended:_____
3. Did you do Form VI?   Yes ☐   No ☐
4. Last year of secondary school: 19
5. What is your age? Less than 20 years ☐ 20–25 years ☐
    25–30 years ☐   More than 30 years ☐
6. Sex: Male ☐   Female ☐
7. Are you married?   Yes ☐   No ☐
8. Have you been divorced?   Yes ☐   No ☐
9. How many children do you have?   ☐
10. (a) Indicate by a tick mark (√) against the region you consider your
       home district

Region	Home district	Region	Home district
Arusha	☐	Morogoro	☐
Coast	☐	Mtwara	☐
Dar es Salaam	☐	Mwanza	☐
Dodoma	☐	Rukwa	☐
Iringa	☐	Ruvuma	☐
Kigoma	☐	Shinyanga	☐
Kilimanjaro	☐	Singida	☐
Lindi	☐	Tabora	☐
Mara	☐	Tanga	☐
Mbeya	☐	Zanzibar & Pemba	☐

   (b) Your permanent residence is in an: Urban area ☐
                                               Rural area ☐
11. Are you a Tanzanian citizen?   Yes ☐   No ☐
12. When you completed you secondary school education, you wanted to
    be:

Natural scientist	☐	Business man & manager	☐
Engineer	☐	Agriculturist	☐
Social scientist	☐	Lawyer	☐

Humanistic professional □   Other □
Health professional □   (specify)
(A list of the fields leading to each profession is appended)

13. (a) Did you get any information on career possibilities before you applied for higher education?   Yes □   No □

    (b) You got it from:

Central Establishment office	□	Other students □
Staff of educational institutions	□	Previous employment you had in the field □
Friends, parents or relatives	□	General information sources, books, newspapers, etc. □
Career master	□	

14. Was the advice: Very satisfactory □
                        Satisfactory □
                        Not satisfactory □

15. Name of the course or degree which you are doing: _____

16. How many years have you been studying on your present course? □

17. Tick the institution you are now attending:
University of Dar es Salaam □
Dar es Salaam College of National Education □
Iringa College of National Education □
Technical College Dar es Salaam □
Institute of Development Management □
Fisheries Institute Dar es Salaam □
Institute of Finance Management □
Olmotonyi Institute of Forestry □
Institute of Land Survey □

18. If you are a university student, your faculty is:
Law □   Arts □   Science □   Agriculture □
Engineering □   Medicine □

19. Why did you undertake post-secondary study/training? (tick one)
Wanted specific professional qualification □
Bursary incentives □
Desire for more study for its own sake □
Better employment opportunities for qualified professionals □
To make yourself available for manpower needs □

20. Was your present course of study your first choice?   Yes □   No □

21. Do you like the course you are now doing?
Much □   Reasonably □   Not at all □

22. If you have changed your field of study during your education, indicate the SINGLE most important reason for the most recent change:

I did not have enough money ☐
My family wanted me to do something else ☐
I later got better information on career possibilities ☐
Someone in my family died, my family moved, etc. ☐
My grades were not good enough ☐
I did not like what I was doing ☐
Another reason (specify) _____ ☐

23. Do your think that your secondary school course was adequate background for your present course of study? Yes ☐ No ☐

24. Are you employed?
Full-time ☐ Part-time ☐ In the vacations ☐

25. Approximately, how much do you earn per year (do not include your bursary)? Shs._____

26. What is the major source of finance for your present education?
Government bursary ☐ Family ☐
Non-government bursary ☐ Own efforts (employment, savings) ☐

27. Are you a boarding student? Yes ☐ No ☐

28. When you have completed your education do you intend to seek employment in your major field of study?
Yes, permanently ☐ Yes, but not permanently ☐ No ☐

29. If you do not expect to be permanently employed in your present major field, why do you remain in this field?
The field gives me good career preparation ☐
I enjoy the field ☐
The field gives me a wider choice of future careers ☐
It was a mistake to choose this field, but it is too late to change ☐
I am bonded to the field ☐

30. If you entered direct employment after secondary school education, how much do you think you would be earning (salary per month before deductions)?
Less than Shs. 250 ☐ Shs. 250–500 ☐ Shs. 500–750 ☐
Shs. 750–1,000 ☐ More than Shs. 1,000 ☐

31. Your guardian is:
Your father ☐ mother ☐ another relative ☐ none ☐

32. Your guardian's occupation is (tick one):

Professional, technical and related ☐   Agricultural, animal husbandry, forestry, fishery ☐
Administrative and managerial ☐   Production and related ☐
Clerical and related ☐   Unemployed ☐
Sales work ☐   Not classifiable ☐
Service work ☐

(Please consult the occupational classification list appended for identification of the exact occupation)

33. What is the highest level of education which your parents have (tick the correct box)?

	Mother	Father
None	☐	☐
St. IV or less	☐	☐
St. VIII or less	☐	☐
Form IV or less	☐	☐
Form VI or less	☐	☐
Post-secondary	☐	☐
Post-graduate	☐	☐

34. What is your guardian's approximate monthly income (before deductions)?
Less than Shs. 250 ☐   Shs. 250–500 ☐   Shs. 500–750 ☐
Shs. 750–1,000 ☐   More than Shs. 1,000 ☐

35. Should your Institution take any interest in the employment possibilities of its graduates?
Yes ☐   No ☐   No opinion ☐

36. Does your Institution seek the co-operation of government, industry and business in getting specialists to inform students about careers and employment opportunities?
Yes ☐   No ☐   No opinion ☐

37. If more detailed occupational guidance had been made available to you, would you have been willing to change your field of study?
Yes ☐   No ☐   No opinion ☐

38. The following list gives four ways of obtaining better knowledge on conditions of work, promotion prospects, etc. Please rank them in order of preference (1 = most preferred, 4 = least preferred):
Practical job experience during a study course ☐
Personally getting information from prospective employers ☐
Reading careers publications ☐
Discussing with workers from particular fields ☐

39. To what extent will choice of career depend on success in your present studies?
Much ☐   Reasonably ☐   Not at all ☐

40. In what sector do you expect to be permanently employed when you have completed your course?
Government service ☐   Private sector ☐
Parastatal ☐   Self employed ☐

41. What factors might induce you to work in rural areas (please indicate how important you think each of these factors is)?

	Very important	Important	Not important
Financial incentives	☐	☐	☐
Promotion prospects	☐	☐	☐
A post of greater responsibility	☐	☐	☐

Opportunity for a free life	☐	☐	☐
Another reason: _____	☐	☐	☐

42. Which of the following factors would discourage you from taking a job in the rural areas (please indicate the importance of each of these factors)?

	Very important	*Important*	*Not important*
Lack of tap-water, electricity, etc.	☐	☐	☐
Communication and transportation difficulties	☐	☐	☐
Separation from friends and relatives	☐	☐	☐
Belief that rural life is dull and slow	☐	☐	☐
No scope for improving competence	☐	☐	☐
Possible delays in promotion	☐	☐	☐
Others: (specify): ...	☐	☐	☐

43. What do you expect to be earning per month when you have finished your course, *before deductions*?

At the start of your career	Shs._____
After about five years	Shs._____
After about ten years	Shs._____
Near retirement	Shs._____

44. How important do you think each of the following factors is
    (1) towards making a job satisfactory, and
    (2) towards meeting career objectives

	Towards making a job satisfactory (1)			Towards meeting career objectives (2)		
	Very imp.	*Imp.*	*Not imp.*	*Very imp.*	*Imp.*	*Not imp.*
Interesting work	☐	☐	☐	☐	☐	☐
Use of special talent	☐	☐	☐	☐	☐	☐
Creative work	☐	☐	☐	☐	☐	☐
No supervision	☐	☐	☐	☐	☐	☐
Further studies	☐	☐	☐	☐	☐	☐
Improve competence	☐	☐	☐	☐	☐	☐

Helpful to others and society	☐	☐	☐	☐	☐	☐
Work with people	☐	☐	☐	☐	☐	☐
Good income	☐	☐	☐	☐	☐	☐
Travel	☐	☐	☐	☐	☐	☐
Supervise others	☐	☐	☐	☐	☐	☐
Better prospects	☐	☐	☐	☐	☐	☐
Secure future	☐	☐	☐	☐	☐	☐
Time for family and hobbies	☐	☐	☐	☐	☐	☐
Use of skill learned in formal schooling	☐	☐	☐	☐	☐	☐

45. I hereby declare that the information contained in this questionnaire is complete and correct to the best of knowledge and belief.

Signed:_____

Date:_____

II. GRADUATE QUESTIONNAIRE

To be completed by employed post-secondary graduates in Tanzania

All answers are confidential

This survey is being carried out by the International Institute for Educational Planning (Unesco), Paris in conjunction with the Ministry of National Education, Dar es Salaam, Tanzania

1. Are you a Tanzanian citizen? Yes ☐ No ☐
2. What is your age? Less than 20 years ☐   20–25 years ☐
   25–30 years ☐   More than 30 years ☐
3. Sex: Male ☐   Female ☐
4. (a) Indicate by a tick mark (√) against the region you live now under (1), and the region you consider your home district under (2)

Region	Live now (1)	Home district (2)	Region	Live now (1)	Home district (2)
Arusha	☐	☐	Morogoro	☐	☐
Coast	☐	☐	Mtwara	☐	☐
Dar es Salaam	☐	☐	Mwanza	☐	☐
Dodoma	☐	☐	Rukwa	☐	☐
Iringa	☐	☐	Ruvuma	☐	☐
Kigoma	☐	☐	Shinyanga	☐	☐
Kilimanjaro	☐	☐	Singida	☐	☐
			Tabora	☐	☐

Lindi ☐ ☐ Tanga ☐ ☐
Mara ☐ ☐ Zanzibar &
Mbeya ☐ ☐ Pemba ☐ ☐

(b) Your permanent residence is in an: Urban area ☐
Rural area ☐

5. Are you married? Yes ☐ No ☐
6. What is the educational level of your husband or wife?
None ☐ Form IV or less ☐
St. IV or less ☐ Form VI or less ☐
St. VII or less ☐ Post-secondary ☐
Post-graduate ☐

7. What is the highest level of education which your parents have (tick the correct box)?

	Mother	*Father*
None	☐	☐
Standard IV or less	☐	☐
Standard VII or less	☐	☐
Form IV or less	☐	☐
Form VI or less	☐	☐
Post-secondary	☐	☐
Post-graduate	☐	☐

8. (a) What is the highest academic qualification you hold?
Diploma —1 year full time ☐
2 year full time ☐
3 year full time ☐
First degree (B.A., B.Sc. gen., ☐
B.Sc. engin., M.B.B.S.) ☐
Post-graduate diploma/certificate ☐
Second degree (M.A., M.Sc., etc.) ☐
Third degree (Ph.D) ☐

(b)

	Where did you get your highest qualification?	*Which other Institutions have you attended?*
University of Dar es Salaam	☐	☐
Dar es Salaam College of National Education	☐	☐
Iringa College of National Education	☐	☐
Technical College Dar es Salaam	☐	☐
Institute of Development Management	☐	☐
Fisheries Institute Dar es Salaam	☐	☐

Institute of Finance
   Management ☐ ☐
Olmotonyi Institute of
   Forestry ☐ ☐
Institute of Land Survey ☐ ☐
Overseas ☐ ☐

(c) If you are a university graduate, please mention the faculty:
Arts ☐   Science ☐   Agriculture ☐   Engineering ☐
Medicine ☐   Law ☐

(d) In what year were you admitted to the Institution which gave you your highest academic qualification?   19_____

(e) In what year did you obtain your highest academic qualification?   19_____

9. (a) When you completed your secondary school education you wanted to be:

Natural scientist ☐   Business man & manager ☐
Engineer ☐   Agriculturist ☐
Social scientist ☐   Lawyer ☐
Humanistic professional ☐   Other (specify) ☐
Health professional ☐

(b) Why did you undertake post-secondary study or training (tick one)?

Wanted a specific professional qualification ☐
Desired study for its own sake ☐
The country needed my talent for manpower
   needs ☐
Better employment opportunities for graduates ☐

10. Are you a teacher?   Yes ☐   No ☐
11. Did you train to be a teacher?   Yes ☐   No ☐
12. If you changed your field of study during your education, indicate your SINGLE most important reason for the most recent change.

I did not have enough money ☐
My family wanted me to do something else ☐
I later got better information on career possibilities ☐
Someone in my family died, my family moved, etc. ☐
My grades were not good enough ☐
I did not like what I was doing ☐
Another reason: _____ ☐

13. How did you get your first employment after graduation?   Indicate the waiting-period.
    ☐ months

Through the institution from which you
graduated ☐
NHLMAC (Central Establishment) ☐
Appointment bureau ☐
Newspaper advertisement ☐

Personal contacts with the employers ☐
Tied to the employment by bonding ☐
Another method (specify) _____ ☐

14. In your own opinion, do you think that the education you received was useful to the needs of your job?
Very useful ☐   Useful ☐   Useless ☐

15. To what extent were your educational qualifications necessary for getting your present job?
Very necessary ☐   Necessary ☐   Not necessary ☐

16.

	Which field did you specialize in for your highest qualifications?	*Which field is the most relevant to your current job?*
Natural sciences	☐	☐
Engineering	☐	☐
Social sciences	☐	☐
Humanities	☐	☐
Health (medicine)	☐	☐
Business and commerce	☐	☐
Agriculture	☐	☐
Law	☐	☐
Administration	☐	☐

17. How important do you consider each of the following factors was in your getting the job?

	Very important	*Important*	*Unimportant*
Academic record	☐	☐	☐
Aptitude tests	☐	☐	☐
Interview	☐	☐	☐
Past experience in a similar type of job	☐	☐	☐
Letters of recommendation	☐	☐	☐
Physical appearance	☐	☐	☐
Marital status	☐	☐	☐
Others (specify) _____	☐	☐	☐

18. Did you ever change your job?   Yes ☐   No ☐

19. (a) If you changed your job, why did you make this change?
Better conditions of service ☐   Lost previous job ☐
Better use of training ☐   Did not get along with
Better prospects for   the people you
promotion ☐   were working with ☐
More suited to   Other reasons ☐

personal talents ☐
  (b) In what sector are you working now?

Government	☐	Private sector	☐
Parastatal sector	☐	Self employed	☐

20. Did the educational institution you attended last have an employment office?   Yes ☐   No ☐
If not, would it have been useful to you if there had been one?
        Yes ☐   No ☐

21. What was the major source of finance for your FIRST post-secondary education?

Government bursary	☐	Family	☐
Scholarships from other agencies	☐	Own efforts (employment savings)	☐

22. How many *hours* approximately do you work *per week*?   [   ]

23. The following list gives four ways of obtaining better knowledge on conditions of work, promotion prospects, etc. Please rank them in order of preference (1 = being the best; 4 = the least)

Practical job experience during the course of study
  (e.g. sandwich courses, practical teaching, vacational employment) ☐
Personally getting information from prospective employers ☐
Reading careers publications ☐
Discussing with workers from particular fields ☐

24. To what extent did choice of career depend on success in your studies.
Very much ☐   Somewhat ☐   Not at all ☐

25. How important do you think each of the following factors is
    (1) towards making a job satisfactory, and
    (2) towards meeting career objectives?

	Towards making a job satisfactory (1)			Towards meeting career objectives (2)		
	Very imp.	Imp.	Not imp.	Very imp.	Imp.	Not imp.
Interesting work	☐	☐	☐	☐	☐	☐
Use of special talent	☐	☐	☐	☐	☐	☐
Creative work	☐	☐	☐	☐	☐	☐
No supervision	☐	☐	☐	☐	☐	☐
Further studies	☐	☐	☐	☐	☐	☐
Improve competence	☐	☐	☐	☐	☐	☐
Helpful to others and society	☐	☐	☐	☐	☐	☐
Work with people	☐	☐	☐	☐	☐	☐
Good income	☐	☐	☐	☐	☐	☐

Travel ☐ ☐ ☐ ☐ ☐ ☐
Supervise others ☐ ☐ ☐ ☐ ☐ ☐
Better prospects ☐ ☐ ☐ ☐ ☐ ☐
Secure future ☐ ☐ ☐ ☐ ☐ ☐
Time for family and
  hobbies ☐ ☐ ☐ ☐ ☐ ☐
Use of skill learned
  in formal schooling ☐ ☐ ☐ ☐ ☐ ☐

26. Which of the following factors might induce you to work in rural areas? (Please indicate the degree of importance)

	Very important	*Important*	*Unimportant*
Financial incentives	☐	☐	☐
Promotional prospects	☐	☐	☐
A post of greater responsibility	☐	☐	☐
Opportunity for a freer life	☐	☐	☐
Low cost of living	☐	☐	☐
Another reason (specify)_____	☐	☐	☐

27. Which of the following factors would discourage you from taking a job in the rural areas? (Please indicate the importance of each of these factors)

	Very important	*Important*	*Not important*
Lack of tap-water, electricity, etc.	☐	☐	☐
Communication and transportation difficulties	☐	☐	☐
Separation from friends and relatives	☐	☐	☐
Belief that rural life is dull and slow	☐	☐	☐
No scope for improving competence	☐	☐	☐
Possible delays in promotion	☐	☐	☐
Others (specify)_____	☐	☐	☐

28. What is your *monthly* gross salary at present?   Shs. ☐

29. What was your *monthly* gross salary when you took up your first permanent job?   Shs. ☐

30. (a) Indicate your guardian's occupation when you were a post-secondary student from the occupational classification list given at the end. |A |

    (b) When you were a post-secondary student, what was your guardian's income *per month*?

      Less than Shs. 250 ☐   Shs. 250–500 ☐   Shs. 500–750 ☐

      Shs. 750–1,000 ☐   More than Shs. 1,000 ☐

31. If the institution you attended for your post-secondary education were to ask for your co-operation, would you be willing to co-operate within your time limits in the following areas?

	Yes	No	No opinion
As a member of an advisory group	☐	☐	☐
Filling out some questionnaires from time to time	☐	☐	☐
Attending some of the meetings	☐	☐	☐

32. I hereby declare that the information contained in this questionnaires is complete and correct to the best of my knowledge and belief.

Signed:_____

Date:_____

III. EMPLOYER QUESTIONNAIRE

To be completed by employers of post-secondary graduates in Tanzania

All answers are confidential

This survey is being carried out by the International Institute for Educational Planning (Unesco), Paris in conjunction with the Ministry of National Education, Dar es Salaam, Tanzania

1. Name of the organization: | | | | | | | | | | | | | | | | | | |
2. Date of establishment: | | | | |
3. Is your organization:
   Government ☐   Parastatal ☐   Private ☐
4. Give the industrial classification of your organization (see the industrial classification list appended) |B| | |
5. Number of employees: Full-time _____   Part-time_____
6. Approximate number of employees having at least one year of education after Form VI._____

7. Number of:

	Tanzanians	Non Tanzanians	Total	(Unfilled) vacancies

Professional, technical and related workers	_____	_____	_____	_____
Administrative and managerial workers	_____	_____	_____	_____
Clerical and related workers	_____	_____	_____	_____
Sales workers	_____	_____	_____	_____
Service workers	_____	_____	_____	_____
Agricultural, animal husbandry, forestry workers and fishermen	_____	_____	_____	_____
Production and related workers, transport equipment operators and labourers	_____	_____	_____	_____

(See the occupational classification list appended)

8. What methods do you use to recruit employees with post-Form VI education (tick the appropriate box in each column)?

	Largest number	*Best employees*
Educational institution authorities	☐	☐
Employment exchange office	☐	☐
Government manpower office	☐	☐
Personal contacts	☐	☐
Bonding students by scholarships	☐	☐
Another method (specify)_____	☐	☐

9. How important do you consider each of the following criteria in selecting employees who have post-Form VI education?

	Very important	*Important*	*Unimportant*
Academic record	☐	☐	☐
Aptitude tests	☐	☐	☐
Interview	☐	☐	☐
Past experience in a job of a similar type	☐	☐	☐
Letters of recommendation	☐	☐	☐
Physical appearance	☐	☐	☐

Marital status	☐	☐	☐
Others (specify)_____	☐	☐	☐

10. What is the SINGLE most difficult problem in describing a job for recruitment purposes?

   No correspondence between the educational institution and the
   employer's needs ☐

   The graduates do not have the training you would like them
   to have ☐

   Good performance in the academic life does not mean better
   job performance ☐

   The jobs are too complex for precise specification of education
   qualifications ☐

   Another (specify) _____ ☐

11. What do you think is the degree of correspondence between academic performance and job performance?

	Diploma	*Graduate*	*Post-graduate*
Very high degree of correspondence	☐	☐	☐
Medium degree of correspondence	☐	☐	☐
No correspondence at all	☐	☐	☐

12. Do you have provision for in-service training facilities in your organization for employees having post-secondary education?
   Yes ☐   No ☐

13. If you DO have in-service training indicate the type(s) from the list below. If you do NOT have such facilities, use the same list to indicate the type you would prefer.
   Staff away from your organization: Full-time ☐   Part-time ☐
   Training conducted in your firm ☐
   Any other type (specify)_____ ☐

14. Do you send any staff abroad for training?   Yes ☐   No ☐

15. If you do NOT have any in-service training programmes, would you like to introduce one?   Yes ☐   No ☐

16. In what ways would you like to see the institutions of higher education become more concerned about your needs?

	Yes	*No*
Formulating their curricula	☐	☐
Choosing the method of instruction	☐	☐
Development of new training programmes	☐	☐
Carrying out research projects related to your organization	☐	☐

17. Would you like the institutions of higher education to have sandwich training programmes?   Yes ☐   No ☐

   Are you interested in offering vacation employment to post-secondary students?   Yes ☐   No ☐

Do you have projects in your organization which could be done by students during their training?　　　　　　　Yes ☐　　No ☐

18. Would you kindly indicate the approximate starting salary *per month* including allowances for an employee with one year of formal education after Form VI.　Shs._____

19. Please give the best estimates you can for the following for your concern:

Fields of specialization	*No. of employees in*			
	1968	*1973*	*1977*	*1981*
Natural sciences				
Engineering				
Social sciences				
Technology				
Humanities				
Health (medicine)				
Business & commerce				
Agriculture				
Law				
Administration				
Others				

20. How important do you think each of the following factors is
    (1)　towards making a job satisfactory for the employees, and
    (2)　towards meeting career objectives of the employees?

	Towards making a job satisfactory (1)			*Towards meeting career objectives* (2)		
	Very imp.	*Imp.*	*Not imp.*	*Very imp.*	*Imp.*	*Not imp.*
Interesting work	☐	☐	☐	☐	☐	☐
Use of special talent	☐	☐	☐	☐	☐	☐
Creative work	☐	☐	☐	☐	☐	☐
No supervision	☐	☐	☐	☐	☐	☐
Further studies	☐	☐	☐	☐	☐	☐
Improve competence	☐	☐	☐	☐	☐	☐
Helpful to others and society	☐	☐	☐	☐	☐	☐
Work with people	☐	☐	☐	☐	☐	☐
Good income	☐	☐	☐	☐	☐	☐
Travel	☐	☐	☐	☐	☐	☐
Supervise others	☐	☐	☐	☐	☐	☐
Better prospects	☐	☐	☐	☐	☐	☐
Secure future	☐	☐	☐	☐	☐	☐

Time for family and hobbies	☐	☐	☐	☐	☐	☐
Use of skill learned in formal schooling	☐	☐	☐	☐	☐	☐

Signature:_____   Date:_____
Title:_____

OCCUPATIONAL CLASSIFICATION LIST

Code	Occupational Area
	Professional, Technical and Related Workers
A01	Physical scientists and related workers
A02	Architects, engineers and related workers
A03	Aircraft and ships, officers
A04	Life scientists and related technicians
A05	Medical, dental, veterinary and related technicians
A06	Statisticians, mathematicians, systems analysts and related technicians
A07	Economists
A08	Accountants
A09	Jurists, lawyers, judges
A10	Teachers
A11	Workers in religion (ministers of religion)
A12	Authors, journalists and related workers
A13	Sculptors, painters, photographers and related creative artists
A14	Composers and performing artists
A15	Athletes, sportsmen and related workers
A16	Professional, technical and related workers not classified elsewhere
	Administrative and Managerial Workers
A17	Legislative officials and government administrators
A18	Managers
A19	Government executive officials
	Clerical and Related Workers
A20	Clerical supervisors
A21	Stenographers, typists and card and tape-punching machine operators
A22	Bookkeepers, cashiers and related workers
A23	Computing machine operators
A24	Transport and communications supervisors
A25	Transport conductors
A26	Mail distribution clerks
A27	Telephone and telegraph operators
A28	Clerical and related workers not elsewhere classified
	Sales Workers
A29	Sales supervisors, technical salesmen, manufacturing agents, shop assistants, etc.
	Service Workers

A30   Cooks, domestic servants, waiters, bartenders, cleaners, hairdressers, etc.

         Agricultural, Animal Husbandry, Forestry Workers and Fishermen

A31   Farm workers, forestry workers, charcoal burners, fishermen etc.

         Production and Related Workers, Transport Equipment Operators and Labourers

A32   Production supervisors and general foremen, miners, tailors, machine tool operators, broadcasting station operators, cinema projectionists, plumbers, printers, photographers, painters, bricklayers, carpenters, construction workers, equipment operators, freight handlers, transport equipment operators, etc.

A33   Undergoing Further Training

INDUSTRIAL CLASSIFICATION LIST

Code   *Industrial Area*

B01   Agriculture
Field crops, orchards, cattle, poultry, forestry, erosion control, wildlife, fisheries, etc.

B02   Mining
Quarries, minerals, precious stones, fuel (coal), etc.

B03   Manufacturing
Food, beverages, tobacco, leather, timber, printing and publishing, chemicals, petroleum, rubber products, china, building materials, metals, other manufacturing industries, etc.

B04   Construction
Building, railway, road, airport, dam constructions, mining works, cementation, construction of shafts, etc.

B05   Electricity and Water
Electric plants and grids, water supply plants, etc.

B06   Trade
Stores and other distribution agencies, etc.

B07   Financial Institutions and Insurance

B08   Real Estate

B09   Transport and Communication
Road, rail and air transport, boats, telecommunications, radio, TV, etc.

B10   Government Administration

B11   Community and Business Services
      Sanitation, social and related community services, education,
      medical and veterinary services, welfare, recreational and
      cultural services, police, fire, etc.

B12   Hotels, Restaurants and Tourism